About the Author

Norman Handy was born in Beckenham in the south east of England. He went to Clare House School and his secondary education was at a mixed boarding school in Cranbrook, Kent. Later he attended courses in Law for Accountants, Business Economics and Accountancy at Southampton University

Even during his studies he travelled as often as he could, such as cycling down the Loire Valley and journeying behind the Iron Curtain. After leaving university, he lived and worked abroad, ending up on a date plantation in the Middle East.

He returned to the United Kingdom and after working in a riding school, followed a career in the financial-services sector based in London. Periods were spent working abroad in Europe, the Middle East and Asia. He published his first book in 2017.

He has two children and is a keen walker, skier, cyclist, horse rider and of course, writer. He spends his time between his homes in West Sussex and travelling.

Baltic Capitals

Norman Handy

Baltic Capitals

Vanguard Press

A CIP catalogue record for this title is
available from the British Library.

ISBN 978 1 83794 071 4

Vanguard Press is an imprint of
Pegasus Elliot Mackenzie Publishers Ltd.
www.pegasuspublishers.com

First Published in 2025

Vanguard Press
Sheraton House Castle Park
Cambridge England

Printed & Bound in Great Britain

Map of the Baltic Capitals

Chapter 1

Arrival in Denmark

I was flying into Copenhagen aboard a Maersk charter flight from my local airport. There were great views of the magnificent Øresund Bridge that connects Denmark by rail and road to Sweden. We were coming into land against some strong cross winds, and I was casually chatting to the pilot in the cockpit as the aircraft was descending and crabbing towards the runway.

We were descending but due to the strength of the wind, the nose of the aircraft was several degrees off true to counter the wind. The plan was to straighten up at the last minute, although this would mean a hard landing, but being straight, we wouldn't rip the tyres off the rims and crash to become a statistic.

All of a sudden, an extra strong gust pushed us off course. Nervous flyers should be reassured as large, modern, commercial passenger jets have complex computer systems to fly a plane to counter all such emergencies. The pilot needs only to enter the departure point and destination and the computers will do most of the rest. The plane I was in was old and small, and therefore cheap, but flown by a pilot of considerable skill and experience.

For planes not using electronic navigation, there is a light system of four vertical lights and four horizontal lights to tell the pilot whether he is at the optimal height and bearing. Four lights is optimal and therefore, unsurprisingly, no lights spell disaster and a visual message to abandon the landing.

The first of the four lights may go off, giving the pilot a chance to regain the initiative to correct his height and direction. As I was chatting to the pilot on our descent, the gust was so strong that it pushed us way off course and all the lights went off. We were flying parallel to the runway but over grass and over aircraft standing on taxiways ready to join the main runway and against all IATA rules.

The correct response is to apply full power and gain height and circle to try again. However, we were too slow and low. We might have gained height but, in a low-powered plane, our undercarriage may have clipped the airport perimeter fencing or smashed into some of the warehouses at the end of the runway.

The pilot applied full power to counter the wind to get us back over the concrete of the main runway. We landed hard and fast and the pilot applied all the brakes. The air brakes screamed and the tyres screeched as the airframe shuddered and creaked, rocking from side to side as the mechanical systems struggled against the momentum. We were thrust forward into our harnesses as the brakes bit and the aircraft finally slowed.

We had shot past the last taxiway exit from the main runway as we were going too fast to make a safe turn. Eventually we slowed on the emergency section at the end of the main runway. The pilot calmly liaised with the control tower and turned the aircraft around to take a turn off the main runway to reach the terminal buildings. He was calm and collected as he apologised for the hard landing.

It was quite disconcerting to hear, over the intercom and through the headset, the desperate but calm instructions from the control tower to several aircraft behind us to abort landings. It was equally unsettling to face those aircraft that had expected to land, just two minutes behind us, being told to turn and go to stack positions as we moved back down the runway in the wrong direction, until we were off the main runway.

The airport is very near the centre of the city and it was just a short metro journey to my hotel. The system was opened in 2002 and has had several extensions built since, and annually transports more than fifty million passengers. I was signing into my hotel before the full force of the recent near-miss incident really struck me, but I was delighted that I was in my first capital and country alongside the Baltic.

Denmark consists of more than one thousand, four hundred and nineteen islands larger than one hundred square metres. Nowhere in Denmark is further from the coast than fifty-two kilometres. The country is flat. The highest point is Møllehøj at one hundred and seventy metres. A sizeable portion of Denmark's terrain consists of rolling plains, whilst the coastline is sandy, with large dunes in northern Jutland. Although once extensively forested, today rural Denmark consists largely of arable land.

From the eighth to the tenth century, the wider Scandinavian region was the source of Vikings. They colonised, raided, and traded in all parts of Europe. The Danish Vikings were active in the eastern and southern British Isles. They conquered and settled parts of England, consequently known as the Danelaw.

The Danish monarchy traces its roots back to Gorm the Old, who established his reign in the early tenth century. The Danes were converted to Christianity around 965 AD by Harald Bluetooth. It is probable that Denmark became Christian for political reasons, to avoid invasion by the rising Christian power in Europe, the Holy Roman Empire, which was an important trading partner. In the early eleventh century, Canute the Great captured and united Denmark, England and Norway for almost thirty years.

In 1397, Denmark entered into a union with Norway and Sweden, united under Queen Margaret I. Thus, much of the next one hundred and twenty-five years of Scandinavian history revolves around this union, with Sweden breaking away and being repeatedly re-conquered. For practical purposes, the issue was resolved on 17th June 1523, as Swedish King Gustav Vasa conquered the city of Stockholm.

The Protestant Reformation spread to Scandinavia in the 1530s, and following the Count's Feud civil war, Denmark converted to Lutheranism in 1536. Later that year, Denmark entered into a union with Norway.

After Sweden permanently broke away from the union, Denmark tried, on several occasions, to reassert control over its neighbour. King Christian IV attacked Sweden in the 1611–1613 Kalmar War but failed to accomplish his main objective of forcing it to return to the union. The war led to no territorial changes, but Sweden was forced to pay a war indemnity of one million silver *riksdaler* to Denmark, an amount known as the Älvsborg ransom.

King Christian used this money to found several towns and fortresses, most notably Glückstadt as a rival to Hamburg and Christiania. Inspired by the Dutch East India Company, he founded a similar Danish company and planned to claim Ceylon as a colony, but the company only managed to acquire Tranquebar on India's Coromandel Coast.

In reality, Denmark's large colonial aspirations were limited to a few key trading posts in Africa and India, plus Greenland and Iceland. While Denmark's trading posts in India were of little note, it played an important role in the highly lucrative transatlantic slave trade through its trading outposts in Fort Cristiansborg in Osu, Ghana, though which 1.5 million slaves were trafficked.

Denmark prospered greatly in the last decades of the eighteenth century, due to its neutral status allowing it to trade with both sides in the many contemporary wars. In the Napoleonic Wars, Denmark traded with both France and the United Kingdom and joined the League of Armed Neutrality with Russia, Sweden, and Prussia. The British considered this a hostile act and attacked Copenhagen in 1801 and 1807, in one case capturing the majority of the Danish fleet, and in the other, burning large parts of the Danish capital.

The union was dissolved by the Treaty of Kiel in 1814, whereby the Danish monarchy renounced claims to the Kingdom of Norway in favour of the Swedish king. Denmark kept the possessions of Iceland (which retained the Danish monarchy until 1944), the Faroe Islands and Greenland. Denmark continued to rule over Danish India from 1620 to 1869, the Danish Gold Coast (Ghana) from 1658 to 1850 and the Danish West Indies from 1671 to 1917.

Denmark peacefully became a constitutional monarchy on 5th June 1849 but it faced war against both Prussia and the Austrian Empire in what became known as the Second Schleswig War, lasting from February to October 1864. Denmark was defeated and was obliged to cede Schleswig and Holstein to Prussia. This loss came as the latest in the long series of defeats and territorial losses. After these events, Denmark pursued a policy of neutrality in Europe.

Industrialisation came to Denmark in the second half of the nineteenth century. The nation's first railways were constructed in the 1850s, and improved communications and overseas trade allowed industry to develop in spite of Denmark's lack of natural resources. There was a considerable migration of people from the countryside to the cities, and Danish agriculture centred on the export of dairy and meat products.

In 1939 Denmark signed a ten-year non-aggression pact with Nazi Germany, but Germany invaded Denmark on 9th April 1940 and the Danish government quickly surrendered. The Second World War in Denmark was characterised by economic co-operation with Germany until 1943.

The Danish resistance performed a rescue operation that managed to evacuate several thousand Jews to safety in Sweden before the Germans could send them to death camps. Some Danes supported Nazism by joining the Danish Nazi Party or volunteering to fight with Germany as part of the Frikorps Danmark.

The earliest historical records of Copenhagen stem from the end of the twelfth century but recent archaeological finds, as part of the work on the city's metro, revealed the remains of a merchant's large house, from circa 1020, near today's Kongens Nytorv. The remains of an ancient church, with graves dating to the eleventh century, have been unearthed near where Strøget meets Rådhuspladsen.

Substantial discoveries of flint tools in the area provide evidence of human settlements dating to the Stone Age. The natural harbour and good herring stocks seem to have attracted fishermen and merchants to the area from the eleventh century. The first houses were probably centred on Gammel Strand.

The earliest written mention of the town was in the twelfth century, when Saxo Grammaticus referred to it as Portus Mercatorum, meaning Merchants' Harbour or, in the Danish of the time, Købmannahavn. Copenhagen's founding has been dated to Bishop Absalon's construction of a modest fortress on the island of Slotsholmen in 1167 where Christiansborg Palace stands today.

The fortress was built in response to attacks by Wendish pirates, who plagued the coastline during the twelfth century. Defensive ramparts and moats were completed, and by 1177 St Clemens Church had been built. Attacks by the Wends continued and after the original fortress was eventually destroyed by the marauders, islanders replaced it with Copenhagen Castle.

As the town became more prominent, it was repeatedly attacked by the Hanseatic League (a fascinating organisation, which will be detailed later in the book) and in 1368 was successfully invaded during the Second Danish-Hanseatic War.

As the fishing industry thrived in Copenhagen, the city began expanding to the north of Slotsholmen. In 1254, it received a charter as a city under Bishop Jakob Erlandsen, who garnered support against the king from the local fishing merchants by granting them special privileges.

With the establishment of the Kalmar Union (1397–1523) between Denmark, Norway and Sweden, by 1416

Copenhagen had emerged as the capital, when Eric of Pomerania moved his seat to Copenhagen Castle. The University of Copenhagen was inaugurated in 1479 by King Christian I, following approval from Pope Sixtus IV. This makes it the oldest university in Denmark and one of the oldest in Europe.

In disputes prior to the Reformation of 1536, the city which had been faithful to Christian II, who was Catholic, had been besieged in 1523 by the forces of Frederik I, who supported Lutheranism. Copenhagen's defences were subsequently reinforced with a series of towers added to the walls. After a siege for a year from July 1535, during which the city supported Christian II's alliance with Malmö and Lübeck, it was finally forced to capitulate to Christian III.

During the reign of Christian IV, between 1588 and 1648, Copenhagen experienced dramatic growth. On his initiative, two important buildings were completed on Slotsholmen: the Tøjhus Arsenal (1593–1604) and Børsen (1625), the stock exchange. The East India Company had been founded in 1616 to foster international trade. To the east of the city, inspired by Dutch planning, the king developed the district of Christianshavn as a fortified trading centre, with canals and ramparts. Christian IV also sponsored an array of ambitious building projects, including Rosenborg Slot and the Rundetårn.

By 1661, Copenhagen had asserted its position as the capital of Denmark and Norway. All the major institutions were located there, as were the fleet and the army. The defences were further enhanced with the completion of the Citadel in 1664 and the extension of Christianshavns Vold with its bastions in 1692, leading to the creation of a new base for the fleet at Nyholm.

Copenhagen did suffer setbacks, such as the loss of twenty-two thousand of its population of sixty-five thousand to the plague in 1711. The city was also struck by two major fires that destroyed much of its infrastructure. The Copenhagen Fire of 1728 was the largest in the history of Copenhagen. It began on the evening of 20th October, and continued to burn for three days, destroying approximately twenty-eight per cent of the city, leaving twenty per cent of the population homeless. Nearly half the medieval section of the city was destroyed. Along with the 1795 fire, it is the main reason that few traces of the old town can be found in the modern city.

A substantial amount of rebuilding followed. In 1733, work began on the royal residence of Christiansborg Palace which was completed in 1745. In 1749, development of the prestigious district of Frederiksstaden was initiated: it now hosts the Amalienborg Palace built in the Rococo style. Major extensions to the naval base of Holmen were undertaken while the city's cultural importance was enhanced with the Royal Theatre and the Royal Academy of Fine Arts.

After the Christiansborg Palace was destroyed by fire in 1794, and another fire caused serious damage to the city in 1795, work began on the classical Copenhagen landmark of Højbro Plads.

On 2nd April 1801, a British fleet under the command of Admiral Sir Hyde Parker attacked and defeated the neutral Danish-Norwegian fleet anchored near Copenhagen. Vice-Admiral Horatio Nelson led the main attack. He famously disobeyed Parker's order to cease fire, destroying many of the Dano-Norwegian ships before a truce was agreed. Copenhagen is often considered to be Nelson's hardest-fought battle, surpassing even the heavy fighting at Trafalgar. It was during this battle that Lord Nelson was said to have put the telescope to his blind eye in order not to see Admiral Parker's signal.

The Second Battle of Copenhagen (or the Bombardment of Copenhagen 16th August – 5th September 1807) was, from a British point of view, a pre-emptive strike on Copenhagen, targeting the civilian population to yet again seize the Dano-Norwegian fleet. From a Danish view point, the battle was a terror bombardment on their capital. Particularly notable was the use of incendiary Congreve rockets containing phosphorus, which cannot be extinguished with water, that randomly hit the city. Few houses with straw roofs remained after the bombardment. Several historians consider this battle the first terror attack against a major European city.

The British landed thirty thousand men who surrounded the city and attacked for the next three days, killing some two thousand civilians and destroying most of the city. The devastation was so great because Copenhagen relied on outdated defence cannons with limited range which could not reach the British ships.

Despite the disasters of the early nineteenth century, Copenhagen experienced a period of intense cultural creativity, known as the Danish Golden Age. In the early 1850s, the ramparts of the city were opened to allow new housing to be built around The Lakes that bordered the old defences to the west. By the 1880s, the western ramparts had been demolished to extend the city limits and the port extended. In 1840, Copenhagen was inhabited by one hundred and twenty thousand people but by 1901, it had increased to four hundred thousand inhabitants.

During the First World War, Denmark was neutral and traded with both sides, while the city's defences were kept fully manned by some forty thousand soldiers for the duration of the war. In the 1920s, there were serious shortages of goods and housing. Plans were drawn up to demolish the old part of Christianshavn and to get rid of the worst of the city's slums, but it was not until the 1930s that five large blocks of flats were actually built.

During the Second World War, Denmark was occupied by Nazi troops in April 1940. Adolf Hitler hoped that Denmark would be a model protectorate and initially the Nazi authorities sought to arrive at an understanding with the Danish government. The 1943 Danish parliamentary elections were allowed to take place with only the Communist Party excluded. However, in August 1943, after the government's collaboration with the occupation forces collapsed, several ships were scuttled in Copenhagen Harbour by the Royal Danish Navy to prevent their use by the Germans. Many Danish officers and Jews escaped to Sweden before the Nazis could retaliate.

In 1945 Ole Lippman, leader of the Danish section of the Special Operations Executive, invited the British Royal Air Force to assist their operations by attacking Nazi headquarters in Copenhagen. Air Vice-Marshal Sir Basil Embry drew up plans for a spectacular precision attack on the Sicherheitsdienst and Gestapo building, the former offices of the Shell Oil Company. Political prisoners were kept in the attic to prevent an air raid, so the RAF had to bomb the lower levels of the building.

The attack, known as Operation Carthage, was on 22nd March 1945, in three waves. In the first wave, all six planes hit their target, but one of the aircraft crashed near Frederiksberg Girls' School. Four of the planes in the two following waves assumed the fire at the school was the military target and aimed their bombs at the site, leading to the death of one hundred and twenty-three civilians (of which eighty-seven were schoolchildren). However, eighteen of the twenty-six political prisoners in the Shell Building managed to escape, while the Gestapo archives were completely destroyed. The city was liberated on 8th May 1945 by Field Marshal Bernard Montgomery, who supervised the surrender of thirty thousand German soldiers around the capital.

With an early commitment by urban planners to develop the city's environmentally friendly credentials, Copenhagen today is recognised as one of the most environmentally friendly cities in the world and has received awards for its green economy. It is ranked as one of the top green cities globally.

Copenhagen aims to be carbon-neutral by 2025. Commercial and residential buildings are to reduce electricity consumption by twenty per cent and ten per cent, respectively. Renewable energy features, such as solar panels, are becoming increasingly common in the newest buildings in Copenhagen. District heating will be carbon neutral by 2025 through waste incineration and biomass. New buildings must now be constructed according to Low Energy Class ratings. By 2025, seventy-five per cent of trips should be made on foot, by bike, or by using public transit. The city is planning for between twenty and thirty per cent of cars to be running on electricity or biofuel by 2025.

Special attention is given to both climate issues and efforts to ensure maximum application of low-energy standards. Priorities include sustainable drainage systems, recycling rainwater, green roofs and efficient waste-management solutions. In city planning, streets and squares are designed to encourage cycling and walking, rather than driving.

Developments have been so advanced in sewage treatment that there is a clean, sandy, public beach at Amager Strandpark, which opened in 2005, an artificial island with a total of 4.6 kilometres of beaches just fifteen minutes by bicycle, or a few minutes by metro from the city centre.

In international surveys, Copenhagen has been ranked high for its quality of life. Its stable economy, together with its education services and level of social safety, makes it a very attractive location. It is one of the world's most expensive cities but it has excellent public transport with facilities favouring cyclists and walkers over motor vehicles. Over eighty-six per cent of the population are of Danish descent. The balance is comprised of immigrants, the top five countries of origin being Turkey, Poland, Syria, Germany and Iraq.

I had arrived in Copenhagen and signed into my hotel, but I was going straight out again to check out the city and to get my bearings. I didn't have a specific plan as I like to build a lot of slack into the travel timetable, just in case of delays, but I always have a plan B.

I wandered along Strøget, Copenhagen's main shopping street, closed to traffic as a pedestrian area since 1964, making it the world's oldest and longest pedestrian street at 3.2 kilometres. It is full of speciality shops, cafés, restaurants and bars and it is always full of life. At times it is like an impromptu circus with musicians, magicians, jugglers and other street performers.

Copenhagen has one of the highest number of restaurants and bars per capita in the world. Denmark has a very liberal alcohol culture and a strong tradition of brewing, although binge drinking is frowned upon and the

Danish Police take driving-under-the-influence very seriously.

I was also looking out for local cuisine and I checked out the menus of every restaurant I passed. I love food and am a sucker for any item claiming to be a traditional dish or local delicacy. Copenhagen has fifteen Michelin-starred restaurants, the most of any Scandinavian city, so finding a good restaurant wasn't difficult, but I was looking for traditional and hopefully medium-priced rather than the high-class, high-priced offerings on the main thoroughfare.

Apart from the selection of upmarket restaurants offering standard international cuisine that I can get at home, Copenhagen offers a great variety of Danish, ethnic and experimental restaurants and it is possible to find modest eateries serving reasonably priced meals, but I would have to check out side streets and out-of-town areas to find the better-value options.

The best known Danish cuisine is Danish pastries that can be sampled from any of the numerous bakeries found in all parts of the city and all around the world. The Copenhagen Bakers' Association dates back to the 1290s and Denmark's oldest confectioner's shop is still operating. Conditori La Glace was founded in 1870 in Skoubogade by Nicolaus Henningsen, a master baker from Flensburg, and is just a short walk off the Strøget. It is worth the effort to find it if you have a sweet tooth and if you are interested in nineteenth-century architecture.

Another well-known Danish culinary option is *Smørrebrød*, a variety of Danish open sandwich made of rye bread piled high with delicacies, usually eaten for lunch. Some of the dishes I was looking for were items such as *frikadeller* (meatballs of veal and pork) and *hakkebøf* (minced-beef patties), or more substantial meat and fish dishes such as *flæskesteg* (roast pork with crackling) and *kogt torsk* (poached cod) with mustard sauce and trimmings. All these can be washed down with Danish beers, such as its market leaders, Carlsberg and Tuborg, or some of the lesser known brands, or akvavit and bitters.

Chapter 2

Cultural Copenhagen

At the far end of Strøget, I made my way to Tivoli Gardens, another well-known Copenhagen attraction. The city has the two oldest amusement parks in the world.

Dyrehavsbakken is a fairground and pleasure park that was established in 1583, located in Klampenborg, just north of Copenhagen in a forested area. Christian IV created it as an amusement park, complete with rides, games and restaurants, and it is the oldest surviving amusement park in the world. Pierrot, a fool dressed in white with a scarlet grin, wearing a boat-like hat while entertaining children, remains one of the park's key attractions. In Danish, Dyrehavsbakken is often abbreviated as Bakken.

The Tivoli Gardens is an amusement park located in central Copenhagen. It was opened in 1843, making it the second oldest amusement park in the world. Among its rides are the oldest, still-operating rollercoaster (Rutschebanen, from 1915), and the oldest Ferris wheel still in use, opened in 1943. Tivoli Gardens also serves as a venue for various performing arts.

It is the city's most visited tourist attraction with its fairground atmosphere, its Pantomime Theatre (opened in 1874, the oldest building in the Tivoli Gardens), its Concert Hall and many rides, stalls, restaurants and fast-food outlets. I had to return at dusk when the ambience picks up and it has something akin to a party atmosphere with bright colourful lights and music.

I was up early and started walking along the waterfront. Many of the sights that I wanted to see opened only mid-morning, so that gave early-risers like me a few hours to see things that don't have opening hours. I crossed the bridge over Nyhavn and through the Amaliehaven Gardens to the Gefion Fountain.

The fountain was donated to the city by the Carlsberg Foundation to celebrate the brewery's fifty-year anniversary in 1897, although it was completed only in 1908. It was originally supposed to be located in the main town square, outside city hall, but it was decided to build it near the Øresund in its current location near the Kastellet, a star fortress.

The fountain depicts the mythical story of the creation of the island of Zealand on which Copenhagen is located. The legend appears in the Ragnarsdrápa, a ninth-century poem recorded in the Prose Edda and in the Ynglinga saga.

According to the Ynglinga saga, the Swedish king Gylfi promised Gefjun all the land that she could plough in a night. She turned her four sons into oxen and the land they ploughed was then thrown into the Danish Sea between Scania and the island of Fyn. The hole became a lake called Lögrinn, but tourist information about the fountain identifies the resultant lake as Vänern, Sweden's largest lake, citing the fact that modern maps show that Zealand and the lake resemble each other in size and shape.

Just a little further up the waterfront is the Statue of the Little Mermaid; Copenhagen's most visited tourist attraction. For something that is so well known and visited, I was surprised that it was so small. The Little Mermaid is a Danish literary fairy tale written by Hans Christian Andersen. The story follows the journey of a young mermaid who is willing to give up her life in the sea as a mermaid to gain a human soul. The tale was first published in 1837 as part of a collection of fairy tales.

Just next door is the Kastellet, a well-preserved, five-pointed star fort built to protect the old harbour. However, it was yet to open, so I made my way further up the waterfront to the modern harbour. Years of substantial investment in sewage treatment have improved water quality in the harbour to an extent that the inner harbour can be used for swimming.

Shipping is an import sector of the economy with Maersk, the world's largest shipping company, which has its headquarters in Copenhagen with some of the largest and most energy-efficient container ships in the world.

They have 4.1 million TEUs (Twenty-Foot Equivalent Units, meaning containers) and seven hundred and five ships capturing seventeen per cent of the market. The contender for second place is the Mediterranean

Shipping Company with 3.9 million TEUs and five hundred and seventy-nine ships. Third is CMA CGM, a French company of which I was aware, as I had flown one of their aircraft in South America with three million TEUs and five hundred and fifty-seven ships with a twelve and a half per cent share of the market battling for position with COSCO, a Chinese company also with three million TEUs but only four hundred and ninety-nine ships. One surprise in the list of top shipping companies was ZIM, an Israeli company which, despite the country's small population came in at ninety-third in world terms, but its shipping company is tenth with four hundred and twenty-seven TEUs and ninety-eight ships.

Copenhagen Port has experienced a resurgence since 1990, following a merger with Malmö harbour with both ports operated by Copenhagen Malmö Port (CMP). The ports act as a hub for freight that is transported onward to the Baltic countries and annually services eight thousand ships.

Copenhagen's economy is based largely on services and commerce, with more than a third of a million workers employed in transport, communications, trade, and finance producing forty per cent of GDP, while fewer than ten thousand work in the manufacturing industries.

Agriculture production provides less than two per cent of GDP but Denmark is a major producer and exporter of pork products. Ranked by turnover, the largest Danish companies mirroring major sectors are A.P. Møller-Mærsk, Novo Nordisk (pharmaceuticals), ISS (facility services), Vestas (wind turbines), Arla Foods, DSV (transport), Carlsberg, Salling Group (retail) and Ørsted (power).

In contrast, the public sector workforce is around a hundred and ten thousand, including education and healthcare, whilst tourism is booming with six hundred and eighty thousand cruise passengers visiting the port in 2015. The city is a must-see destination and was given a boost in 2019 when Copenhagen was ranked first amongst Lonely Planet's top ten cities to visit.

I crossed some railway lines and walked on through a delightful park with several lakes, which also houses the Statens Museum for Kunst. It wasn't on my list of things to see but the building was attractive and perhaps I had misjudged Kunst's work. There were two temporary exhibitions on offer.

I allowed myself a short deviation from the schedule to visit it. The façade was interesting but internally, it was much like many other large, open spaces to house exhibits. Kunst's work was modern and colourful but not in keeping with the façade and whilst all the collections exercised my sense of what art should be, it was just a little too modern to make me linger too long and I was soon heading for the nearby Palm House of the Botanical Gardens The design takes its inspiration from the London's Crystal Palace originally built in Hyde Park for the Great Exhibition in 1851 but was subsequently moved to Sydenham Hill and with extensions, completed there in 1854. Another inspiration was the Kew Gardens Hot House in London, completed in 1863. The Palm House in Copenhagen is as magnificent as its inspirational forebears.

Just a few hundred metres away, I was back on schedule and visiting the Rosenborg Castle, a Dutch Renaissance-style castle originally built as a country summerhouse in 1606. It is an example of Christian IV's many architectural projects and although it has the word 'castle' in its name, it has no protecting outer wall. With numerous windows on the ground floor, it is more of a palace than a traditional castle and overlooks the oldest royal gardens.

It was used as a royal residence until 1710. After the reign of Frederik IV, Rosenborg was used only twice and on both occasions during emergencies. The first time was after Christiansborg Palace burned down in 1794 and the second was during the British attack on Copenhagen in 1801.

Located on the third floor, the Long Hall was completed in 1624. It was originally intended as a ballroom. Around 1700 it was used as a Royal Reception Room and for banquets. It was not until the second half of the nineteenth century that it became known as the Knight's Hall and houses a large collection of mainly seventeenth-century silver.

Christian V had the hall modernised with twelve tapestries depicting the King's victories in the Scanian War (1675–1679). The stucco ceiling seen today is from the beginning of the eighteenth century. It shows the Danish Coat of Arms surrounded by the Orders of the Elephant and of Dannebrog. There are other reliefs that depict historical events from the first years of the reign of Frederik IV.

Among the main attractions of Rosenborg are the coronation chair of the kings and the throne of the queens, with the three silver lions standing in front. Other exhibits include the Royal Collections and the treasury displaying the Crown Jewels.

It was then time to return to Kastellet, which would now be open. King Christian IV initiated Kastellet's construction in 1626 with the building of St Anne's Redoubt on the north coast of the city to guard the entrance to the port, together with a blockhouse that was constructed north of Christianshavn, which had just been founded on the other side of the strait between Zealand and Amager. At that time the fortifications reached only as far north as the present day Nørreport station, and then returned south east to meet the coast at Bremerholm. However, part of the king's plan was to expand the area of the fortified city by abandoning the old East Rampart and instead, extending the rampart directly north to connect it to St Anne's Redoubt. This plan was not completed until the mid-1640s.

After the Swedish siege of Copenhagen (1658–1660), the Dutch engineer Henrik Rüse was called in to help rebuild and extend the construction. The fortification was named Citadellet Frederikshavn, but it is better known as Kastellet (Citadel). The Kastellet was renovated 1989–

1999 with funds from the A.P. Møller and his wife Chastine McKinney Møller's General Fund.

The Kastellet has two gates, the King's Gate on the south side, facing the city, and the Norway Gate on the north side, both of which date from 1663 and are part of the original citadel. They are built in the Dutch Baroque style. The King's Gate is decorated with garlands and pilasters, and a bust of King Frederik III.

The former earthworks of the bastions now serve as a greenspace. It is a big space to walk about and there is plenty to see with guard rooms, barracks, the Commander's House, stables, storerooms, the Powder House, blacksmiths, a church and even a windmill built in 1847 to replace a 1718 post mill, which was destroyed during a storm.

There is also a prison, where English explorer and pirate John Norcross (1688 – 1758) was incarcerated for the longest period, a total of thirty-two years, half of them in a wooden cage. He was a Jacobite who had fled when the rebellion failed and served under Swedish pirates Lars and Ingela Gathenhielm. He was captured in 1727 and sentenced to life imprisonment. While he was released from the prison in 1745, he was confined to the castle until his death.

The citadel is still an active military base that belongs to the Ministry of Defence. Occupation includes use by the Home Guard, Defence Intelligence Service, the Judge Advocate Corps, and the Royal Garrison Library. There is a midday changing-of-the-guard ceremony at the Central Guard House every day.

From some of the higher points, there are views over the city, and over the water are the towers of the Øresund Bridge. A little nearer are the turbines of the Middelgrunden offshore wind farm, built in 2001, with twenty turbines with a rating of 40MW, which provides four per cent of the city's power. This was novel and innovative at the time, but miniscule by modern standards.

The largest currently operational wind farm is Hornsea 1 in the United Kingdom with one hundred and seventy-four turbines, rated at a total of 1,218MW. Second is Borssele in the Netherlands with one hundred and seventy-one turbines, rated at 1,483MW. This is followed by East Anglia ONE UK with one hundred and two turbines rated at 714MW, and all built in the last few years. The London Array plans to have one hundred and seventy-five turbines but is only rated at 630MW.

Other energy sources include large deposits of oil and natural gas in the North Sea but Denmark ranks at number thirty-two in the world among net exporters of crude oil, and produces a quarter of a million barrels of crude oil a day. Denmark is a long-time leader in wind power, which produces more than forty per cent of the country's electricity consumption.

I started the next day at the Copenhagen Cathedral, known as the Church of our Lady. Christianity is the dominant religion in Denmark with three quarters of the population members of the Church of Denmark, the officially established church, which is Protestant in classification and Lutheran in orientation. Membership, however, has been falling since the 1970s and yet only three per cent of the population regularly attend Sunday services.

Archbishop Absalon (1128–1201) started building the Church of St. Mary in 1187 and it was consecrated in 1209, but destroyed by fire in 1314. It was rebuilt in red brick. A school was built next door in 1479 and became the Copenhagen University. There was a troublesome period when Denmark chose to follow Lutheranism, but the Roman Catholic faithful tried to maintain it as a Roman Catholic church. However, its name was changed to satisfy Lutheran sensitivities, regarding including the word 'Saint' in the name of the church.

The cathedral was destroyed by a four-day-long conflagration in October 1728, destroying a third of the city, but it was rebuilt yet again in brick. That building didn't last long as it was destroyed in September 1807 during the bombardment of Copenhagen by the Royal Navy, under Admiral James Gambier, during the Napoleonic Wars.

The British had demanded the surrender of the Dano-Norwegian fleet to stop it falling into the hands of Napoleon. The Danes refused, but with most of the army on the Schleswig-Holstein border, the city lacked adequate forces. Royal Navy gunners used the tower of the church for range practice, setting it ablaze, which in turn burned the church to the ground, along with nearby sections of the city. Copenhagen surrendered and the fleet was turned over to the British.

Yet another church was built and completed in 1829 but controversially included a tower; not standard style for Neo-Classical styles, but the citizens demanded and got a tower. It is sixty metres high and contains four bells, the largest being the Stormklokken, cast in 1828, which is the heaviest bell in Denmark at four tons. The oldest bell in Denmark also hangs there, cast in 1490, taken from the former Antvorskov Kloster in Slagelse.

I walked on to the City Hall, an impressive building that was inaugurated in 1905 to replace a series of former buildings on the site that had been destroyed. It was designed in the National Romantic style, but with inspiration from the Siena City Hall. It is dominated by its richly ornamented front, the gilded statue of Bishop Absalon just above the balcony, and the tall, slim clock tower which, at over one hundred and five metres high, is a distinctive feature of the Copenhagen skyline which houses Jens Olsen's World Clock.

I walked along Hans Christian Andersen Boulevard, past the Tivoli Gardens and the Ny Carlsberg Glyptopek, to cross the central harbour to reach the Christianshavn district and its canal.

The area was developed by Christian IV in the early seventeenth century. Impressed by the city of Amsterdam, he employed Dutch architects to create canals within its ramparts. The canals, lined with houseboats, are one of the area's attractions. Another interesting feature is Freetown

Christiania, a fairly large area which was initially occupied by squatters during student unrest in 1971. Today it still maintains a measure of autonomy. The inhabitants openly sell drugs on Pusher Street, as well as their arts and crafts. Buildings of interest in Christianshavn include the magnificent Rococo Christian Church and the North Atlantic House, which displays culture from Iceland and Greenland and houses the Noma restaurant, known for its Nordic cuisine. I would check this out another time, but I was on my way to visit the Church of Our Saviour.

When Christian IV planned Christianshavn in 1617, it was intended as an independent merchants' town on the island of Amager. It therefore needed a church but construction did not start until 1682. It was designed in a Dutch baroque style.

The church opened in 1695, but the temporary altar was not replaced until 1732. The plans for the spire were altered and not completed until 1752. It used a novel design of a tower topped by a spiral spire, making it very distinctive. Visitors can climb up the inside to gain some marvellous views.

The black and golden spire reaches a height of ninety metres and the external staircase turns four times counter-clockwise around it. Inspiration for the design came from the spiral lantern of Sant'Ivo alla Sapienza, in Rome, which turns the same way.

There are a total number of four hundred steps to the top of the spire, the last one hundred and fifty being outside, though not open to the public. The spire is topped by a vase-like structure, carrying a gilded globe with a four-metre-tall figure of Christ Triumphant holding a banner. It has an infamous reputation for being the ugliest sculpture in Copenhagen, but it is intentionally constructed with exaggerated proportions because it is meant to be seen only from long distances.

There is an urban legend that the architect killed himself, by jumping from the top of the spire, when he realised that the spiral turns the wrong way (anti-clockwise). But it is an urban myth: the architect died in his bed seven years after it was completed.

The huge organ with Christian V's gilded monogram and a bust was built by the Botzen Brothers from 1698-1700 and is mounted on the wall and supported by two elephants. It has more than four thousand pipes with the original cymbelstern tinkling in the background during a special part of a musical piece. The church arranges between fifteen and twenty concerts every year, together with musical church services on Sundays.

The tower has a concert carillon, dating from 1928, that was rebuilt in 1980 and consists of forty-eight bronze carillon bells that have a musical range of four octaves, making it the largest carillon in Northern Europe. The largest bells weigh over two tons and the smallest, ten kilograms. They chime every hour.

For the rest of the day, or what was left of it, I wandered along the parks, across the bastions and ramparts of the eastern defences.

Chapter 3

Roskilde

During my walks in the city, I had passed a travel agent's along Strøget and had booked a day trip outside the capital: a whistle stop tour of Roskilde. I could have taken the train or a bus for the thirty-five-kilometre journey but I had decided to join a tour to get the benefits of a tour guide. I would enjoy the ease of getting about without the need to check timetables or work out my own itinerary.

I was picked up outside the front of my hotel and as I was the first person, I had a choice of seats and sat in the front. Then the minibus took a tour of the city, stopping at different hotels to pick up guests before heading out of the city to the countryside.

Almost all of Denmark's primeval temperate forests have been destroyed or fragmented, chiefly for agricultural purposes, during the last millennia. The deforestation has created large swathes of heathland and devastating sand drifts. In spite of this, there are several, larger, second-growth woodlands in the country and, in total, almost thirteen per cent of the land is now forested. Beech trees are common but Norway spruce is the most widespread tree.

Roe deer occupy the countryside in growing numbers and large-antlered red deer can be found in the sparse woodlands of Jutland. The forests are home to smaller mammals, such as polecats, hares and hedgehogs.

Large marine mammals include populations of Harbour porpoise, growing numbers of pinnipeds and occasional visits of large whales, such as blue whales and orcas. Cod, herring and plaice are abundant and form the basis for a large fishing industry.

Roskilde was developed as the hub of the Viking land and sea trade routes over a thousand years ago and is one of Denmark's oldest cities. From the eleventh century until 1443, it was the capital of Denmark: hence, on my theme of visiting the Baltic capitals, I just had to visit.

By the Middle Ages it had become one of the most important centres in Scandinavia. Roskilde was founded in the 980s by Harald Bluetooth on high ground overlooking the harbour. In 1997 archaeologists found the remains of Viking ships, the oldest of which is dated to 1030.

Harald was buried in the wooden church he had built on the site of today's Roskilde Cathedral. Bishop Absalon had a brick church built on the site of Harald's church in 1170. Today's cathedral was completed in 1275. Coins were minted there from the eleventh to the fourteenth century, increasing the city's importance.

In 1150, Sweyn Grathe built a moat around the city. In 1151, a religious confraternity was founded for the defence of the town against Wendish pirates. The Reformation brought Roskilde's development to an abrupt stop. While the cathedral continued to be the preferred location for the entombment of the Danish monarchs, most of the other religious institutions disappeared. For the next three centuries, the city suffered a series of disasters, including the effects of the Dano-Swedish War which ended with the Treaty of Roskilde in 1658, plagues in 1710 and 1711 and a series of fires in 1730. Conditions improved in 1835, when the city hosted the Assembly of the Estates of the Realm and in 1847, with the railway connecting Copenhagen and Roskilde.

Roskilde became an important hub for traffic with Copenhagen. In the 1870s, the harbour was extended, attracting industrial firms to the area. By the end of the century, there were tobacco factories, iron foundries and machine shops, but as ships increased in size, the harbour was too small and shallow for navigation, so development occurred elsewhere.

Our first stop was at Ledreborg Castle and despite having the word castle in the title, it is a stately home. In 1663, the statesman Henrik Müller purchased eight farms and five houses in Lejre and presented the property to his daughter Drude and her husband, statesman Thomas Finke, who built a house called Lejregård.

In 1739, Johan Ludvig Holstein bought the property and developed the modest building into one of the country's finest mansions. He commissioned Johan Cornelius Krieger to extend the building to the east and west. Krieger also added a chapel and a monumental staircase designed by Jacob Fortling. In 1745, Niels Eigtved developed the interior, including the Rococo banqueting hall, while Lauritz de Thurah decorated the inner courtyard with two pavilions and added obelisk-shaped lampposts.

Also designed by Krieger from 1742 until the mid-1750s, the terraced Baroque park extends from the mansion down the steep slopes of the Kornerup Valley. In the wooded area to the east, the Dyrehaven was laid out between 1757 and 1762, with paths leading past sculptures and obelisks.

After visiting the castle we were driven to the harbour, which is where the Viking Ship Museum is located. This is a museum exhibiting seafaring artefacts and has the remains of five, well-preserved, eleventh-century Viking ships. These were excavated from the fjord, twenty kilometres north of the city, in the 1960s.

The ships were scuttled there in the eleventh century to block a navigation channel to protect the city – then the Danish capital – from seaborne assault. The five Viking ships represent several distinct classes, such as the Longship and Warship, and smaller fishing and ferry boats. The ships on display range from three to fifteen metres. The museum's boatyard safeguards the Viking-boat building tradition by building and exhibiting full-scale replica ships on site.

I could have stayed longer but it was just a brief visit before reboarding the minibus. We were dropped off opposite the railway station and walked past the Roskilde Jars: three huge jars surrounded by shallow water. They are five metres high and weigh twenty-four tons. The jars are the work of the Danish abstract sculptor Peter Brandes (born 1944) and were commissioned by Elsebeth Stryhn of Stryhns Leverpostej, a local meat-paste producer. They were presented to the city in 1998 to celebrate Roskilde's thousandth anniversary.

We had a walk through the city centre with various locations pointed out, such as the Convent, Roskilde Museum, several old buildings and restaurants for lunch. One of the oldest restaurants in Roskilde is the Raadhuskælderen, in a building dated to 1430, noted for its salmon steak with tartare sauce and grilled chicken and cream sauce dishes. Also of note is La Brasserie on Algade, the Gimle Musikcafe on Ringstedgade, which is an English-style pub-restaurant with live music, and Restaurant Toppen at the top of a former water tower, eighty-four metres high, built in 1961, with fine views of the town.

The old town of Roskilde is centred around the main square, Stændertorvet, just south of the cathedral. The original street plan is preserved in nearby Skomagergade, Algade and Hestetorvet, although most of the buildings were rebuilt after fires in the eighteenth century. The area is flanked to the north by two large parks, Byparken and Folkeparken, which stretch down to Roskilde Fjord and the harbour.

We had some free time for lunch but were under strict instructions to assemble outside the cathedral for the afternoon visits. I was tempted by the menu and seafood choices at Raadhuskælderen. I can eat at any time but this was my first time in Roskilde, so I grabbed a sandwich from a supermarket and made my way back to the Roskilde Museum.

The museum has several branches but this branch is housed in two listed buildings, the Sugar House and the Liebe House. The Sugar House was built by a consortium led by Johan Jørgen Holst to process raw sugar from the Danish West Indies. The company also had its own ship, Roskilde Ark. Large vessels had only been able to travel as far up Roskilde Fjord as Frederikssund, where goods had to be transferred onto smaller boats to reach Roskilde harbour.

After pressure from the sugar company, the city agreed to construct a new pier and some dredging took place, which enabled their ship to continue all the way to Roskilde. Roskilde Ark brought raw sugar and coal to the factory and shipped processed sugar to other ports, continuing until the factory closed in 1779.

Next door is the Liebe House. In 1804, Jacob Borch constructed a large house on the site. It replaced a modest house with timber framing and a straw roof dating from the seventeenth century. The name of the building refers to the Liebe family who owned the property for two generations later in the century.

On the death of the last Liebe in 1900, he left the entire building complex to the Roskilde Municipality. Roskilde Local History Museum was founded in 1929 on the ground floor of the Liebe House. Meanwhile, in 1908, the Sugar House was used as a fire station, but when the fire station moved to new premises in 1989, Roskilde Museum took over the Sugar House.

I was dutifully outside the cathedral along with the other members of the group, at the appointed time, to be met by our guide. We went into the Roskilde Cathedral of the Lutheran Church of Denmark. This is the most important church in Denmark as it has been the official royal burial church of the Danish monarchs since the fifteenth century.

It shows eight hundred years of European architectural styles and is one of the earliest examples in Scandinavia of a Gothic cathedral to be built in brick. Constructed during the twelfth and thirteenth centuries, the cathedral incorporates both Gothic and Romanesque architectural features, but it has been significantly extended and altered over the centuries.

King Harald Bluetooth named Roskilde the new capital of Denmark around the year 960AD. The king had previously resided in Jelling, in Jutland, but after uniting the Danes and Norwegians, a move was necessary to enable the monarch to stay close to the centre of power in the new kingdom.

The construction of a simple stone church began in 1026, although construction of a cathedral was started by

Bishop Wilhelm after 1060 and was completed by his successor in 1080.

With the new cathedral completed, there was a desire to obtain a relic for it. Two canons were dispatched to Rome to find something suitable. Legend claims that while they were resting after their arrival, St Lucius, who had been Pope from 253AD to 255AD, appeared before them and told them that he had been chosen to be the patron saint of Roskilde.

The next day, the two canons were taken to Santa Cecilia in Trastevere to choose from the many relics there. They saw a skull shining brightly: the skull of St Lucius. On their return, their ship came under attack from a powerful demon that lurked in Danish waters. The crew drew straws and the lot fell on the canon carrying the skull of St Lucius. He offered a prayer to the saint, washed the skull three times, threw the water in the ocean, and jumped overboard. To everyone's surprise, the canon was able to walk on the water. The demon disappeared screaming into the depths, never to be seen again.

It is not known for certain which year the relic arrived in Roskilde, only the date – 25th August – as it is on that day that the relic's arrival has always been celebrated. The first written mention of the relic dates to Ælnoth, a monk in Odense, who described it in a work on the life of Canute the Holy in 1122. Another item, a seal carved from a walrus tusk, depicting St Lucius between the twin towers of the cathedral, has been dated to the same period.

Soon after Absalon became Bishop of Roskilde in 1157, he began to expand the cathedral. In 1160, the art of firing bricks was brought to Denmark from Italy by monks and the new material was employed. It was decided to build a new cathedral around the existing one, allowing services to continue during construction.

When he was forced to surrender his position as Bishop of Roskilde in 1191, only the two floors of the apse – the choir towers and part of the transept – had been completed. His successor, Peder Sunesen, embracing the new French Gothic style, made significant changes to the plans, tearing down the choir towers and reducing the width of the transept.

The choir was completed and inaugurated in 1225, allowing services to begin there, and the old cathedral was demolished. Work on the nave continued for the next fifty-five years, limited by funds and the lack of kilns to fire the bricks. With the exception of the two towers on the west facade, the cathedral was completed by 1280, and work on the interior proceeded, though slowed by a fire in 1282. Several chapels were also added to the cathedral, and in 1405, work on the towers was completed.

When Margrethe I died in 1412, she was buried in her family's chapel at Sorø Klosterkirke. But the following year, bishop Peder Jensen Lodehat, who had been the Queen's chancellor and religious advisor, brought her body to Roskilde Cathedral. The monks in Sorø were outraged, due partly to the loss of prestige but more likely to the significant loss in income from requiems, which would attract a fee; and for a queen, such requiems would probably have been conducted on a regular basis in perpetuity.

On 14th May 1443, a fire swept through Roskilde, destroying most of the city. The fire was so intense that the glass windows cracked, and the lead roofing melted. In order to help with its reconstruction, the bishops of Denmark each signed a letter granting forty days of indulgence to whomever would contribute to its cost. The reconstruction was helped by the decision of Christian I to build the Chapel of the Magi and together with the sarcophagus of Margrethe I and the remains from the previous churches, it marks the earliest royal burials. It was not until 1463 that the bishop could rededicate the cathedral.

While the cathedral suffered financial hardship, as its treasures and possessions were confiscated, including one in every four farms on Zealand and thirty large estates, it was endowed with a variety of gifts from Christian IV. These included a royal box in 1600, the pulpit in 1610, his own burial chapel in 1614, the altarpiece in 1623, the construction of the iconic twin spires in 1633 and finally, a grand Renaissance sandstone entrance portal in 1635.

In 1806, the cathedral sold its inventory of items from its Catholic days at a notorious auction. Among the items sold was a grand crucifix, which went to a local coppersmith. While he was sawing the crucifix into firewood, the head of Jesus split open and a small, golden cross fell out. It was hollow and hidden inside was a splinter from Christ's cross. Rumour of the find quickly reached the Royal Art Collection, later the National Museum of Denmark, which immediately purchased it.

There are many side chapels to see and the tour took longer than had I been by myself, but that is just one of the drawbacks on joining a tour. At last, the final anecdote had been told, the last chapel visited and we were making our way to the last site on the agenda – the Royal Mansion, also known as the Yellow Palace.

The building seen today replaced a bishop's palace, which had stood at the site since the Middle Ages. Commissioned by King Christian VI, the new building was constructed to provide a residence for the royal family when they visited Roskilde. Lauritz de Thurah had recently been engaged as royal master builder: he was charged with its design in 1733 and the palace was completed in 1736.

During the English siege of Copenhagen in 1807, the mansion served as the headquarters of General Wellesley, the future Duke of Wellington. Later in the century, it provided a venue for the so-called Assembly of the Estates, a key event leading up to the adoption of the constitution in 1849.

Built in the Baroque style, with yellow-painted masonry and a red-tiled roof, the four-winged complex consists of a two-storey main wing, two one-storey lateral wings and a curved gate wing opening onto the Stændertorvet.

The facade of the main wing has pilasters and a median risalit tipped by a triangular pediment decorated with the royal coat of arms. Dating from the thirteenth century, the Gate of Absalon, which connects the mansion to the apse of Roskilde Cathedral, is the only surviving part of the former bishop's palace.

Since 1924, one of the wings has been home to the office and official residence of the Bishop of Roskilde. The rest of the complex houses the Roskilde Museum of Contemporary Art, founded in 1991, as well as the Roskilde Art Association and the Palace Collections.

The next day I made my way by public transport to Lyngby, just north of Copenhagen, to the Open Air Museum. I just can't get enough of these museums. For me such a visit ticks so many boxes: the countryside, a pleasant walk, architecture, history, culture, the atmosphere, the furniture, the gardens and the animals. And despite the numbers that I have visited and the number that I planned to visit over the next three months, I never tire of them.

The buildings have been collected from all over the country to represent different styles, periods and trades. There are old breeds of domestic animals in the fields and many of the buildings have flower and vegetable gardens.

Chapter 4

Castles and cemeteries

I made my way to Frederiksberg Slot, the Frederiksberg Palace. By some international conspiracy, many museums around the world are shut on a Monday, but I had checked and unusually, this one was open. As crown prince, Frederick IV broadened his education by travelling abroad: he was particularly impressed by the architecture in Italy. On his return to Denmark, he asked his father, Christian V, for permission to build a summer palace on Solbjerg Hill in Valby. Construction started in 1699.

The original building was designed and completed in 1703 as a small, one-storey summer residence. The first major extension occurred in 1709, when it was converted into a three-storey, H-shaped building, giving the palace an Italian Baroque appearance. It was Lauritz de Thurah who executed the third and final extension, between 1733 and 1738, when the palace received extensions to the lateral wings, linked by a semi-circular building creating the courtyard.

In 1716, Frederick IV received the Russian Tzar Peter the Great at the palace and in 1721, shortly after the death of his first wife, Queen Louise, he married his mistress Anne Sophie Reventlow there.

Frederick VI liked the palace so much that he lived there both as crown prince and as king. After Frederick VI's dowager wife Queen Marie died at the palace in March 1852, the building lay empty and fell into disrepair. In 1868, it was transferred to the War Ministry and the following year it became the Officers' Academy.

The building has twice undergone significant restoration work, first from 1927 to 1932 and again from 1993 to 1998. The chapel was designed in the Baroque style and consecrated in 1710. When the palace was taken over by the Officers' Academy, the chapel's furnishings, including the impressive pulpit, were dismantled. However, they were returned in the 1930s.

The palace is surrounded by the Frederiksberg Gardens created for the original palace in 1703. It was designed as a symmetrical Baroque garden with waterfalls and rows of linden trees. From 1795 to 1804, it was re-developed as an English landscape garden, with winding paths, lakes, islands, canals and the Chinese Summerhouse, to create the gardens that can be seen today.

Next door to the palace is Copenhagen Zoo with its black tower and observation platform at the entrance. It attracts 1.2 million visitors a year. In 2014, it was involved in a controversy. A healthy, young, male giraffe, Marius, was put down on the recommendation of the European Association of Zoos and Aquaria, and the meat was fed to the zoo's lions. The scientific director defended the cull, saying that the giraffes at the zoo bred very well, so some might have to be culled for space and to ensure that only the best genes were passed down.

I wasn't interested in visiting a zoo. I was heading off in the opposite direction to look around Assistens Kirkegård, the Assistens Cemetery (meaning an assistance cemetery) to satisfy my passion for funereal architecture. An assistenskirkegård was originally a generic term in Danish used to refer to cemeteries which were created to complement existing burial sites.

In 1666, the Naval Holmen Cemetery was moved from its original cramped location to a site outside the Eastern City Gate as the first burial facility to be located outside the city. An outbreak of plague in 1711, which killed twenty-three thousand citizens put the existing burial sites under so much pressure that up to five coffins were sometimes buried on top of each other. This led to the establishment of five new cemeteries on the periphery of the city but just inside the city walls, while the military Garrison Cemetery was relocated to a site next to that of Holmen Cemetery.

In 1760, the City Council opened a large new cemetery outside the city walls. The cemetery was intended as a burial ground for paupers. In 1785, an affluent citizen, writer and First Secretary of the War Chancellery, Johan Samuel Augustin, made a specific request to be interred at the cemetery. He was soon followed by other leading figures from the elite, and the cemetery soon developed into the most fashionable burial ground of the city.

Around that time, excursions with picnic baskets to the cemetery became a popular activity. A commission established in 1805 issued instructions prohibiting the consumption of food or drink, as well as music or any other kind of cheerful behaviour in the cemetery.

The gravediggers, who lived on the premises, were to enforce these restrictions but they seem to have taken their duties lightly: legislation was introduced in 1813 to prohibit them selling alcohol to visitors. Despite these efforts, the desired peace and quiet was a long time coming. For particularly grand funerals, crowds of spectators would gather and people would climb the cemetery walls to get a better view. There was talk of introducing admission fees to reduce visitor numbers but this was never carried out. Many leading figures, such as Hans Christian Andersen, Søren Kierkegaard, Christoffer Wilhelm Eckersberg and Christen Købke, are buried here.

Late in the nineteenth century, as the cemetery filled up, a number of new cemeteries were established around Copenhagen, but it continued to attract notable people. Among the latter were the Nobel Prize-winning physicist Niels Bohr and a number of American jazz musicians who settled in Copenhagen during the 1950s and 1960s, including Ben Webster and Kenny Drew. The cemetery covers more than twenty-five hectares and is still used as a green space for picnics, exercise and a quiet place to read a book in the shade of some of the many trees.

I walked down Åboulevard to Søpavillonen, Lake Pavillion, an historic building completed in 1895 to a Historicist design set on the embankment between Peblinge Lake and Sankt Jørgens Lake, both part of the former defences of the city that were decommissioned and left to civilian authorities in 1868.

I walked on to Ørsteds Park, another remnant of the city's former defences. The park was named after the Ørsted brothers, the politician and jurist Anders Sandøe Ørsted and the physicist Hans Christian Ørsted, who are both commemorated with monuments in the park.

I was making my way towards Torvehallerne, a well-known food market in the city. I wanted to see the sights and smells of a local market. I was a bit disappointed in the architecture as the building was completed only in 2009. I had hoped for a traditionally built old market.

There are two, covered market-hall areas with a partially covered area in between. There are more than eighty stall holders. It was late in the day but many of the stalls were still open, displaying their wares. It was a colourful display but it has moved upmarket from just a group of green grocers. There are crowded, fast-food stalls doing a roaring trade and plenty of options available from all over the world.

Until you visit, you never know whether it is a functional vegetable market or an upmarket site selling a whole range of produce including clothes, bric-a-brac and souvenirs. Although this was a functional vegetable market to serve the city, there were also many stalls selling manufactured upmarket products, from clothes to scented candles.

I moved on to my last, scheduled tourist stop of the day at the Rundetårn, the Round Tower. It was one of the many architectural projects instigated by Christian IV in the seventeenth century, built as an astronomy observatory in a Dutch Baroque design in 1637. The building is known for its equestrian staircase, a 7.5-turn helical corridor leading to the platform at the top at 34.8 meters high, to give expansive views over the city. On clear days, the Øresund Bridge and Sweden can be seen in the distance.

The tower is part of the Trinitatis Complex which provided university scholars with the Trinitatis Church and the first Copenhagen University Library. It is Europe's oldest functioning observatory. Astronomy had grown in importance in seventeenth-century Europe, due to countries establishing colonies abroad to expand their influence, empires and trade. Longer voyages created the need for accurate navigation across the oceans. Many national observatories were therefore established, the first in 1632 at Leiden in the Dutch Republic.

The existing, timber-framed houses on the site were demolished and the foundations were created using stone recycled from the city ramparts. Bricks were imported from the Netherlands as local manufacturers could not meet the high-quality standards required. The design called for alternating layers of yellow and red bricks, the colours of the Oldenburgs, the ruling house.

The tower was completed in 1642 but the church and library were completed only in 1657. There were several breaks in the construction timetable due to shortages of funds, made up by asking every church throughout Denmark and Norway for a proportion of their income to fund the project to completion.

Every year, in the spring, a unicycle race is held in the Round Tower. The contestants have to cycle up and down the tower. The world record, set in 1988, is one minute and 48.7 seconds.

I walked through the early-morning crowds along Strøget and across Kongens Nytorv, exiting the square along Bredgade. When I was level with Frederiks Kirke, I turned to reach the Amalienborg Palace Museum.

Christian IV had acquired land outside Copenhagen's old, walled city and the first palace built on the site was called Sophie Amalienborg, commissioned by Queen Sophie Amalie, consort to Frederick III. Other parts of the estate were used for Rosenborg Castle, Nyboder, and the new, eastern fortified wall around the old city. It included a garden, a replacement for the Queen's Garden, which had been located beyond the city's western gate, but had been destroyed during a siege by Sweden in 1659.

Work on the new garden began in 1664 and the palace was built between 1669 and 1673. The King died in 1670, and the Queen Dowager lived there until her death in 1685. In 1689, Sophie Amalie's son, King Christian V, celebrated his forty-fourth birthday at the palace with a German opera, but a stage decoration caught fire, causing the theatre and the palace to burn to the ground with the deaths of one hundred and eighty people. The remaining buildings were demolished.

The second Amalienborg palace was built by Frederick IV, at the beginning of his reign, as a summerhouse with a central pavilion boasting orangeries and arcades on both sides. On one side of the building was a French-style garden, and on the other were military drill grounds. The project consisted of four, identical mansions to be built to house four, distinguished, noble families from the royal circles, placed around an octagonal square.

When the Royal Family found itself homeless following the Christiansborg Palace fire of 1794, the palaces had been empty for long periods throughout the year, with the exception of the Brockdorff Palace, which housed the Naval Academy.

The noblemen who owned them were willing to part with their mansions for promotion and money. Immediately after the Christiansborg Palace fire, Christian VII purchased the Moltke and a few days later, the Schack Palace was acquired. Since that date, successive royal family members have lived at Amalienborg as a royal residence.

The four palaces were renamed and Moltke's Palace became Christian VII's Palace; Levetzau's Palace became Christian VIII's Palace; Brockdorff's Palace became Frederick VIII's Palace and Schack's Palace became Christian IX's Palace.

A colonnade was added in 1794 to connect the king's palace, known as the Christian VII Palace, with that of the Crown Prince's palace, now called Christian IX's Palace.

According to Eigtved's master plans for the four major buildings surrounding the plaza, they were to have identical exteriors but the interiors differed. The sites on which the nobility could build were given to them free of charge and they were exempted from taxes and duties. The only conditions were that the palaces should comply exactly with the Frederikstad architectural specifications and that they should be built within a specified time. Building of the palace on the western side of the square started in 1750 and the last palace was completed in 1760.

Currently, only the palaces of Christian VII and Christian VIII are open to the public. Christian VII's Palace was originally built for Lord High Steward Adam Gottlob Moltke. Moltke's Palace was built from 1750 to 1754. It was the most expensive of the four palaces at the time and had the most extravagant interiors. Its Great Hall featured woodcarvings by Louis August le Clerc, paintings by François Boucher and stucco by Giovanni Battista Fossati, and is acknowledged widely as perhaps the finest Danish Rococo interior. Since 1885, it has accommodated prominent government guests and receptions, and used for ceremonies.

After his death in 1808, Frederick VI used the palace for his Royal Household. The Ministry of Foreign Affairs used parts of the Palace in the years 1852-1885. For short periods of time in the intervening years, the palace has housed various members of the royal family while restoration took place on their respective palaces.

Christian VIII's Palace was originally built for Privy Councillor Count Christian Frederik Levetzau in 1750–60. It is the north-western palace and was the home of Crown Prince Frederik until 2004. On Levertzau's death, the palace was sold, but the family set a condition, when they sold the building, that the Count's coat of arms should never be removed from the building. It can still be seen beside that of the monarch's today.

Christian VII's half-brother, Frederik, bought the palace in 1794 and modernised the interiors in the new French Empire style. The palace was named Christian VIII's Palace after his son, Christian Frederik, who took over the building in 1805 upon the death of his father, and would become king in 1839.

Christian VIII died young in 1848 and after the Queen Dowager, Caroline Amalie, died in 1881, the Ministry of Foreign Affairs used parts of the palace from 1885 to 1898.

In the 1980s, the palace was restored and used as a residence for the Crown Prince, storage facilities for the Queen's Reference Library and a museum for the Royal House of Glücksborg. The museum features private royal apartments from 1863 to 1947, including original fittings and furnishings.

Amalienborg is guarded day and night by the Royal Life Guards in their colourful full-dress uniform and bearskin hats. The guard marches daily from Rosenborg Castle at eleven thirty a.m. through the streets of

Copenhagen and celebrates the changing of the guard in front of Amalienborg at noon. A smaller ceremony to rotate guard duties, known as post replacement, is conducted every two hours.

Between the Amalienborg and the waterfront is the Amaliehaven Gardens. It was created in 1983 as a gift from the A.P. Møller and Chastine McKinney Møller Foundation to the citizens of Copenhagen. After the grandeur of a tour through the palaces, it makes a nice change for some fresh air and a break from the intense culture. There are trees for shade, several marble statues, a central fountain and a chance to sit and have a packed lunch and look across the water to the Copenhagen Opera House; that ugly building in sharp contrast to the traditional styles of the palaces.

Along the waterfront, I came to the Nyhavn canal, which stretches up to the spacious square of Kongens Nytorv, which was laid out by Christian V in 1670. Important buildings include Charlottenborg Palace, famous for its art exhibitions; the Thott Palace (now the French embassy); the Royal Danish Theatre and the Hotel D'Angleterre, dating from 1755. The canal is lined with colourful houses from the seventeenth and eighteenth centuries, many now converted to lively restaurants and bars. Hans Christian Andersen lived here for a while.

I was giving myself a strong dose of culture as I made my way along the waterfront to the Ny Carlsberg Glytotek, an art museum. Ny means new in Danish whilst Glyptotek is a portmanteau word which comes from the Greek root glyphein (to carve) and theke (storing place).

The display is built around the personal collection of Carl Jacobsen, 1842–1914, the son of the founder of the Carlsberg Breweries. He was an obsessive collector of antique sculpture but there are also many modern sculptures and paintings in the collection, as his interests spread to include French impressionists, post-impressionists, Danish Golden Age paintings, and all the bronze sculptures of Degas.

When his private villa was extended in 1882 and its winter garden opened to the public, sculptures soon outnumbered plants. In the following years, the villa was expanded on a number of occasions to meet the need for more space for his steadily growing collections. By 1885, his 'house' had grown to a total of nineteen galleries, a re-design of the gardens and some of the collection was on display in the brewery. A larger premises was required.

In 1888, Carl Jacobsen donated some of his collection of modern art to the Danish State and the City of Copenhagen on condition that they provided a suitable building for its exhibition. Copenhagen's old fortifications had recently been decommissioned and a site was chosen on a ravelin facing the city ramparts, just south of the Tivoli Gardens.

Carl Jacobsen chose the name for the museum inspired by Bavarian Ludwig I's Glyptothek in Munich. The museum was opened in 1897. In 1899, Jacobsen donated his collection of antique art to the museum, thereby necessitating an expansion, inaugurated in 1906.

The museum not only houses a number of great pieces of art but is also of architectural merit. The Dahlerup Wing is the original part of the museum, built in a lavish Historicist building. The façade is red brick with polished granite columns in a Venetian Renaissance style. It houses the French and Danish collections.

There were other wings added as the museum expanded, such as the Kampmann Wing built in a neo-classical style with a central auditorium used for lectures, concerts and poetry readings and noted for its good acoustics. The two wings are connected by the Winter Gardens with mosaic floors, tall palms, a fountain, and topped by a dome made in copper and wrought iron.

There are many other wings and collections on display including Egyptian, Greek, Roman, the Etruscan collection which is the largest outside Italy. The largest by far is the French collection, comprising nineteenth-century French paintings and sculptures.

The French painting collection contains works by such painters as David and Manet, as well as a large collection of Impressionist painters, including Monet, Cézanne and Bonnard. Paul Gauguin is represented by more than forty works. The museum also holds a large collection of French, nineteenth-century sculpture by artists such as Carpeaux and Rodin, the Rodin collection being the largest in the world. The Danish Collection holds an impressive collection of Golden Age paintings by artists including Eckersberg, Købke and Lundbye. It also contains the largest representation of Golden Age sculpture in the country.

Late night opening is Thursday. It wasn't a Thursday, it was getting late and I was becoming tired. I had already seen a lot of culture so some of the galleries I just walked through, looking to left and right but not stopping to linger unless something really gripped my imagination. I had intended this just as an add-on to my day, but hadn't realised how much there was to see and should have made it a focus of a major day of culture rather than just as an 'extra'.

I was looking forward to moving on to the next leg of the trip but I had one, last, full day in Copenhagen to visit the Christiansborg Slot, Christiansborg Palace, which lies on Slotholmen, surrounded by a canal on three sides and the main water front on the fourth side. It is a former palace, the seat of the Danish Parliament, housing the Danish Prime Minister's Office and the Supreme Court. Some areas are also still used by the monarch. The palace is unique, as it houses all three supreme powers of government: the executive, the legislative and the judicial powers.

The present building is the third to be built on the site since the first castle was built in 1167. The first two were destroyed by fires in 1794 and 1884. The current building was finished in 1928, in Neo-baroque style, although the chapel dates from 1826 and is in a neoclassical style and the showgrounds were built from 1738-46.

On Absalon's death in 1201, possession of the castle and city of Copenhagen passed to the bishops of Roskilde. However, there was a long feud for two centuries between the church and monarchy over ownership, not helped by frequent attacks by pirates and the Hanseatic League, as it controlled access between the Baltic and North Seas. From 1249, it was plundered and occupied for the next decade.

In 1369, King Valdemar IV of Denmark was defeated by the Hanseatic League, who demolished the original castle. A new castle with ramparts was built. It was only in the middle of the fifteenth century that the castle became the principal residence of the Danish kings and the centre of government.

In the 1720s, Frederick IV entirely rebuilt the castle, but it was so heavy on the soft grounds that the walls began to crack. Christian VI recognised the need for a new design. Work began in 1731 to replace the castle with the first Christiansborg palace, which was completed in 1745, becoming the largest palace in northern Europe at the time. The kings didn't have much time to enjoy it, as it was destroyed by fire in 1794. The king moved to Amalienborg Palace and construction on the second palace started in 1803 in a French Empire style. When it was completed in 1828, King Frederik VI decided not to move in and only King Frederik VII lived in the palace between 1852-1863. This building was also destroyed by fire in 1884.

The current and third palace was constructed between 1907-1928. This time it was built of reinforced concrete with a granite facade and a copper roof, although some of the ruins were incorporated into the design. A weather vane with two crowns was later added to the tower and at one hundred and six metres, it became the tallest tower in the city.

During the groundworks to create the foundation, some ruins of Absalon's original castle were discovered. It was decided to make them publicly accessible and the ruins and a historical exhibition opened to the public in 1924. Several parts of the palace are open to the public.

Despite being a recent construction, the Royal Reception Rooms located on the ground floor and first floor are richly adorned with furniture and works of art rescued from the two earlier palaces, as well as contemporary designs by some of the best Danish artists. The rooms are used for the monarch's official functions, such as banquets, state dinners, diplomatic accreditations, audiences and meetings of the council of state.

Visitors are taken through the Hall of the Halberdiers, the Audience Chamber, the King's Stairway, and the Tower Hall with its tapestries. The Tower is open to the public to give views across the city. Other magnificent rooms include the oval Throne Room and the Great Hall, which is over forty metres long with a gallery.

The first floor of the Parliament Wing is structured around the Lobby. At each end of the Lobby are the chambers of Rigsdagen, the former bicameral parliament; the Folketing and the Landsting chamber, although this has been unused since 1953 when the Folketing became the sole legislative assembly.

The tour continues via some of the ruins, the chapel and the extensive Royal Stables, home to the many carriages used for ceremonies. There is a lot to see and a lot to remember and endless stories and anecdotes. It is expensive but it is also fascinating.

I didn't realise that there was so much to see and therefore how long it would take. There were some other visits planned whilst I was in the area, but I was feeling a little overawed and tired after being on my feet for so long. I walked through the Danish War Museum but I just walked past the outside of the other two venues that I had planned to visit, such as the 1640 Borsen Stock Exchange, which is a beautiful building. The other building was the Royal Library which, disappointingly, was a modern steel, glass and concrete box. Founded in 1648, it is the largest library in the Nordic countries with an almost complete collection of all printed Danish books since 1482. I headed back to the hotel to pack.

Chapter 5

Train to Sweden

It was a short walk from the hotel towards the Tivoli Gardens and the railway station just beyond it. I was catching the train to Stockholm. Air travel is quicker from point A to B, except for the time that you need to get to the airport, pass through security and sit around waiting for your flight to take off, not to mention the process at the other end to collect your luggage, the journey into the centre of the city and the carbon footprint.

Rail travel is often from one city centre to another, without the long time in airport security queues, waiting lounges and onward travel. Pricing is also an issue as aircraft fuel, by international convention, is not taxed when flying between signatory states, thus distorting pricing and the consumers' choice between more carbon-friendly rail and air travel.

We all like low prices but it is about time that consumers were more concerned about their actions for the benefit of the whole of society. After the damage to economies caused by COVID restrictions and the huge amounts of spending by government-support programmes, it should be time that governments worked together to tax aviation fuel to both generate revenue and cut carbon emissions to meet their carbon-reduction obligations. It is our responsibility to support them for the benefit of the planet, rather than selfishly continuing to contribute towards massive global warming.

I love rail travel: you don't need all that time for security scans and for baggage handling issues, while the rail ticket is instantly transferable to the next departure and you can see so much more of the countryside. The train pulled out of the station and soon passed through several tunnels as it picked up speed. It skirted the northern end of the Copenhagen airport and dived into a tunnel which forms part of the Øresund Bridge.

I had planned to observe it from the water on a boat tour, but after viewing it from both the Rundetårn and the Christiansborg Palace Tower, I had seen enough of it to cut the boat tour out of my schedule, but I still had to have the experience of crossing it for myself.

The start of the crossing to Malmö in Sweden is the four-kilometres-long Drogden Tunnel from the Danish island of Amager to Peberholm, an artificial island. At Peberholm the eastern portal of the Drogden Tunnel emerges and there is a massive combined rail and road bridge across the Øresund strait between Sweden and Denmark. It was the longest, combined road and rail bridge connection in Europe, running nearly eight kilometres from Peberholm, in the middle of the strait, to the mainland in Sweden, until Vladimir Putin illegally annexed the Crimea and built the Kerch Strait Bridge to connect occupied Ukrainian Crimea to mainland Russia.

The Øresund Bridge was the final link for the road and rail networks to directly connect Sweden, via several Danish islands, to the Jutland Peninsula and ultimately to the rest of Europe. The expensive twin-tunnel/bridge design was required to avoid interfering with air traffic from the nearby Copenhagen Airport, where the northerly flight-path take-offs cross the route and prohibited the building of a tall suspension bridge required to cross the gap. The tunnel also provides a clear channel for ships, even in bad winter weather, and prevents ice floes from blocking the strait.

There is a strait between Helsingør in Denmark and Helsingborg in Sweden further north, less than half the distance of the Øresund strait, between Copenhagen and Malmö. That option was soon discarded: it would have required a vast amount of investment in infrastructure to reach it and a journey back to Malmö of over sixty kilometres, with a significant increase in both costs and journey times.

Construction of the Øresund crossing began in 1995. Several connections had been proposed over the past decades but this was the one that got the finance and go-ahead to be built. Despite two potential setbacks, such as the discovery of sixteen unexploded Second World War bombs on the seafloor, and an inadvertently skewed tunnel segment, the bridge-tunnel was finished three months ahead of schedule and opened to traffic in 2000.

The bridge company is jointly owned by the Danish and Swedish states. The construction was financed by loans guaranteed by the governments to be repaid by toll income. The cost for the Øresund bridge, including motorway and railway connections on land, was DKK 30.1 billion or USD4.85 billion.

Taxpayers have paid for neither the bridge nor the tunnels, but tax money has been used for the land connections. On the Danish side, the land connection has domestic benefits, mainly to connect the airport to the railway network. The Malmö City Tunnel has the benefit of connecting the southern part of the inner city to the rail network and allowing better train connections with the Swedish rail network.

Traffic levels have increased as people move out of expensive city centres to live on the other side of the Øresund and choose to commute further to work. About sixty per cent of passengers cross by road and the balance by train, with annual numbers of crossings of over four million continuing to rise.

At seven thousand eight hundred and forty-five metres, the bridge covers half the distance between the two countries. The structure has two railway tracks beneath four road lanes. On both approaches to the central cable-stayed bridge section, the track bed is supported every hundred and forty metres by concrete piers.

The two pairs of free-standing, cable-supporting towers are two hundred and four metres high, allowing shipping fifty-seven metres of headroom under the main span of four hundred and ninety-one metres, but most ships' captains prefer to pass through the unobstructed Drogden Strait, above the Drogden Tunnel, with more room to manoeuvre in case of difficulties.

The connection between Copenhagen and Peberholm is by the four thousand and fifty metre-long Drogden Tunnel. It comprises a three thousand five hundred and ten metre immersed tube, plus two hundred and seventy metre entry tunnels at each end. The tube tunnel is made from twenty, prefabricated reinforced concrete segments, some of the largest in the world at fifty-five thousand tonnes each, laid in a trench dug on the seabed. Two tubes in the tunnel carry railway tracks, two carry roads and a small fifth tube is provided for emergencies.

The tunnel emerges on Peberholm (Pepper Islet). The name was chosen to complement the natural island of Saltholm (Salt Islet), just to the north. Peberholm is a designated nature reserve built from rock, sand and mud dredged up during the bridge and tunnel construction. The island is four kilometres long and an average width of fifty metres and up to twenty metres high.

Trains run on the left in Sweden and on the right in Denmark. Initially the switch was made at Malmö Central Station. After the 2010 inauguration of the Malmö City Tunnel connection, a flyover was built at Burlöv, north of Malmö, where the two southbound tracks cross over the northbound pair.

Both Sweden and Denmark are signatories to the Schengen Agreement, which removes border and passport controls between participant countries. However, in January 2016, during the European migrant crisis, Sweden was granted a temporary exemption under the terms of the Schengen Agreement in order to mandate that all travellers across the bridge had photographic proof of identity.

Therefore, travellers into Sweden must show a valid passport or national ID card and entry visa, if required. The move marked a break with sixty years of passport-free travel between the Nordic countries. Passengers from Sweden do not have to go through checks to enter Denmark: the checks take place on board.

There were a couple of stops before reaching the Copenhagen airport station. The train then entered the Drogden Tunnel and exited on Pederholm to cross the bridge. Seventeen minutes later came the next stop at Hyllie station in Sweden. Three quarters of an hour after leaving Copenhagen, I had arrived in the Malmö main station where I was due to change trains.

The journey time between Copenhagen and Stockholm by train is about five and a half hours, faster if you take the (more expensive) express. The time to change trains, if you are in a hurry, is only a few minutes but I had purposefully taken an early train to have several hours in Malmö, Sweden's third city after Stockholm and Gothenburg, but still arrive in the capital during daylight hours.

My plan was a walking tour around the city. I had visited it years before but I couldn't remember very much and it was just a fleeting visit between trains. Before the bridge was built, the journey times were a lot longer, as passengers needed to take the slow ferry and it was an all-day journey compared with the just-over-an-hour option by air.

My first stop was Sankt Petri Kyrka, (St Peters Church), a brick-built church inaugurated in 1319 that was the largest parish church in what was then part of Denmark. It suffered as one of only four occurrences of violence due to iconoclasm during the Danish Reformation when, in 1529, Claus Mortensen led the destruction of the ornamentation in the church, deemed as too Catholic by the Reformer. In later years, the interiors were whitewashed. Today, much of the ornamentation has been reintroduced.

I walked past Stortorget, a square where building started in 1538 and through Little Torg, originally an open market but it became fashionable with substantial half-timbered and brick-built town houses and is an architectural gem. It has many restaurants spilling out into the square. After walking through the Kingsparken and Slottsträdgården, both beautiful and colourful parks overlooking the moat around Malmöhus Slott (Malmö Castle), and past an old windmill in the Slottsträdgården, I reached the causeway entrance into the castle.

The first castle was founded in 1434 by King Eric of Pomerania. This structure was partially demolished in the 1530s and a new one was built in its place by King Christian III of Denmark, to become one of Denmark's strongest fortresses.

It has a connection with British history as it was used as the prison for James Hepburn, fourth Earl of Bothwell for the period 1568–1573; the third husband of Mary, Queen of Scots. The earl was taken into custody when his ship ran aground in Bergen, Norway, during a storm. He was sent to Malmö Castle to be imprisoned, although he had previously been released from the Tower of London for lack of evidence regarding the murder of Mary's second husband, Henry Stuart, Lord Darnley. The king had hoped for a ransom to be paid for his release. He was later transferred to Zealand and died there in 1578.

The train left Malmö station on its four and a half-hour journey to Stockholm. Although I was travelling second class, the seats were luxurious. The special glass in the windows kept the heat of the sun out of the carriage, assisted by efficient air conditioning.

I had made sure that I reserved a window seat facing the direction of travel, so I could stare at the scenery as it sped by. After leaving the marshalling yards outside the station, there is straight track, where the train picked up speed towards Lund. With new rolling stock, engines and some straightening of the track, an hour has been knocked off the travel time to Stockholm.

After leaving the urban area, there were fields that we whizzed past. The route passed the northern shores of Ringsjön. We stopped only at major settlements and shot through several small, local stations. As we headed north, the fields slowly gave way to forest. We skirted several lakes with their brilliant blue surfaces shimmering and sparkling in the summer sun.

We slowed as we passed Glan, a lake outside Norrköping, as the railway took several turns to cross the river Motala that flows out of Glan into the Baltic and cuts across some hills. After leaving the main station in Norrköping, we passed along part of the estuary of the Motala and I was on the last leg of the journey to Stockholm. We crossed several bridges over some of the fourteen islands on which Stockholm is located, on the estuary of the river that runs out of Lake Mälaren, Sweden's third largest lake to the main station.

I walked back across the bridge that I had just crossed on the train to find my hotel in Gamla Stan (Old Town). From archaeological evidence, the original settlers here are thought to have been Vikings in 1000AD, although the settlement of present-day Stockholm appears only in written records as late as 1252.

The first part of the name (stock) means log in Swedish, whilst the second part of the name (holm) means islet. According to legend, the previous capital of Sweden was located in Sigtuna, sixty kilometres to the north, which was continually raided by Karelians.

The situation became untenable and there was a need to find a new location for the capital. The leaders in Sigtuna took a tree trunk, hollowed out the centre, filled it with gold and pushed it into the water. The log drifted with the currents for several days and was then washed up on an island: this was where the new capital was to be built.

It had the advantage that an island is easier to defend and it was nearer the sea for trade.

Dendrological examinations of logs found on Helgeandsholmen, just north of Stadsholmen in 1978–1980, concluded that these trees were cut down during the period 970–1020, suggesting that this was when a settlement was first founded here. The city originally developed as a result of the Baltic trade with the Hanseatic League. Stockholm developed strong economic and cultural links with other major trading cities, such as Lübeck, Hamburg, Gdansk and Riga.

The strategic and economic importance of the city made Stockholm an important contributor within the three crowns of the Kalmar Union of present day Denmark, Norway, Sweden, including, at the time, Finland plus Norway's overseas colonies. These included Iceland, Greenland, the Faroe Islands, and the Northern Isles of Orkney and Shetland from 1397 to 1523.

In 1520, a massacre of opposition figures, called the Stockholm Bloodbath, took place when Swedish noblemen were murdered by the Danish King Christian II. The following revolt and civil war led to the dissolution of the Kalmar Union and independence for Sweden.

The seventeenth century saw Sweden grow into a major European power. In 1634, Stockholm became the official capital of the Swedish empire. From 1610 to 1680, the population multiplied sixfold and trading rules were passed that gave Stockholm an essential monopoly over trade between foreign merchants and other Scandinavian territories. However, the economic development was damaged in 1710 when a plague killed twenty thousand, over a third of the population.

The Swedish Empire had expanded to include present day Finland, parts of Norway and Russia, around St Petersburg, Estonia and some possessions in Germany. It was at its largest extent in 1658. But Sweden could not hold on to all of their disparate empire.

The Great Northern War (1700–1721) was fought between Russia and Sweden, with a host of Russian allies (including the Polish Lithuania Commonwealth, Denmark, Prussia and Hanover), who battled against Sweden's allies (including the Ottoman Empire, the Crimean Khanate and the Dutch Republic).

Allies can be fickle, depending upon where their national interests lie, and can be bought off. Several allies withdrew or changed sides, including Britain who firstly supported Russia, yet swapped in 1719 to support Sweden. Sweden was overwhelmingly defeated by Russia and lost a lot of its possessions, ceasing to be a significant European power. But having an extensive empire also meant wealth and history, which is reflected in some of the grand buildings seen today.

Russia gained land at the extreme east of the Baltic on which St Petersburg stands today, and an ice-free harbour that it had always wanted. Stockholm's population growth halted and its economy stagnated.

By the second half of the nineteenth century, Stockholm had regained its leading economic role. New industries emerged and Stockholm was transformed into an important trade centre. The population grew dramatically during this time, mainly through immigration. At the end of the nineteenth century, less than forty per cent of the residents were Stockholm-born and even today, nearly a third of the city's population were not born in Sweden.

Stockholm became a modern, technologically advanced, and ethnically diverse city in the latter half of the twentieth century, with more than eighty-five per cent of the working population employed in service industries. The almost total absence of heavy industry and fossil fuel power plants makes Stockholm one of the world's cleanest metropolises.

The city was granted the 2010 European Green Capital Award by the EU Commission, which was the first time that the award was made, making Stockholm Europe's first green capital. Applicant cities were evaluated taking into account climate change, local transport, public green areas, air quality, noise, waste, water consumption, wastewater treatment, sustainable utilisation of land, biodiversity and environmental management.

Out of thirty-five participant cities, Stockholm faced some strong competition from seven other finalists, namely Amsterdam, Bristol, Copenhagen, Freiburg, Hamburg, Münster and Oslo. As an aside, Stockholm is twinned with twenty-three other cities, and as I looked down the list, I realised that I had visited eighteen of them.

Chapter 6

Swedish Palaces

I went for a walk, in the late afternoon, around Gamla Stan. Many historical buildings were demolished during the modernist and functionalist era, 1930-35, including substantial parts of the historical district of Klara, but many buildings in the old centre survived. The area dates back to the thirteenth century and is a mass of medieval alleyways with cobbled streets. North German architecture has had a strong influence and there are many tall, narrow town houses painted in distinctive colours, a feature of many northern European cities.

I made my way to Stortorget, which is the large Medieval square in the centre, surrounded by old merchants' houses and the former Stockholm Stock Exchange Building. It was originally a small market but expanded following a fire in the early fifteenth century. The square was the site of the Stockholm Bloodbath.

I walked north to the cathedral, which claims to be the oldest church in Stockholm, inaugurated in 1306. The exterior of the church is Baroque as the result of extensive changes made in the eighteenth century. Inside, it maintains much of its late medieval appearance with a vaulted ceiling supported by brick pillars. During the Middle Ages, it was dedicated to Saint Nicholas, but after the Reformation it became a Lutheran church, not formally dedicated to any saint.

For a long time, the building was the only church in Stockholm and from an early date it was connected with the Swedish royal family. It has been the scene of historical events on numerous occasions and was used as a coronation church for centuries. Royal weddings and military victories, as well as national tragedies, have been commemorated here and it is still used for funerals of public figures. The church contains several important works of art and furnishings: among these is a late medieval sculpture of St George and the Dragon, and Vädersolstavlan, a painting of one of the earliest images of Stockholm.

I continued west towards the Bonde Palace, a prominent monument to the era of the Swedish Empire, completed in 1667 as the private residence of the Lord High Treasurer Gustaf Bonde (1620–1667). It later housed the Stockholm Court House and since 1949, it has been the home of the Swedish Supreme Court.

Next door is the Riddarhuset (House of Nobility), built in the seventeenth century and where the Riksdag of the Estates met, the second highest authority in the kingdom after the king. In 1866, the Riksdag was replaced by the new Parliament of Sweden. From then on, the building served as a quasi-official representative body for the Swedish nobility. Maintaining records, it acts as an interest group on their behalf. It was still open and despite being near to closing time, on the spur of the moment, I entered for a quick walk through. The walls of the Session Hall are decorated with the two thousand three hundred and twenty-six coats of arms of the Swedish aristocracy.

I crossed the bridge onto Ridderholmen, a small but separate island to the east of Gamla Stan, to visit the Riddarholmskyrkan, (Riddarholmen Church), dating from the late thirteenth century, making it just a bit older than the cathedral. This church is Stockholm's only surviving medieval abbey and is the final resting place of Swedish monarchs, with the exception of Queen Christina, but all subsequent rulers of Sweden from Gustav II Adolf (d. 1632) to Gustaf V (d. 1950) are buried here. Some kings from the Middle Ages are also interred here, such as Magnus Ladulås and Karl Knutson Bonde (d. 1470).

I walked along the waterfront of Gamla Stan. Across the water in Södermalm, I could see the spire of the Sta Maria Magdalena Kyrka, (St Mary Magdalene Church) and behind it Söder Torn, a eighty-six-metre-tall residential tower with its strange structure on the roof.

I cut inland to wander through some of the streets to make my way back to the main square. From the nineteenth century, Gamla Stan was considered a slum, but it has become a tourist attraction due to the charm of its medieval and Renaissance architecture.

As the city started to become overcrowded in the fourteenth century, new buildings were built on the shores outside the city wall and over the water. The main streets had stipulations about width, but people started building out into the streets, so some are just narrow, twisting alleys, which are characteristic for the old town.

Archaeological excavations have shown that the oldest streets were covered with wood, the oldest being found under the northern end of Västerlånggatan from around 1250–1300, and up to three metres below current levels.

During the latter part of the fourteenth century, stone paving formed the streets and the archaeological deposits above them contain few finds. Waste was often simply poured out into the alleys and streets. A few medieval subterranean wooden tubes and vaulted underground chambers have been found, but few traces remain of the sort of sophisticated system of sewers found, for example, in Visby and Bergen.

The present alleys give only a vague glimpse of life in the medieval city. Without a sewer system, waste was thrown into the streets to add to household waste and although the numbers of animals were restricted inside the city, they also added to the filth on the streets and the smells of dung, fishing, forges and leather tanning could not be disguised by breweries, food and seasonal spices.

I passed Den Gyldene Freden (The Golden Palace) a restaurant located on Österlånggatan. It has been in business since 1722 and according to the Guinness Book of Records, it is the longest operating restaurant with an unchanged environment and is one of the oldest restaurants in the world. It is now owned by the Swedish Nobel Academy who have their 'Thursday luncheons' there every week.

Claiming to be the oldest restaurant is a crowded market, with Restaurante Botín in Madrid making a bid, but operating from only 1725. It was immortalised by frequent patron Ernest Hemingway in his book 'The Sun Also Rises'. Another contender is Zum Franziskaner, located in south east Gamla Stan. It specialises in German and Swedish cuisine, and the current location dates back only to the turn of the twentieth century. However, the menu remains much the same as it was when German monks established the restaurant back in 1421.

It was getting late but it was still sunny and warm. Stockholm lies further north than mainland Britain on similar latitudes as Oslo, Helsinki and St Petersburg. With an average of just over eighteen hundred hours of sunshine per year, the city is one of the sunniest in Northern Europe, receiving more sunshine than several other major European cities at more southerly latitudes. At the height of summer, the nights are relatively short in contrast to about eighteen hours of daylight. In the bright sunlight of an early evening, I made my way to Zum Franziskaner for my evening meal.

Despite the sun shining for eighteen hours a day, the city still works on a nine-to-five basis and I was awake early and ready for another day. I had seen several communal bike stands the previous day and so I spent a little time researching.

From April to October, it is possible to rent a Stockholm City Bike by purchasing a bike card online or through retailers. Cards allow users to rent bikes from any Stockholm City Bike stand across the city and return them to any stand. There are two types of cards; either the Season Card or a short-period, three-day card. When their validity runs out, they can be reactivated and are therefore reusable. It is typical of the Swedes to choose a green option, so I rearranged my planned visits to make use of the three-day card to its fullest.

Not only is there an international conspiracy to close museums on a Monday, but very few museums open early: ten a.m. seems to be a commonly accepted time. No good to some of us early birds, but at least some stay open late into the evening. I always looked for things to do early in the morning.

I wandered around some of the back streets and on my way to the Royal Palace, I found Bollhustäppa (The Ball House Patch) – home to a fifteen-centimetre-tall, wrought-iron statue called Järnpojke (Iron Boy). For some reason it is called Little Boy Looking at the Moon in English, the smallest statue in Stockholm created by Liss Eriksson in 1967. It is colloquially called Olle.

The statue is caressed by crowds of tourists every year, as the shiny head shows, and it is given coins for good luck. Stockholmers knit scarfs and caps for the boy to wear during winter. The coins that tourists give to the sculpture are periodically collected by the Finnish Church.

I was first in the queue to enter Kunglika Slottel (Royal Palace). The first building on this site was a fortress with a tower, built in the thirteenth century by Birger Jarl, to defend Lake Mälaren. The fortress grew to a castle, eventually named Tre Kronor due to the main tower's spire top decorated with three crowns. This building was destroyed by a fire in 1697, except for the recently constructed northern walls, which are still standing.

The site was cleared and building work started on a palace measuring one hundred and fifteen by one hundred and twenty metres. Building started during the reign of Charles XII, but the costly campaigns during the Great Northern War slowed progress. Charles XII was defeated at the Battle of Poltava in Ukraine in 1709, and that same year the construction of the palace came to a complete halt with just the ground-floor walls completed. The palace remained in limbo until 1727, when the Riksdag granted funds to continue the work, but construction would continue until 1771.

The State Apartments were completed in 1753 and the Royal Family moved from the Wrangel Palace on Riddarholmen to their new residence. Several major changes were made to the colour of the facade but eventually the light-yellow brick facade was painted over during the reign of Oscar II (1829 - 1907) until a decision was made to return to the original architects' choice of red.

Oscar II ordered a number of additions, improvements and modernisations to the palace. Most of the empty facade niches were filled with sculptures. He had the palace's installations updated, such as installing piped water in 1873, electricity in 1883, telephone in 1884 and central heating in 1900.

The palace is made of brick and sandstone from Gotland and roofed with copper. The facades of the palace were each given their own design. A triumphal arch in splendid Baroque style frames the entrance. Ever since the palace was built, the weathering of the sandstone has been a problem and this has accelerated since the oil-based paint was removed from the stone during the renovation in the 1890s. In 2008, a comprehensive study was commissioned to make a long-term plan for maintenance of the palace.

The study showed that the Gotlandic sandstone was in worse condition than expected. A number of stones were cracked and loose. The biggest facade renovation in the history of the palace started in 2011 and is planned to take twenty-two years. In order to provide matching stone for the project, a sandstone quarry on Gotland was re-opened and a new masonry school opened.

It is a huge place to visit, but I had my audio guide and dutifully stopped and listened to the commentary at every numbered stop. There are four floors to see and a mezzanine, numerous state apartments, museums, furnishings and exhibits.

What piqued my interest most were the many stories of the palace ghosts. One of them is the Gubben Grå (Old Grey Man), who, according to tradition, lives in the cellar ruins of the old Tre Kronor Castle. He is considered to be a kind of guarding spirit for the palace and he is able to predict the future. According to other legends, it is the ghost of Birger Jarl.

The most noted of the palace's ghosts is the Vita Frun (White Lady). A similar ghost is sighted in many castles throughout Europe. According to legend, the White Lady is a messenger of death for someone in the royal family, and appeared when someone was about to die. She is tall and wears a white, silk dress and only the rustle of the silk is heard as she approaches. There are several theories as to who she might be and where she comes from.

According to one theory, she is the Duchess Agnes of Merán, a German noble lady from the House of Hohenzollern, who lived in the 1200s. She was married to Count Otto of Orlamünde until he died in 1293. She murdered both her children by him in order to marry Albrect, a Count from Nurnberg, but he abandoned her. She died in prison and has, since then, been appearing in Hohenzollern castles in connection to important family events.

Other sources claim that the White Lady is Perchta von Rosenberg, daughter of Ulrich II von Rosenberg, a German noble woman from the fifteenth century, who was unhappily married against her will to Jan of Liechtenstein. She also allegedly appears in the Český Krumlov Castle in southern Czech Republic.

Deaths of members of the royal family have occurred in connection with the appearance of the White Lady in the palace. In March 1871, Princess Eugenie saw the ghost and three days later, Queen Louise died. The White Lady appeared again in 1907 and shortly after that, King Oscar II died. The last time she was seen was in 1920, when Princess Margaret lay dying. A guard is said to have seen the White Lady on the roof: two hours after this, the princess died.

After a long visit to the royal palace, I crossed the bridge and walked around Riksplan, some gardens on an island in front of the palace. It was lunch time and it seemed to be crowded with people. Stockholm is ranked as the tenth most visited destination in Europe, with over ten million overnight stays per year, so it is not surprising that the parks are busy at the height of summer.

Opposite the Riksplann is the Medeltidsmuseet (Medieval Museum). It is a small but modern museum that opened in 1986 and won the European Museum of the Year Award. The artefacts were found whilst digging an underground car park and the plans were changed to make way for the museum. The museum enables visitors to experience medieval Stockholm, with its brick houses and booths, workshops, harbour, gallows and part of the city walls. It relates the medieval history of the city from the 1250s to the 1520s.

I walked back over the bridge past the palace and cathedral to the Stock Exchange, although they moved out in 1999. It is a beautiful building, built from 1773 - 1778 and looks more like a palace than a trading floor. Now, a small part of it houses the Nobelmuseet (Nobel Prize Museum), while other areas are home to the Swedish Academy and the Nobel Library.

I was visiting as much to see the architecture as the exhibits, but my interest was piqued as I couldn't imagine what might be on show. I was familiar with the story of how the family rose to prominence, manufacturing dynamite and guns, but when described as the 'merchant of death', Alfred established the Nobel Peace Prize. The museum showcases information about the prize and prize winners, as well as information about the founder of the prize, Alfred Nobel (1833–1896). The museum's permanent display includes many artefacts donated by Nobel Laureates.

I picked up my bike and cycled onto the mainland, heading north to reach Östermalms Saluhall. It is a marketplace for the public to buy food and delicacies, plus there are a number of cafes. The three thousand square-metered hall was built in just six months and opened in 1888. The facade is built of red brick with lots of fine, decorative brick work. The building is dominated by a corner tower with a slate roof crowned by a lantern. Behind is a complicated cast-iron structure of pillars supporting the roof with roof lights.

From here I cycled out of the city and across the bridge to reach the island of Lidingö. I was making my way to Millesgården, an art and sculpture museum garden and the former home of sculptor Carl Milles (1875–1955) and his wife, artist Olga Milles (1874-1967).

They built the house in 1908 and from the beginning, there was a plan that the house would be based around art. In 1936, Millesgården was transformed into a foundation which was handed over as a gift to the Swedish people. The Woodland Chapel was added in the late 1940s and is the burial site of both Carl and Olga Milles. I am always in two minds about modern art, but I like to challenge myself.

My next outing by bike was to cycle to Skansen on the island of Djurgården, the first open-air museum and zoo in Sweden, opened in 1891 by Artur Hazelius (1833–1901) to show the traditional rural way of life.

Society was rapidly changing to an urbanised and industrialised society and many feared that the country's traditional customs and occupations might be lost to history. Artur Hazelius was inspired by the open-air museum founded by King Oscar II in Kristiania in 1881. Skansen became the model for other early open-air museums in Scandinavia and elsewhere.

After extensive travelling, Hazelius bought around one hundred and fifty houses from all over the country (as well as one structure from Telemark in Norway) and had them shipped, piece by piece, to Skansen, where they were rebuilt to provide a unique picture of traditional Sweden. Only three of the buildings in the museum are not original and were painstakingly copied from examples he had found.

Skansen attracts more than 1.3 million visitors each year. It was crowded but I was in my element and I checked out every building. The many exhibits over the thirty-hectare site include a nineteenth-century village in which craftsmen in traditional costume, such as tanners, shoemakers, silversmiths, bakers and glass-blowers, demonstrate their skills. There are gardens growing vegetables, rare breeds of farm animals and displays of folk dancing and traditional folk music.

There is also a zoo containing a range of Scandinavian animals, including bison, brown bear, moose, grey seal, lynx, otter, reindeer, wolf, and wolverine, plus some non-Scandinavian animals because of their popularity.

My third cycling trip was back to the same island but this time to visit the Vasamuseet, (Vasa Museum), which displays the only, almost fully intact seventeenth century ship that has ever been salvaged; namely the sixty-four-gun warship Vasa that sank on her maiden voyage in 1628. The museum opened in 1990.

The main hall contains the ship itself and various exhibits related to the archaeological finds of early seventeenth-century Sweden. The conserved Vasa has been fitted with the lower sections of all three masts, a new bowsprit, winter rigging, and has had certain missing or heavily damaged parts replaced. The replacement parts have not been treated or painted and are therefore clearly visible against the original material that has been darkened after three centuries underwater. The ship can be seen from six levels, from her keel to the very top of the stern castle. Around the ship are numerous exhibits and models portraying the construction, sinking, location and recovery of the ship.

The museum also features four other ships moored in the harbour, such as the ice breaker Sankt Erik (launched in 1915); the lightvessel Finngrundet (1903); the torpedo boat Spica (1966); and the rescue boat Bernhard Ingelsson (1944). I moved on to the Nordiskmuseet (Nordic Museum), which I had seen from Skansen the day before.

Opened in 1873, it is a substantial building, founded by the same Artur Hazelius connected with the later Skansen attraction, and dedicated to the cultural history and ethnography of Sweden from 1520. Hazelius bought or begged donations of objects like furniture, clothes and toys from all over Sweden and the other Nordic countries.

Hazelius hoped for government support. None came, initially, but he received widespread support and donations, particularly in 1898 from the Society for the Promotion of the Nordic Museum. Parliament eventually allocated funds in 1891 and doubled the amount in 1900.

The present building was completed in 1907 after a nineteen-year construction process using granite and red brick. Originally, it was intended to be a national monument housing the material inheritance of the nation. However, it was not completed to the extent originally planned at three times the present size. It takes its style from Dutch-influenced Danish Renaissance architecture (similar to the Frederiksborg Palace), rather than any specifically Swedish historical models.

At the core of the building is a huge hall, one hundred and twenty-six metres long, rising the height of all storeys up to the roof and dominated by the enormous sculpture of King Gustav Vasa, who founded Sweden. The museum has over one and a half million objects in its collections.

There is a research library and the museum archive houses an extensive collection of documents and approximately six million photographs dating from the 1840s.

I didn't return straight away, but cycled the short distance to the Abba Museum, just to see what it looked like. It was a non-descript building but popular with fans to see the waxworks, costumes, caricatures and artefacts. For a non-fan, it was expensive but I walked through quickly, not stopping to gaze in awe or read any of the signs and trying not to listen to the constant round of Abba hits being played over the tannoy.

I was soon on the bike again and cycled to the central bus station, parked the bike and handed in my pass to be reused. I checked times and fares for the next day's excursion and then filled in time before my evening meal. I was close to the iconic landmark of the Stockholm City Hall, built 1911–1923.

It is built of twelve million red bricks, has two courtyards and a one hundred and six-metres high tower at one corner, with three hundred and sixty-five steps to ascend, with the Swedish three-crowns symbol at the pinnacle. It is famous for its Blue Hall, although there are no blue decorations due to a change in the design during construction.

The organ in the Blue Hall, boasting ten thousand two hundred and seventy pipes, is the largest in Scandinavia. Above the Blue Hall lies the Gyllene Salen (Golden Hall), named after the decorative mosaics made of more than eighteen million tiles recalling events from Swedish history. The building also displays a sculpture of the log that floated ashore on Gamla Stan, which was the founding of the city.

I had originally planned to cycle to Dottningholm Palace for the exercise: the rented bicycles are okay for short trips around the flat city landscape but, as I had discovered on my trip to Millesgården, they are heavy and poorly geared as compared with my carbon fibre racing bike at home. I hadn't found a city-bike stand nearby Dottningholm Palace on the internet, so I changed my plans and I was at the central bus station early in the morning for an alternative mode of travel.

Drottningholms Slott (Drottningholm Palace) is the private residence of the Swedish royal family, located on Lovön Island. It was built in the late sixteenth century and served as a regular summer residence to the Swedish royal court for most of the eighteenth century. It is built of yellow stone under a grey slate roof and is a spectacular, sprawling building overlooking Lake Mälaren.

The name Dottningholm (Queen's Islet) came from the original Renaissance palace built in 1580 by John III of Sweden for his queen, Catherine Jagellon. The Queen Dowager Regent Hedwig Eleonora bought the building in 1661 but it was destroyed by fire. She engaged architects and work started in 1662, taking more than two decades to complete.

Hedwig Eleonora ruled as regent for the underage king, Charles XI of Sweden, from 1660 to 1672. Sweden had grown to be a powerful country after the Peace of

Westphalia that ended the Thirty Years' War (1618 - 1648) (between Sweden, Bohemia, Savoy, Dutch Republic, Denmark, Prussia, and later France, against the Habsburg Monarchy, Spanish Empire and Bavaria, plus a host of smaller allies on either side) brought calm, closing a calamitous period of European history that killed approximately eight million people. Her position as queen of an important European power demanded an impressive residence located conveniently close to the capital.

The court was often present, using it for hunting, whilst Hedwig Eleonora used the palace as a summer residence, ruling Sweden during the absence of Charles XII during the Great Northern War until her death in 1715.

In 1744, the palace was gifted from King Frederick I to the then Crown Princess, later Queen of Sweden, Louisa Ulrika of Prussia when she married Adolf Frederick of Sweden, who became King of Sweden in 1751. During Louisa Ulrika's ownership of Drottningholm, the interior of the palace was transformed into a more sophisticated French Rococo style.

During the reign of Charles XIV (r. 1818–1844), the palace was abandoned. The King regarded it as a symbol of the old dynasty and Drottningholm was left to decay. Oscar I of Sweden took an interest in the palace and although he preferred Tullgarn Palace as a summer residence, he took care to preserve the palace by doing the first repairs in 1846.

Both Oscar I and Oscar II were criticised for modernising the palace and adjusting it to contemporary fashion, rather than restoring it to its original state, and it was not until the reign of Gustav V that the palace was reconstructed to its eighteenth-century appearance.

The current Swedish royal family have used the west wing of Drottningholm as their primary residence since 1981. Since then, the palace has also been guarded by the Swedish Military in the same fashion as Stockholm Palace.

The Drottningholm Palace Theatre is the opera house located there. It is still in use and its summer opera festivals are popular. The Chinese Pavilion, located on the grounds of the Drottningholm Palace park, is a Chinese-inspired royal pavilion built in 1763–1770.

The back of the building overlooks extensive gardens, established in stages and resulting in different styles of parks and gardens. There is a baroque garden with tree-lined avenues and several statues taken by the Swedish army as spoils of war from the Wallenstein Palace in Prague, while the two marble lions at the main gate of the palace were taken from the Ujazdów Castle in Warsaw.

Chapter 7

Hanseatic League and Lübeck

It was time to move on, so I walked to the central train station. I had taken the train to reach Stockholm but to get back to Copenhagen, I was going to fly so I was here to catch the Arlanda Express to the airport. I went back to the same hotel where I had started my Baltic Capital journey. My plan was to hire a car but when I enquired, the insurance would not cover me to drive across the border unless I paid a large extra fee and returned the car to Denmark. There are no border controls but if I had an accident, the insurance would be invalid. So, I took the train to Lübeck in Germany.

I had taken the train on this route before but this time the journey was very different. Denmark consists of the mainland called Jutland and a series of islands. In the past, the passengers would get off and the train was shunted onto the ferry. It was functional and interesting to watch but time-consuming.

Now, there is a tunnel and bridge connection, like the Øresund connection, across the strait between Zealand (where Copenhagen sits) and Funen, and a bridge between Funen and Jutland, cutting hours off the journey.

I had to change trains in Hamburg. It was an eighteen-minute break if you are in a hurry, but I had taken an early train from Copenhagen to purposefully spend a few hours in Hamburg but still arrive in Lübeck during daylight hours.

I had visited the city several times, though not recently. It wasn't a capital, so I didn't intend to spend much time here. I walked around the city centre and although I recognised the main station, I didn't recognise anything else. Either it had changed, or my memory wasn't accurate. It could be just that I didn't walk down the right streets, so I was disappointed. I boarded the train to Lübeck.

After just half an hour, I was crossing bridges across two separate branches of the Trave Canal and into the Altstadt (Old Town) in Lübeck to find my hotel. The astute reader will notice that I didn't stop in Hamburg, as it isn't a capital, so why was I stopping in Lübeck? Simply because Lübeck was the capital of the Hanseatic League.

The Hanseatic League was a commercial and defensive confederation. It grew from a few North German towns in the late 1100s to dominate trade for three centuries across the Baltic and the North Sea, along the coast of Norway, into Russia and westwards to France and England.

Its aim was to protect their economic interests, guilds and diplomatic privileges. The Hanseatic cities had their own legal system and operated their own armies, creating a powerful economic and defensive alliance that left a great cultural and architectural heritage, such as its brick, Gothic-style monuments of Stralsund's St Nikolai Church and its city hall. Despite this, the organisation was not a state, nor could it be called a confederation of city-states as only a very small number of the cities were free cities.

Scandinavians led international trade in the Baltic before the Hanseatic League, establishing major trading hubs at Birka, Haithabu, and Schleswig by the ninth century. The later Hanseatic ports, along the German coast between Mecklenburg and Königsberg, (present-day Kaliningrad), originally formed part of the Scandinavian-led Baltic trade system.

Historians generally trace the origins of the Hanseatic League to the 1159 rebuilding of the north German town of Lübeck by the powerful Henry the Lion, Duke of Saxony and Bavaria. German cities achieved domination of trade in the Baltic with striking speed during the thirteenth century and Lübeck became a central hub in the seaborne trade that linked the North and Baltic seas.

Long before the term Hansa appeared in a document in 1267, merchants in different cities began to form guilds with the intention of trading with other towns. The towns raised their own armies with each guild required to provide levies, a form of conscription, when needed. The Hanseatic cities were obliged to come to the aid of one another and commercial ships were often used to carry soldiers.

Visby had functioned as the leading centre in the Baltic before the Hansa. Visby merchants established a trading post at Novgorod (Gutagard) in 1080. Merchants from northern Germany also stayed there until they established their own trading station nearby, known as Peterhof, after they were granted privileges that made their positions more secure in 1229.

Hansa societies worked to remove restrictions on trade for their members. The earliest recorded example was in 1157, when the merchants of the Hansa in Cologne convinced King Henry II of England to exempt them from all tolls in London and allow them to trade at fairs throughout England. Hamburg became a free imperial city in 1189, as did Lübeck in 1226, where traders were required to trans-ship goods between the North Sea and the Baltic.

In 1266, King Henry III of England granted the Lübeck and Hamburg Hansa a charter for operations in the country and it became the largest Hansa operation in England.

Existing territorial governments, who had failed to provide security for trade, were surpassed by the Hansa, who promoted co-operation for security covering their major trade routes. The principal city remained Lübeck, where the first general diet of the Hansa was held in 1356, when the Hanseatic League acquired an official structure.

Lübeck's location on the Baltic provided access for trade with Scandinavia and Veliky Novgorod (Great Newtown) in Russia, placing it in direct competition with the Scandinavians who had previously controlled most of the Baltic trade routes. A treaty put an end to this competition and Lübeck merchants gained access to the inland Russian port of Novgorod, where they built a trading post known as a Kontor (Office).

The league never became a closely managed, formal organisation. Assemblies of the Hanseatic towns met irregularly in Lübeck for a Hansatag (Hanseatic Day), from 1356 onwards, but many towns chose not to attend, and decisions were not binding. A network of alliances grew to include a flexible roster of between seventy to one hundred and seventy cities, as some joined, and others left.

The league succeeded in establishing additional Kontors in major centres, such as Bruges and Bergen. These Kontors became significant enclaves. The London Kontor was established in 1320 and stood west of London Bridge, near Upper Thames Street, on the site now occupied by Cannon Street station. It grew into a significant, walled community with its own warehouses, church, offices and houses, reflecting the importance and scale of trading activity on the premises.

Starting with trade in coarse woollen fabrics, the Hanseatic League had the effect of bringing both commerce and industry to northern Germany. As trade increased, newer and finer woollen and linen fabrics, and even silks, were manufactured in northern Germany. The same refinement of products out of cottage industry occurred in other fields, such as armour production, engraving, wood-turning and carving. Their century-long monopolisation of sea trade ensured that the Renaissance arrived in northern Germany long before it did in the rest of Europe.

In addition to the major Kontors, individual ports had a representative merchant and warehouse. In England this happened in Boston, Bristol, Bishop's Lynn (now King's Lynn, which features the sole, remaining Hanseatic warehouse in England), Hull, Ipswich, Norwich, Yarmouth (now Great Yarmouth) and York.

The league's early primarily traded items from the Baltic included timber, wax, amber, resins, furs, flax, honey, wheat and rye, brought to ports by barge from farms inland from the east, with cloth and manufactured goods going in the other direction. Metal ores, principally copper and iron, plus herring, came southwards from Sweden.

The cities' strategic locations along trade routes were a great advantage. At the height of their power in the late-fourteenth century, the merchants of the Hanseatic League succeeded in using their economic power and, sometimes, used their military might to protect ships and trade routes and to influence imperial policy.

The league wielded power overseas in its collective interests. Between 1361 and 1370, it waged war against Denmark. Initially unsuccessful, the Hanseatic towns in 1368 allied with the Confederation of Cologne, and collectively sacked Copenhagen and Helsingborg forcing Valdemar IV, King of Denmark, and his son-in-law Haakon VI, King of Norway, to grant the league fifteen per cent of the profits from Danish trade in the subsequent peace treaty of Stralsund in 1370, thus gaining an effective trade and economic monopoly. This treaty marked the height of Hanseatic power.

The Hansa also waged a vigorous campaign against pirates. Between 1392 and 1440, the league's maritime trade faced danger from raids of the Victual Brothers and their descendants, privateers hired by Albert of Mecklenburg, King of Sweden, against Margaret I, Queen of Denmark.

In the Dutch–Hanseatic War (1438–1441), the merchants of Amsterdam sought and eventually won free access to the Baltic, and broke the Hanseatic monopoly. As an essential part of protecting their investment in ships and their cargoes, the League trained pilots and erected lighthouses. Lübeck has the second tallest lighthouse at one hundred and fourteen metres.

Most foreign cities confined the Hanseatic traders to certain trading areas and to their own trading posts. They seldom interacted with the local inhabitants, except when doing business. Many locals envied the power of the League and tried to diminish it. For example, in London, the local merchants exerted continuing pressure for the revocation of privileges. The refusal of the Hansa to offer reciprocal arrangements to their English counterparts exacerbated the tension. The very existence of the League, with its privileges and monopolies, created economic and social tensions. The league wasn't always triumphant. Tsar Ivan III of Russia closed the Hanseatic Kontor in

Novgorod in 1494. In 1597, Queen Elizabeth of England expelled the League from London.

The economic crisis of the late fifteenth century did not spare the Hansa. It was also known as the Great Bullion Famine and was caused partially by poor harvests and the famines of 1457 - 1464 reducing tradable goods, increasing prices and the outflow of precious metals, mainly gold and silver but also copper, used to trade with the Middle East and Asia. This was not matched by mining output.

Other innovations were threatening the Hansa's prominence, such as bills of exchange, an accounting idea from Italy, where double-entry book-keeping was invented in 1492 and outpaced the Hansa economy in which silver or gold coins changed hands to buy goods.

Kraków, then the capital of Poland, had a loose association with the Hansa but the trading of grain was an important commodity. The lack of customs borders on the River Vistula, after 1466, helped to gradually increase Polish grain exports, from ten thousand tons per year in the late fifteenth century to over two hundred thousand tons in the seventeenth century, making Danzig (now Gdańsk) one of the Hansa's largest cities.

A major economic advantage for the Hansa was its control of the shipbuilding market, particularly in Lübeck and in Danzig. The Hansa sold ships everywhere in Europe. When the Dutch started to become competitors of the Hansa in shipbuilding, the Hansa tried to stop the flow of shipbuilding technology from Hanseatic towns to

Holland. Danzig, a close trading partner of Amsterdam, attempted to forestall the decision. Dutch ships sailed to Danzig to take grain from the city directly, to the dismay of Lübeck. The Dutch also circumvented the Hanseatic towns by trading directly with north German princes in non-Hanseatic towns. Dutch freight costs were much lower than those of the Hansa, and the Hansa were excluded as middlemen.

When Bruges, Antwerp and Holland all became part of the Duchy of Burgundy, they competed with the monopoly of trade from the Hansa. The Dutch merchants aggressively challenged the Hansa and met with much success. Hanseatic cities in Prussia and Livonia (circa present-day Lithuania and Latvia) supported the Dutch against the Hansa in northern Germany. After several naval engagements, Amsterdam gained the position of the leading port for Polish and Baltic grain from the late fifteenth century onwards.

At the start of the sixteenth century, the Hanseatic League found itself under pressure. In the Swedish War of Liberation (1521-1523), the Hanseatic League was successful in protecting the trade in the mining and metal industries in Bergslagen, the main mining area of Sweden in the sixteenth century.

However, the Hanseatic League ended up on the wrong side, in 1536, after Christian III's victory in the civil war in Scania and Denmark. With its wealth gone, the Hanseatic League's influence in the Nordic countries was over. After that, Denmark and Sweden only ever viewed the Hanseatic League as an unwanted competitor.

Later in the sixteenth century, the Swedish Empire took control of much of the Baltic Sea. Denmark had regained control over its own trade and the Kontor in Novgorod had closed. The Kontor in Bruges had become effectively moribund. The individual cities making up the League had also started to put self-interest before their common Hanseatic interests. Finally, the political authority of the German princes had started to grow, constraining the independence of the merchants and Hanseatic towns.

The league attempted to deal with some of these issues, but they proved unable to prevent the growing mercantile competition, so a long period of decline commenced. The Antwerp Kontor closed in 1593, followed by the London Kontor in 1598, although the Bergen Kontor continued until 1754.

By the late seventeenth century, the league had imploded and could no longer deal with its own internal tensions. The social and political changes that accompanied the Protestant Reformation included the rise of Dutch and English merchants and the pressure of the Ottoman Empire upon the Holy Roman Empire and its trade routes.

In 1666, during the Great Fire of London, the London Kontor burned down. The manager sent a letter to Lübeck appealing for immediate financial assistance for a reconstruction. Hamburg, Bremen and Lübeck called for a

Hansetag in 1669. Only a few cities participated and those who attended declined to contribute to the reconstruction. It was the last formal meeting. Only three members (Lübeck, Hamburg and Bremen) remained until its demise in 1862, with the creation of the German Empire under Kaiser Wilhelm I.

Despite its collapse, several cities maintained the link to the Hanseatic League. Five Dutch cities, including Groningen, Deventer, Kampen, Zutphen and Zwolle, and ten German cities including Bremen, Demmin, Greifswald, Hamburg, Lübeck, Lüneburg, Rostock, Stade, Stralsund and Wismar still call themselves Hansa cities (their car licence plates are prefixed H, such as HB for Hansestadt Bremen). Hamburg and Bremen continue to style themselves officially as free Hanseatic cities.

The legacy of the Hansa is remembered today through several names, such as the German airline Lufthansa (Air Hansa); F.C. Hansa Rostock; Hanze University of Applied Sciences in Groningen, Netherlands; the Hansa Brewery in Bergen; Hansabank in the Baltic states (until it was rebranded into Swedbank); and Hansa-Park, a large theme park in Germany.

In 1980, former Hanseatic League members established a new Hanse in Zwolle. This league is open to all former Hanseatic League members and cities that share a Hanseatic Heritage. In 2012, the New Hanseatic league had one hundred and eighty-seven members. This includes twelve Russian cities, including Novgorod, and King's Lynn joined in 2006, followed by Hull and Boston. The new Hanse fosters and develops business links, tourism and cultural exchange with headquarters of the new Hanse in, where? In Lübeck, of course.

I had been a tourist in Lübeck before and had recently visited many of the top sights. It is a beautiful city and there is a lot to see: however, I was not going to revisit the major sights but see some of those that I had missed. My first stop was on the northern tip of the island on which Altstadt stands. Here is the Burgtor, the entrance into the old city, built in 1444 in late Gothic style, which is the oldest surviving gate into Hanseatic Lübeck. The other is the more famous, yet younger Holstentor, a beautiful red-brick building consisting of two round towers with conical spires.

Nearby is the Europäisches Hansemuseum (European Hansemuseum), dedicated to the history of the Hanseatic League. It is the largest museum in the world specifically dedicated to the subject. I was hoping to see the museum housed in a traditional building of the era, but it is an ugly modern monstrosity.

Planning for a museum began in 2004, but completion was delayed due to essential archaeological discoveries and opened only in 2015. It exhibits original historical objects, has interactive elements and stages historical scenes from some of the Hansa's former major trading ports, such as Novgorod, Bruges, Bergen, London and Lübeck. Its collection includes paintings, plus gold and silver coins.

I crossed the bridge over the Trave and walked along the far side of the river Wakewnitz to Dräger Park. Then I crossed over the Moltkebrücke back into the Altstadt. Picking up my hire car, I drove to the edge of the city. I was on a nostalgia trip. Many years before I had cycled across northern Europe, at Easter, to cross into what was then East Germany. I planned to cycle over the border with one night's camping and stay a few nights in a hotel in the small market town of Schwerin. I recall the story in another book, 'A Freshman's Travels'.

I had cycled up to the border but I was not allowed across as the campsites were closed and I wasn't permitted to bush camp, so I had to take the train. Lübeck had expanded right up to the barbed-wire border, but beyond it was empty: just the north German plain and wheat on the gentle, rolling countryside, without any hedges or fences, for as far as the eye could see. With re-unification and the removal of the border, the city had expanded. I drove around but couldn't positively identify where that border used to be.

I drove on the Bad Kleinen, where all those years before I had changed trains en route to Schwerin. It was bigger than it used to be, but I recognised some bits. I moved on to Schwerin, overlooking a large lake called Schweriner Innensee.

On the internet, I had found the same hotel that I had stayed in all those years before, although it had changed its name and been refurbished. It was a large, tall, rectangular, Stalinist-style concrete structure but it was central. Despite a lot of better-looking hotels, more rustic and sometimes cheaper options, I had booked a room there for the sake of nostalgia. I couldn't remember the exact room number but I specified a room on the fifth floor overlooking the square.

I had a few days to look around the city. The time difference and development hadn't changed the city centre too much and I recognised the central square, the castle, the church, the waterfront and many other buildings and parks. Where I thought the communist multi-storey, but empty, department store stood, it had been replaced with a row of new but old-style buildings.

I drove back to Lübeck and dropped off the hire car, then took the train to spend a night in Hamburg. I bought a ticket for the 08.34 train to Warsaw and went to the local supermarket to stock up with supplies for the journey. It would be an eleven-hour journey with a change of trains in Berlin and Katowice, before arriving in Warsaw.

The distance from Warsaw to Kaliningrad, my next Baltic capital, was less than half the distance compared to Hamburg to Warsaw, but the train journey was over eighteen hours due to no direct connection and the need to go via Lithuania and make several changes of trains. There were long waiting periods in between, as the train timetables weren't co-ordinated, so I chose to go by coach.

For my one evening in Warsaw, I went to the bus station to buy a ticket to Kaliningrad. I don't speak Polish and firstly asked in English, which earned me a blank stare and a shake of her head. I tried Russian but again I got a blank stare and a shake of the head. I started in German but the ticket seller waved a hand indicating for me to wait and disappeared.

She returned with a colleague who spoke excellent English, who checked that I had a valid Russian visa (a free electronic visa for a short, tourist visit), reserved my preferred seat and sold me my ticket. Then I made my way to the local supermarket for supplies for the journey.

In the morning, I made my way to the bus station to catch the coach to Kaliningrad. It would have taken under five hours to drive the three hundred and seventy-five kilometres, and a little extra for border formalities, but the coach stopped at several towns en route and intermediate stops at motorway service stations. It took more than eight hours, in all, but I was rewarded with a lot of views of the Polish countryside before reaching the border.

Chapter 8

Sambian Peninsula

At the border, we all had to get off to reclaim our luggage, walk through security, border control and customs. Russians returning home were through in no time, but foreigners were given a more thorough search and interrogation.

I was of especial interest to them, possibly as I was a regular visitor to Russia when they checked their computer systems. Also, why was I crossing a land border from Poland when I could fly direct? Where had I come from – a long story of Denmark, Sweden, Denmark, Germany and Poland and then going on to where? Lithuania, Latvia, Estonia, Finland and St Petersburg. They obviously didn't get many overlanders on long trips. I was the last person to get back on to the coach and I apologised to my fellow passengers for the delay.

At last, I was into the Russian exclave of Kaliningrad. It is bordered by Lithuania and Poland and access to Russia proper is via a second country, such as Latvia or Belarus. The astute reader will notice that, once again, I might have reached a major city, but as Kaliningrad is part of Russia and the capital of Russia is Moscow, it is not a current capital. However, there is some historical basis. Kaliningrad is the regional capital of the exclave and under its former name, Königsberg, it was the capital of Prussia until it was moved to Berlin in 1701.

The first recorded settlement at the site of the present city was an Old Prussian fort called Twangste (Oak Forest). During the conquest of the area by the Teutonic Knights in 1255, Twangste was destroyed and replaced with a new fortress and renamed Königsberg.

The Teutonic Knights' official title was the Order of Brothers of the German House of Saint Mary in Jerusalem, a military Catholic religious order founded in 1192 in Acre, then part of the Kingdom of Jerusalem. Its aim was to protect Christians on their pilgrimages to the Holy Land and to establish hospitals. With the loss of the Holy Land, they turned their attentions to areas nearer to home and used Königsberg as a base for campaigns against pagan Lithuania.

Königsberg joined the Hanseatic League in 1340 and developed into an important port, prospering after the Teutonic Order's victory over Lithuanians following the 1348 Battle of Strawen. However they didn't have it all their way and in 1454, the Prussian Confederation rebelled against the Teutonic Knights and formally asked the Polish King Casimir IV Jagiellon to incorporate Prussia into the Kingdom of Poland as a fief. This started a long chain of changes of control over the centuries.

The rebellion marked the beginning of the Thirteen Years' War (1454-66) between the Teutonic Order and Poland. At the Second Peace of Thorn (1466), parts of Prussia were transferred to victorious Poland.

The city flourished through the export of wheat, timber, hemp, furs, pitch and tar. The population also threw off their Catholic faith and became Protestant or Lutheran. After several changes of rulers, the Treaty of Oliva 1660, ending the Second Northern War (1655-1660), marked the high point of the Swedish Empire and peace was made between Sweden, the Polish–Lithuanian Commonwealth, the Habsburgs and Brandenburg-Prussia and confirmed Prussian independence.

Königsberg Castle witnessed the coronation of Elector Frederick III, who then became Frederick I, King in Prussia in 1701. It heralded the birth of a new nation with Königsberg as its capital, although the monarchy's main residences were in Berlin and Potsdam.

After Prussia's defeat at the hands of Napoleon Bonaparte, in 1806, and the subsequent occupation of Berlin, King Frederick William III of Prussia fled with his court from Berlin to Königsberg.

It served as the capital of the united Province of Prussia from 1824 to 1878, when East Prussia was merged with West Prussia. The extensive Prussian Eastern Railway linked the city to many other major trading centres. The city became part of the German Empire in 1871 during the Prussian-led unification of Germany.

At the start of the First World War, in August in 1914, the Germans managed a spectacular victory at the Battle of Tannenberg, one hundred and forty kilometres south of the city. The Russians had two hundred and thirty thousand soldiers, in two armies, facing one hundred and fifty thousand German soldiers. Using their extensive railway network to move their troops, the Germans concentrated their forces and defeated one army, then moved the same troops to defeat the second army. The Russians lost half their soldiers, killed or captured, plus a lot of equipment, and had to retreat. The Germans lost just ten per cent of their strength.

At the end of the First World War, the Hohenzollern monarch, Kaiser Wilhelm II, abdicated and Imperial Germany was replaced with the democratic Weimar Republic. However, Königsberg and East Prussia were separated from the rest of Weimar Germany by the creation of the Polish Corridor to allow otherwise landlocked Poland access to Danzig and therefore to the Baltic.

Prior to the Nazi era, Königsberg was home to a third of East Prussia's thirteen thousand Jews. Under Nazi rule, the Jewish and Polish minorities were classified as Untermensch and persecuted. The city's Jewish population shrank from three thousand two hundred in 1933, a year after Hitler came to power, by over a thousand by October 1938, boosted by the destruction of the synagogue during Kristallnacht in November 1938, when another five hundred Jews fled the city.

After the Wannsee Conference in January 1942, Königsberg's Jews began to be deported to Nazi concentration camps. The SS sent the first group of Jewish deportees, comprising four hundred and sixty-five Jewish men, women and children, from Königsberg to the Maly Trostenets extermination camp near Minsk in June 1942. Most were murdered soon after their arrival. Additional transports from Königsberg to the Theresienstadt ghetto and Auschwitz took place until 1945.

In 1944, Königsberg suffered heavy damage from British bombing attacks and burned for several days. The historic city centre, surrounding districts and the old harbour were destroyed, indicating to me that there may not be much old architecture to see.

As the Red Army advanced towards the city in October 1944, many people fled, spurred on after word spread of the brutal Soviet rape and massacre of civilians, plus French and Belgium POWs, at Nemmersdorf. In early 1945, Soviet forces, under the command of the Polish-born Soviet Marshal Konstantin Rokossovsky, besieged the city that Hitler had envisaged as the home for a museum holding all that the Germans had looted from Russia.

In Operation Samland, General Baghramyan's First Baltic Front, now known as the Samland Group, captured Königsberg in April. Although Hitler had declared Königsberg an invincible bastion of German spirit, the Soviets captured the city after a three-month-long siege. A temporary German breakout had allowed some of the remaining civilians to escape via train and naval evacuation from the nearby port of Pillau. Königsberg, which had been declared a fortress by the Germans, was fanatically defended.

On 21st January, during the Red Army's East Prussian Offensive, the Nazis gathered Polish and Hungarian Jews, from various concentration camps, in Königsberg. Up to seven thousand of them were forced on a death march to Sambia. Those that survived were subsequently executed at Palmnicken.

On 9th April, one month before the end of the war in Europe, the German military commander of Königsberg, General Otto Lasch, surrendered the remnants of his forces after the siege by the Red Army. For this act, Lasch was condemned to death, in absentia, by Hitler. At the time of the surrender, military and civilian dead in the city were estimated at forty-two thousand, with the Red Army claiming over ninety thousand prisoners.

About one hundred and twenty thousand survivors remained in the ruins of the devastated city. These survivors, mainly women, children and the elderly, were held as slave labourers until 1949. The vast majority of the German civilians left in Königsberg, after 1945, died from disease, deliberate starvation, or in revenge-driven ethnic cleansing. The remaining twenty thousand German residents were expelled in 1949–50. At the Potsdam Conference, northern Prussia, including Königsberg, was annexed by the USSR.

The fortifications of Königsberg consist of numerous defensive walls, forts, bastions and other structures. They make up the First and the Second Defensive Belt, built in 1626–1634 and 1843–1859, respectively. The fifteen-metre-thick First Belt was erected due to Königsberg's vulnerability during the Polish–Swedish wars. The Second Belt was largely constructed on top of the first one, which was in a bad condition. The new belt included twelve bastions, three ravelins, seven spoil banks and two fortresses, surrounded by a water moat. Ten brick gates served as entrances, and passages through defensive lines were equipped with retractable bridges.

There was a Bismarck tower just outside Königsberg, on the Galtgarben, the highest point on the Sambian peninsula. It was built in 1906 but destroyed by German troops in January 1945, as the Soviets approached.

As a major transport hub, with sea and river ports, the city is home to the headquarters of the Baltic Fleet of the Russian Navy and is one of the largest industrial centres in Russia. It was recognised as the best city in Russia in 2012, 2013 and 2014, according to Kommersant's magazine, The Firm's Secret.

On 4th July 1946, the Soviet authorities renamed Königsberg as Kaliningrad, following the death in June 1946 of the Chairman of the Presidium of the Supreme Soviet of the USSR, Mikhail Kalinin, one of the original Bolsheviks.

In October 1945, only about five thousand Soviet civilians lived in the territory. Between October 1947 and October 1948, about one hundred thousand Germans were forcibly expelled and replaced by four hundred thousand

Soviet civilians and the city's official language was changed from German to Russian.

The town of Baltiysk to the east of Kaliningrad, sitting on the Baltic coast, is the only Russian Baltic Sea port said to be ice-free all year round. The region hence plays an important role in maintenance of the Baltic Fleet. The Soviet Baltic Fleet was headquartered in the city in the 1950s and because of its strategic importance, Kaliningrad was closed to foreign visitors.

Due to the collapse of the Soviet Union in 1991, Kaliningrad became an exclave, geographically separated from the rest of Russia. This isolation from the rest of Russia became even more pronounced politically when Poland and Lithuania became members of NATO and subsequently the European Union in 2004. All military and civilian land links between the region and the rest of Russia have to pass through members of NATO and the EU.

Today, the overwhelming majority of Kaliningrad's residents are of Russian ethnicity, settled after 1945. A minority of the population is comprised of other Slavic people, with communities of Ukrainian, Belarusian, Tatar, Armenian, Polish and Lithuanian origins.

The pre-war city centre (Altstadt and Kneiphof) currently consists of parks, broad avenues, a square on the site of the former Königsberg Castle and two prestigious buildings, Dom Sovyetov (House of Soviets) and the restored Königsberg Cathedral on the Kneiphof island (now known as Kant island). Immanuel Kant's grave is situated next to the cathedral. Many German-era buildings in the historic city centre have been preserved or rebuilt, including the reconstruction of the Königsberg Synagogue. The new city centre is concentrated around Victory Square. The Cathedral of Christ the Saviour, consecrated in 2005, is located on that square.

Also worth seeing are the former Stock Exchange, the surviving churches and the remaining city gates. The Dohna Tower houses the Amber Museum and the Wrangel Tower remains as a reminder of the former Königsberg city walls.

Notable monuments include the statue of Immanuel Kant in front of the Immanuel Kant State University of Russia. The original statue was made by sculptor Christian Daniel Rauch and unveiled in 1864. It was destroyed in 1945 but recreated in 1992.

Other statues and monuments include the statues of Duke Albert, Friedrich Schiller, Tsar Peter the Great, the Cosmonaut monument, which honours the Kaliningrad cosmonauts Alexei Leonov and Yuri Romanenko, and the Monument for the twelve hundred Guardsmen, remembering the Battle of Königsberg.

Kaliningrad has imported its culinary traditions from wherever the population came after 1945. Borscht and okroshka may be served, as in the rest of Russia, but there are many international cuisines available all over the city.

In 1996, Kaliningrad was designated a Special Economic Zone. Manufacturers based there get tax and customs duty breaks on the goods they send to other parts of Russia. That policy means that the region is now a manufacturing hub. One in three televisions in Russia are made in Kaliningrad, including the Ericsson brand Telebalt and Polar. It is also home to Cadillac and BMW car plants.

The European Commission provides funds for business projects under its special programme for Kaliningrad. In the early twentieth century, it experienced an average GDP growth of more than ten per cent per year. Kaliningrad grew faster than any other region in Russia, even outstripping the success of its EU neighbours.

There were several things that I wanted to see but getting there by public transport was going to be time-consuming and might mean retracing my steps several times. I abandoned the idea of arranging it myself and booked a couple of day tours. I was picked up from my hotel and had a short drive to our first destination on the outskirts of the city.

This was the Juditten Church, originally built as a Roman Catholic church between 1276 and 1298. It claims to be the oldest building in Kaliningrad. A separate and free-standing tower was built in 1400, but it was connected to the nave via a barrel-vaulted vestibule in 1820.

The church was converted to Lutheranism in 1526. It escaped the heavy bombing of the city in 1944 but was plundered by Soviet forces in April 1945. The building was refurbished and re-consecrated in 1985 as a Russian Orthodox Church.

There were a few stalls nearby and we had some extra time to explore. I was not interested in the goods on offer but where there are people, there are often food stalls. It was still early in the morning and not long after breakfast, but I bought a Königsberger Klopse: a Prussian speciality of veal meatballs with anchovy and breadcrumbs in a white sauce with capers.

We had a journey of nearly an hour to the next stop at Baltiysk. Baltiysk was originally the site of an Old Prussian fishing village that was established on the coast of the Vistula Spit in the thirteenth century. It was named as Pil from Old Prussian, meaning fort.

It was conquered by the Teutonic Knights and the name evolved into Pillau. In 1497, a storm surge breached the spit, widened by another storm to create the navigable Strait of Baltiysk in 1510. It is the channel that ships can use to pass through the spit across the bay and reach Kaliningrad.

During the Thirty Years' War, the harbour was occupied by Sweden. King Gustavus Adolphus landed there with his army in 1626. After a ceasefire in 1629, the Swedes retained Pillau and started upgrading the fortifications, constructing a star fort which remains one of the town's landmarks. In 1635, the citizens of Pillau paid a ransom and Swedish forces handed over the settlement to Brandenburg.

In 1807, Pillau was stormed by Napoleon's Grande Armée, during the Napoleonic Wars, and no outstanding historical events occurred there during the rest of the nineteenth century, except that the entire fortress was updated by the Prussians in 1871. We looked at it from the outside only, and didn't go in.

Until around 1900, only ships drawing less than two metres could cross the lagoon from Pillau to moor in Königsberg. Vessels had to anchor at Pillau (now Baltiysk), where cargo was transferred to smaller vessels. In 1901, a 6.4 metre-deep shipping canal opened, linking Pillau to Königsberg, along the north shore of the Vistula Lagoon, thus avoiding the shallow waters of the lagoon. Pillau's economy had been heavily based on large shipping vessels being forced to dock in the town to unload cargoes to shallow draft vessels, or trains, for onward transport. As a result, Pillau's economy declined.

In April 1945, the German submarine U78 was sunk by Red Army artillery while docked in Pillau port. It was the only U-boat sunk by land-based forces in the war. As the Red Army entered East Prussia, more than four hundred and fifty thousand refugees were evacuated from Pillau to Germany.

After the war, Pillau and the northern part of East Prussia were annexed by the Soviet Union, the last remaining German inhabitants were expelled and place names changed to Russian versions. During the Russification campaign, the town's name was changed from Pillau to Baltiysk in 1946.

In 1952, the Soviet authorities inaugurated a naval base for the Baltic Fleet of the Soviet Navy, at Baltiysk, and it became a closed town with access forbidden to non-locals. Pillau and Kaliningrad are the only northern Russian ports that are ice-free throughout the year.

We took the ferry across the Strait of Baltiysk, which links the Baltic to the Vistula Lagoon, to visit the abandoned aerodrome at Neutief.

It was constructed in the 1930s by Germany but it was rarely used. It was damaged by Allied bombings and after the war, it was used occasionally by the Soviet Air Force as a forward interceptor base for both land and seaplane operations until the 1990s when the site was abandoned following the dissolution of the Soviet Union. There are several hangars, several other buildings, and the long but now overgrown runway.

We took the ferry back across the Strait of Baltiysk and drove across the Sambian peninsula to reach the Curonian Spit National Park. The Curonian Spit stretches from the Sambia Peninsula in the south to its northern tip, where there is a narrow strait, and across the water is the port city of Klaipėda on the mainland of Lithuania.

The spit is nearly one hundred kilometres long and has a width of between four hundred metres and 3.8 kilometres. The southern half is Russian, but the northern half is Lithuanian. The spit creates the Curonian Lagoon behind it.

According to Baltic mythology, the Curonian Spit was formed by a giantess, Neringa, who was playing on the seashore and created it to make a safe place for local fishermen against horrible sea monsters. Neringa appears in other myths and is sometimes depicted as a strong, young woman and in others as a child.

Deforestation of the spit started in the seventeenth century due to overgrazing and timber felling, initially for the building of boats for the Battle of Gross-Jägersdorf (1757) when a Russian army defeated a small Prussian force. The lack of trees led to the development of dunes, which were slowly moved, driven by the wind, to bury several settlements.

Alarmed by these problems, the Prussian government sponsored large-scale reforestation, starting in 1825. Owing to these efforts, much of the spit is now covered with forests, but there are still many sand dunes today. The spit is home to the highest moving sand dunes in Europe: their average height is thirty-five metres but some attain sixty metres.

One of the sand dunes is named Parnidis sand dune and rises fifty-two metres above sea level. Local residents claim that the interpretation of the name is from the phrase meaning 'passed across Nida' because this wind-blown dune has allegedly passed through the village of Nida several times. It is a well-known dune and a popular activity is to climb to the top. Scientists estimated that each person climbing or descending the steep dune slopes moves several tons of sand, so hikers are allowed to climb up only designated paths.

These are high for Europe but you might be amazed to discover that the highest sand dune in the world is La Duna Federico Kirbus in Argentina: from its base it reaches a height of one thousand two hundred and thirty metres. The second highest is Cerro Blanco, in Peru, at one thousand one hundred and seventy-six metres and the third is the much more modest El Medanoso Dune in Chile at five hundred and fifty metres.

From the late nineteenth century, the dune landscape around Nida became popular with landscape painters from the Kunstakademie Königsberg arts school. The painters attracted other people in the art world. Thomas Mann had a summer house on the spit from 1930-32 until he was forced to leave Nazi Germany. When the area was captured and annexed by Nazi Germany in 1939, his house was seized on the orders of Hermann Göring and served as a recreation home for Luftwaffe pilots.

From 1901 to 1946, the village of Rossitten (Rybachy), became the site of the pioneering Rossitten Bird Observatory, the world's first, founded by German ornithologist Johannes Thienemann. Located on a major migratory route, it is frequently visited by migratory waterfowl. Up to twenty million birds fly over during spring and autumn migrations and many pause to rest here.

One item that the guide didn't mention, until I prompted him after borrowing a pair of powerful binoculars from a birdwatcher, was an offshore drilling rig. This was the Kravtsovskoye D6 oilfield, discovered in 1983. Extraction of oil started in 2004, operated by Lukoil. The oil field lies twenty-two and a half kilometres off the Russian coast but just four kilometres from the Lithuanian border and the prevailing northward currents meant that the Lithuanian coastlines would receive much more potential damage in case of an oil leakage..

Local environmentalists in both Russia and Lithuania protested against plans to exploit the oilfield, objecting to the great damage from a potential oil spill to the local unique environment and tourism, a major part of the local economy in both local areas. These concerns were ignored by the government of Russia, so development went ahead unimpeded.

The next day I was on a minibus tour going back along the same roads to Baltiysk. We stopped at the monument to Peter the Great standing on a tall square plinth. His plinth was next to the red and white-painted lighthouse which stands over thirty-one metres high. We walked along the Baltiysk Embankment and I heard many of the stories that I had heard the day before.

Yesterday, I had been shown only the outside of the fortress and a brief history. Today's tour was going into the fort to view its defences and some of the exhibits in the museum. We had a long tour of the structure with its overlapping killing grounds, and some of the interiors with their structures built into the low, squat ramparts to protect them from cannon fire, with wide flat tops to allow movement of horse-pulled cannon.

Afterwards, we walked along the seafront to see the Monument to Empress of Russia Elizabeth Petrovna sitting on a horse, on a plinth, at the northern end of the Straits of Baltiysk.

Also known as Elizaveta Petrona (1709 – 1762), she was the second-eldest daughter of Tsar Peter the Great and she lived through the confused successions of her father's many short-lived descendants until she seized the throne, with the backing of the army, in 1741. She then reigned as the Empress of Russia until her death. She was one of the most popular Russian monarchs because of her decision not to execute a single person during her reign, her numerous construction projects, which employed many people, and her strong opposition to Prussian policies.

Elizabeth led the Russian Empire during two major European conflicts: the War of Austrian Succession (1740–48) and the Seven Years' War (1756–63). She formed an alliance with Austria and France during the first conflict but indirectly caused the second. Russian troops enjoyed several victories against Prussia and briefly occupied Berlin, but when Frederick the Great was finally considering surrender in January 1762, the Russian Empress died.

We drove up the coast to stop at the Amber Pyramid set on a ridge looking out to sea. Between the pyramid and the shore is a large, open-cast mine, where they dig for amber. Kaliningrad has about ninety per cent of the world's reserves of amber. I had expected something a little more interesting, but it is a hollow pyramid, about four metres square, with two benches inside. Nearby is the inevitable souvenir shop that we had half an hour to visit before going back to Kaliningrad.

Chapter 9

Kaliningrad

My first stop in the city centre was going to be the Museum of the World Ocean, located down by the river front in the centre of the city. I knew it had six ships moored there but I was unprepared for some of the other exhibits. Visitors can wander around the main building and its grounds but must join a guided tour to see inside the ships. I bought a series of timed tickets with enough time in-between to walk along the front or to see the exhibits. In the main hall, suspended from the ceiling, was the skeleton of a sperm whale. There were also many other finds and even a small aquarium with live fish, although the only one I recognised from my tropical-fish-breeding days was the Scorpion Fish.

In the grounds were more artefacts, several marine mines, a twin-engine sea plane, diving bells, a midget submarine, a cruise missile and a missile launcher. There was also a giant globe that towered above the masts of the ships nearby and a metal lattice-work sculpture of a dolphin.

Along the front were several ships, such a nineteenth-century wooden fishing boat, known as SRT 129. Next to it was the Irbensky Lightship; followed by the Vityaz research ship; the Space communication vessel Cosmonaut Viktor Patsaev with its exhibits connected with space; and furthest away from the main building, Submarine B-413, a pre-atomic era, diesel-powered submarine, home to three hundred sailors when it was operational. I was in two minds whether I wanted to go into a cramped space with only two exits, but if it held three hundred submariners, I thought that it might be all right. Space on a submarine is at a premium and it was cramped: I was only too happy to be back on dry land.

A sixth vessel forms part of the museum: the 1916-built icebreaker, Krassin, which was the first purpose-built icebreaker in the world, but this is moored in St Petersburg. I had seen the first atomic-powered icebreaker, Lenin, moored in Murmansk, so I was interested to compare it to a conventionally powered vessel. Therefore, I carefully saved my ticket for when I reached St Petersburg the next month.

The need to wait to join a guided tour for each of the ships meant that I stayed a lot longer in the museum than I had planned. Kaliningrad's museums are visited by more than a million people and in terms of museum attendance, Kaliningrad region (although small, at about half the size of the Midlands) ranks seventh among the most visited regions of Russia. I suspected that most of them had chosen to visit the Museum of World Oceans on the same day that I did. I was only too delighted to get away from the crowds that swarmed around the museum.

The museum visit had cut into my planned schedule, so I had a bit of catching up to do, or needed to think about which visit I might abandon. It was late in the day but I walked along the river front to cross onto Kneiphof Island, in the river, on which stood the cathedral. The roof and spire were destroyed by fire in August 1944 by the RAF, during the Second World War, to support the Russian advance. Rebuilding started only in 1992, so much of it is not original.

A small Catholic cathedral was erected in the Königsberg Altstadt between 1297 and 1302. However, when the bishop acquired the eastern part of Kneiphof island from the Teutonic Knights, in 1322, he had a larger cathedral built on the site. The first church was demolished and construction on the new, larger cathedral started in 1330.

The site on which the cathedral was to be built was marshy, so hundreds of oak poles were piled into the ground before the construction began. The cathedral was largely completed by 1380, except for the interior frescoes which took another two decades.

It has an unusual façade with a circular tower and spire on one side and a gable roof on the other. Albert, Duke of Prussia, and some of his relatives, as well as other dignitaries, are buried in the cathedral. The tomb of the philosopher Immanuel Kant, known as the Sage of

Königsberg, is today in a mausoleum in the northeast corner of the cathedral.

In 1995 a new clock was put in place. The clock has four bells (1,180 kg, 700 kg, 500 kg & 200 kg), all cast in 1995. The clock chimes every quarter of an hour. On the hour, the clock chimes by playing the first notes of Beethoven's Symphony No. 5, followed by monotonic chiming to indicate the hour.

As I walked through the streets of Kaliningrad, I stopped at every restaurant to read the menu. I was looking for anything that claimed to be a local dish.

Königsberg was well known within Germany for its unique regional cuisine. It was a bit of a haphazard search, as the original German population had been expelled and the new Russian immigrants brought their own cuisine with them from wherever they originated. There were some dishes that I was specifically looking for.

One was *Stroganina*, from Siberia, consisting of long, thin, sliced strips of frozen fish and served with onion, salt and pepper. The fish is cut in such a way that it forms ribbon curls and is served still partly frozen. It tastes a whole lot better than it sounds and is a perfect accompaniment to a glass of chilled vodka.

Sucharyki are slices of fried black bread, typically *Borodinsky* bread, covered with garlic and melted cheese. *Königsberger Fleck* is a bovine tripe soup and yet another culinary specialty from the former Königsberg, but since tripe is one of the few foods that I cannot stomach, I wasn't about to choose my restaurant on that basis.

Drinks native to the city include *Bärenfang*, a honey flavoured liqueur; *Kopskiekelwein*, a wine made from either blackcurrants or redcurrants; and *Polugaris*, which is a bread-based spirit. Tsar Alexander III banned it in 1895 and had ordered all the copper stills to be destroyed, leaving a monopoly for government-owned distilleries, so people started making vodka instead. When the Rodionov family wanted to reintroduce the drink at the beginning of the twenty-first century, the legislation still prohibited its production, so they distilled it in Poland.

Other drinks include *Ochsenblut* (literally 'ox-blood'), a champagne-burgundy cocktail developed originally by the Blutgericht bar, which no longer exists as it was situated within the Königsberg Castle that was destroyed during the Second World War. I hoped to find someone else who served it. Kaliningrad also has its own beer and vodka brands – Stari Königsberg and Ostmark, respectively.

In the cool of the morning, I walked through the park and along the edge of two lakes known simply as the Lower Pond and the Upper Pond. I arrived dead on opening time at the Königsberger Marzipan Museum, located not far from the zoo. I was here as much for architecture as for the marzipan, another food item for which the city is famous.

It is housed in part of a modest stately home with some gardens and surrounded by a moat. Inside are a series of models of churches, castles, animals and all sorts of items all made out of coloured marzipan by skilled confectioners.

I walked around the Upper Pond and entered the Amber Museum, housed in a red-brick, circular fortress. Although it looks old, construction was started in 1972 and the museum opened in 1979, modelled on a fortification built during the Napoleonic Wars.

There is an explanation to how amber was created and its properties. Among the more than fourteen thousand pieces, some dating back to the seventeenth century, are all sorts of amber art, jewellery and carved pieces, including the world's second-largest piece of amber and a 1.2 metre-tall vase.

I walked back alongside the Lower Pond, towards the city centre, to the Bunker Museum. It is located in a small park off Prospekt Leninskiy and might be easily missed. There is only a small sign and a flight of steps disappearing into the ground, flanked by two artillery pieces.

The Russians had blunted the German advance deep into Russia and was on the offensive and sweeping through Poland and towards Germany.

The bunker was constructed in March 1945, shortly before the Battle of Königsberg took place. It acted as the headquarters for the Axis forces during the siege of the city. The city's last German commander, General Otto von Lasch, capitulated to the Soviets from this subterranean command post on 9th April 1945, just a month before the end of the war in Europe.

The bunker was opened to the public in 1967 to share its historical significance. The museum provides details of the encirclement and fall of Königsberg and life in the bunker. Exhibits include wartime photographs, films, detailed dioramas of the battle in various parts of the city and a display of mannequins in uniform in the room where Lasch surrendered, directly disobeying Hitler's orders.

As a result of Lasch's surrender, Hitler sentenced him, in absentia, to death by hanging and his family was arrested. Lasch went into Soviet captivity and was convicted as a war criminal in the Soviet Union and sentenced to twenty-five years in a corrective labour camp. He was released in 1955.

In the far corner of the park is a monument to Immanuel Kant (1724 – 1804), standing on a two metre-high plinth, with an outstretched arm. The statue was designed by the German sculptor Christian Daniel Rauch. Kant was a German philosopher and one of the central Enlightenment thinkers. His comprehensive and systematic works in epistemology, metaphysics, ethics, and aesthetics have made him one of the most influential figures in modern Western philosophy.

The original monument was erected in the nineteenth century but was destroyed during the Second World War. It was recreated in 1992 and Putin has praised Kant, which is a point of pride for many Russians in Kaliningrad.

My last tourist site for the day was Königsberg Castle, just a short walk from the bunker. The site of the castle was originally the Old Prussian fort known as Twangste.

Following the 1944 bombing of Königsberg by the Allies in the Second World War, the castle was burnt down. However, the thick walls were able to withstand both the aerial bombing and the Soviet artillery during the Battle of Königsberg, allowing the ruins of the castle to stay standing until they were blown up on Leonid Brezhnev's personal orders in 1968. Now it is just a ruin.

Across the Central Square, the House of Soviets building was started in 1970, designed to be a twenty-one-storey administration block for the city's government, constructed in a typically concrete brutalist style, nicknamed 'The Monster' by locals.

Various archaeological digs have taken place in the ruins of the castle, financed by Der Spiegel. There is a faint hope that various buried treasures of the previous castle museum may be uncovered and possibly evidence of the Amber Room, since this was where it was originally sent after being stolen from Catherine's Palace.

I was pleased with myself: after some early morning starts and packing in a full schedule, I was getting back on track, and I might not have to miss anything off my schedule. The visit to the castle was so much quicker than I had envisaged.

I had time to visit the Altes Haus. It is situated some distance northwest from the city centre, and it would have taken time to walk to it. Working it into a schedule was difficult as there was nothing else en route that I wanted to see. On a spur of the moment decision, I caught the tram. The tram system was started in 1881 and was electrified in

1895, making it the oldest tram system in Russia. It dropped me just a short distance from the Altes Haus and it wasn't easy to find down a street of similar non-descript buildings.

I was just in time to join the last tour of the day. Tours in English are available if you pre-book but I was happy to join a Russian-language tour: I might not understand everything but it was good practice. This may seem an unusual option for a tour but it had piqued my interest.

It is a tour of an apartment in a 1912-built block of flats but renovated to show how people lived in that decade. It is surprisingly large for an apartment, but it has been painstakingly recreated to show how merchant and grocery store-owner Gustav Grossman and his family might have lived.

One point that was unusual for a museum was that, as visitors, we were not restricted from touching or holding the objects. We were able to sit on the chairs, at the tables, pose for photos, look inside drawers and cabinets and try to use the implements in the kitchens. I was so happy not to have dropped this from my schedule. . . and I still had time.

I walked down to the waterfront of the Pregolya River to traverse the harbour front on my way back to the city centre. I made my way to my choice of restaurant that evening to select my option of a local dish.

I crossed the Pregolya River to visit Fort Fredrichsburg. Construction of the original fort, by Frederick William of Brandenburg-Prussia, began in 1657 during the Second Northern War and formed part of the ring of fortification around Königsberg constructed from 1626–34.

The interior of the fort contained a command building, barracks, warehouses, a church and a prison. It had a small permanent garrison of about one hundred and fifty men but could host a stronger force if need be. The fort was extensively remodelled in 1852.

By the end of the nineteenth century, the fort was used only for military storage. In order to allow the construction of a new railway, the castle was sold to the Prussian Eastern Railway and partially demolished in 1910. It was restored at the start of the twenty-first century but it is hard to see what is original and what is new, yet built to look old.

I walked to the Brandenburg Gate, the same name as the famous giant structure in Berlin, but this one is older. It is one of seven gates into the city but the only one still used as a gate. It was built in 1657 as part of the strengthening of the city walls at the same time that Fort Fredrichsburg was being built.

The original gate was just a wooden structure due to a lack of funds. It was more than a century later before this was replaced by King Frederick II of Prussia with the current red-brick structure. During restoration work in 1843, the gate was significantly altered with decorative pediments, sandstone trim on the tops, coats of arms and medallions.

'Statues' of Field Marshal Hermann von Boyen (1771–1848), a war minister and reformer of the Prussian army, and Lieutenant-General Ernst von Aster (1778–1855), chief of the engineering corps, and one of the initiators of the second strengthening of the city walls, were added, as well.

After the Brandenburg Gate, I walked along some of the surviving original defences, ravelins, moats and walls. I had had enough of sightseeing, so I cut out the planned visit to the Museum of Miniatures and the Friedland Gate Museum and returned to the hotel.

For my last day in the city, I made my way through the streets, catching a local bus and taking a long walk to reach Fort XI Dönhoff on the outskirts of the modern city.

This is the best preserved of fifteen forts that surrounded the city, largely due to the fact that it escaped the main Russian advance, which was concentrated on Fort V on the other side of the city.

The red-brick structure was built from 1877-1881 and surrounded by a moat. It was originally called Fort Seligenfeld, but in 1894 it was renamed in honour of Friedrich Reichgraf von Dönhoff (1639-1696), from a noble Prussian family, who rose to be the Governor-General of Memel, present day Klaipeda, Lithuania.

In the course of the Russian offensive to gain Königsberg, it was captured on 7th April 1945. In this battle, two sergeants of the Guards Army, Elizarov and Andrusenko, were killed but commemorated as heroes and buried within the walls of the captured Fort. A grave with a headstone is preserved within the grounds.

There was a tour of the interiors with their firing positions, connecting tunnels and rooms containing furniture to re-create the atmosphere of the building when it was in use. There are a few small exhibitions of war-time photography, weapons and ammunition in these rooms, as well as some furniture and photos of a battle-scarred Königsberg during the Second World War.

Climbing up and through the fort, I saw the remains of the lift systems used to bring shells from the ammunition bunkers in the depths of the fortifications to supply the heavy guns spread across the top of the embankments.

Chapter 10

Lithuania

I boarded my coach for the trip from Kaliningrad to my next destination – Kaunas, the temporary capital of Lithuania. It was two hundred and sixty kilometres, so if I were driving myself, it would be perhaps under a four-hour drive, plus some time at the border. The coach schedule included three stops in the Kaliningrad, a long stop at the border and two stops in Lithuania before reaching Kaunas.

People buying tickets, including crossing the border, have to show their passports and visa before they are sold a ticket. I couldn't buy a ticket online and had had to go to the ticket office to display my passport.

The coach schedule indicated that the trip was over seven hours. Leaving Russian Kaliningrad was easy for some of us, but there was another careful scrutiny of passports and visas for those who needed visas to enter Lithuania before we could get back on the road.

Neither Kaunas or Vilnius are on the Baltic yet I have stretched the point once again, as the three Baltic states of Lithuania, Latvia and Estonia are often lumped together.

Also, I had to go through both cities en route to my next true Baltic capital of Riga in neighbouring Latvia.

The modern state of Lithuania is a recent creation but it has a long history. The first record of Lithuania is in the 1009 story of Saint Bruno in the Quedlinburg Chronicle. From the ninth to the eleventh centuries, coastal areas were subjected to raids by the Vikings and the kings of Denmark collected tribute. During the tenth and eleventh centuries, Russian rulers such as Yaroslav the Wise invaded Lithuanian territories and extracted tributes from 1040.

From the mid-twelfth century, it was the Lithuanians who were invading Russia and even the distant and powerful Novgorod Republic was repeatedly threatened by the excursions of the emboldened Lithuanian forces.

In the 1230s, the Lithuanian lands were united by Mindaugas, who was crowned as King of Lithuania in 1253. After his assassination in 1263, pagan Lithuania was a target of the Christian crusades of the Teutonic Knights and the Livonian Order. Despite this devastating century-long struggle, the Grand Duchy of Lithuania expanded rapidly. In 1362, they captured the former Russian principality of Kiev.

In 1385, the Grand Duke Jogaila accepted Poland's offer to become its king. Jogaila established a union between Poland and Lithuania and a gradual Christianisation of Lithuania. At its peak, when Vytautas the Great became the Grand Duke of Lithuania in 1392, Lithuania was the largest state in Europe. Its strength lay in its toleration of different cultures and religions. At the height of its expansion, it might have had only a small shoreline on the Baltic, but it had spread east to the borders of Moscow and south through Ukraine to the Black Sea.

In 1410, the armies of Lithuania and Poland achieved a massive victory over the Teutonic Knights at the Battle of Grunwald (also known as the First Battle of Tannenberg, a site which would witness several battles over the centuries, due to its strategic position) which was the largest battle of medieval Europe. Their victory effectively ended the Teutonic Knights' aspirations regarding Eastern Europe.

Lithuania was forced to seek a closer alliance with Poland, when the growing power of the Grand Duchy of Moscow threatened Lithuania's eastern principalities and sparked the Muscovite–Lithuanian Wars and the Livonian War.

At the Battle of Orsha in 1514, the much smaller Poland–Lithuania army of fewer than thirty thousand soldiers defeated a force of eighty thousand Muscovite soldiers, capturing their camp and commander. A fragile ceasefire and peace developed until the Polish–Lithuanian Commonwealth invaded Moscovy in 1605.

The Polish–Lithuanian Commonwealth was created in 1569 by the Union of Lublin. As a member of the Commonwealth, Lithuania retained its institutions, including a separate army, currency and laws. Eventually, the increasing Polish influence affected all aspects of Lithuanian life, such as politics, language, culture and national identity. From the mid-sixteenth to the mid-seventeenth centuries, culture, arts, and education flourished, fuelled by the Renaissance and the Protestant Reformation, but another influence was the Golden Liberties awarded to the nobles, which created anarchy.

The Commonwealth held its own against Sweden, Russia and the Ottoman Empire, and even launched successful expansionist offensives against its neighbours. In several invasions during the Time of Troubles, Commonwealth troops entered Russia and managed to capture Moscow and hold it for more than two years, from 1610 to 1612, when they were driven out after a siege.

Their power was under pressure from a number of events. In 1655, Vilnius was captured by the Russian army who looted the city, killing ten thousand citizens. The city burned for seventeen days and the Russians occupied it for the next six years, while the territory was fought over by Russian and Swedish armies.

It had a brief period of respite until the Great Northern War, during which hostilities, famine and plague caused the death of forty per cent of the population. The Commonwealth's influence was whittled away by incursions of the Russian Empire, Prussia and the Habsburg Monarchy, and by 1795 it ceased to exist and became part of the Russian Empire.

During the Great War, in 1915, after a year of fighting and a successful German summer offensive, the Russian armies, outnumbered and inadequately supplied, marched rearwards during the Great Retreat, evacuating large salients in Poland and Galicia to shorten their front lines, and Germany occupied Lithuania.

An independent, democratic state of Lithuania was created in 1918 with Vilnius as its capital. However, they were not unchallenged. Lithuania fought three wars of independence; firstly against the Bolsheviks who proclaimed the Lithuanian Soviet Socialist Republic, then against the Bermontians, (a West Russian Volunteer Army in the Baltic provinces of the former Russian Empire) during the Russian Civil War in 1918–20, who were supported by Germany to maintain their influence in the area; and finally, against the newly recreated state of Poland.

In October 1920, Poland invaded the Vilnius Region, annexing it in 1922. Lithuania continued to claim Vilnius as its capital but used Kaunas as the temporary capital. Relations with Poland remained particularly tense and hostile for the entire inter-war period. In January 1923, Lithuania staged the Klaipėda Revolt and captured the Klaipėda region from Germany. In March 1939, Lithuania was handed an ultimatum by Nazi Germany and the region was returned to Germany.

When Nazi Germany and Soviet Union concluded the Molotov–Ribbentrop Pact, Lithuania was initially assigned to the German sphere of influence, but was later transferred to the Soviet sphere. At the outbreak of the Second World War, Lithuania declared neutrality.

In October 1939, Lithuania was forced to sign the Soviet–Lithuanian Mutual Assistance Treaty. Vilnius was returned to Lithuania, captured by the Soviets from Poland in return for the creation of five Soviet military bases with twenty thousand troops in Lithuania.

Delayed by the Winter War with Finland, the Soviets issued an ultimatum to Lithuania on 14th June 1940 to replace the Lithuanian government. The government decided that, with Soviet bases already in Lithuania, armed resistance was impossible. It accepted the ultimatum and a further two hundred thousand Soviet Red Army soldiers crossed into Lithuania.

Between twenty thousand and thirty thousand of Vilnius' inhabitants were subsequently arrested by the NKVD and sent to gulags in the far eastern areas of the Soviet Union. Identical ultimatums were presented to Latvia and Estonia. The Baltic states were occupied and incorporated into the Soviet Union.

Nazi Germany attacked the Soviet Union on 22nd June 1941 and the three Baltic states changed hands again. By December 1941, over one hundred and twenty thousand Lithuanian Jews, more than ninety per cent of the pre-war Jewish population, had been killed. Nearly one hundred thousand Jews, Poles, Russians and Lithuanians were murdered at Paneriai.

About thirteen thousand men served in the Lithuanian Auxiliary Police Battalions, with ten of the twenty-six Lithuanian Auxiliary Police Battalions working with the Nazi Einsatzkommando and involved in the mass killings. Others were forced to fight for Nazi Germany or used as forced labour.

The Soviets recaptured Lithuania in late 1944 and re-established control, with massive deportations to Siberia, whilst Soviet immigration was promoted, although there was armed resistance for nearly a decade.

In March 1990, Lithuania regained its independence, the first former Soviet state to do so. The Soviets introduced an economic blockade and used troops against unarmed protestors, causing casualties, and even backed a coup, but Lithuania did not renounce the declaration of independence, and the last units of the Soviet Army pulled out of Lithuania in August 1993.

The journey had been interesting. We had passed through some farming areas but forests cover more than a third of the country and timber-related industrial production accounts for more than a tenth of total production in the country.

There were also a lot of storks' nests on pylons, churches and on anywhere high. They looked like haphazard piles of sticks, but storks return to the same nest every year and add a few more sticks, so you can judge the age of the nesting pair by the size of the nest. The White Stork is the national bird of Lithuania and the country has the highest-density stork population in Europe.

Lithuania has a wide range of natural ecosystems. A third of the country may be forest but eight per cent is designated as wetland and a lot of migratory birds pass through the country.

The most prolific, large, wild animals are the various species of deer, totalling one hundred and seventy-five thousand, followed by wild boar at fifty-five thousand and foxes, at twenty-seven thousand. The wolf is often mentioned, but it is more ingrained in legend and mythology than reality: there are just eight hundred. Even rarer are the lynxes, at under two hundred.

The coach arrived in Kaunas in the afternoon. I dropped my luggage in the hotel. I discovered that I had done some sloppy planning. Vilnius was the intended capital but Kaunas was the de facto capital while Poland occupied Vilnius.

I hadn't found much that I wanted to see in Kaunas but just a glance at the brochures in the tourist leaflet display in reception showed that I had made a mistake. The country hosts more than 1.5 million foreign tourists, for a country of just 2.8 million. The majority emanate from Germany (fourteen per cent), followed by Belarus (thirteen per cent) Russian (twelve per cent), and Poland (ten per cent). Great Britain comes in at just four per cent. I can't explain my poor planning, despite trying to analyse it in my head as I went to see the cathedral and to check out restaurants.

Kaunas is the country's second largest urban area, producing twenty per cent of the country's GDP compared with the capital, Vilnius, at forty-two per cent. The proportion of the population at risk of poverty or social exclusion (AROPE) has decreased since Lithuania joined the EU in 2004, although it remains among the highest in the EU (29.6% in 2017, compared to the EU average of 22.4%).

By the tenth century, a settlement had been established on the site of the current Kaunas old town, at the confluence where the Neris River joins the Neman River. Kaunas was first mentioned in written sources in 1361, when the brick Kaunas Castle was constructed. In 1362, the castle was captured after a siege and destroyed by the Teutonic Order. It was one of the largest and most important military victories of the Teutonic Knights against Lithuania in the fourteenth century. The Kaunas castle was rebuilt at the beginning of the fifteenth century.

In 1441, Kaunas joined the Hanseatic League and a Kontor was opened; the only one in the whole of the Grand Duchy of Lithuania.

The country had a turbulent history. In 1665, the Russian army attacked the city several times, and in 1701 the city was occupied by the Swedish Army. Plague struck the area in 1657 and 1708, killing many residents, while fires destroyed parts of the city in 1731 and 1732.

After the third and final partition of the Polish–Lithuanian state in 1795, the city was taken over by the Russian Empire. During the French invasion of Russia in 1812, the Grand Army of Napoleon passed through Kaunas twice – once to invade Russia, and again during the long retreat from Moscow, devastating the city each time.

My first tourist sight of the day was the Kaunas Castle, located on the elevated banks above the confluence of the rivers. The precise date of construction is unknown but archaeological evidence suggests the middle of the fourteenth century, to protect trade routes and support the capital one hundred kilometres further inland.

In 1362, the castle was besieged by the Teutonic Order. The walls were eleven metres high and garrisoned by four hundred Lithuanians. The Teutonic Knight constructed a siege tower and siege machinery to penetrate the walls. After just three weeks, they captured the castle with only thirty-six Lithuanians surviving.

The castle was repaired, but in 1384 it was re-captured by the Teutonic Knights. At this time, Grand Master Konrad Zöllner von Rotenstein began reconstruction of Kaunas Castle and renamed it Marienwerder. The presence of the Knights in Kaunas meant that the entire defensive system of castles along the Neman River, linking Vilnius to the Baltic, was threatened.

Confronting this situation, the Lithuanians launched an attack on the castle later the same year and recaptured it, deploying cannons and trebuchets, although the trebuchets were destroyed by cannon fire from the cannons recently installed by the Knights to defend the castle.

After the Battle of Grunwald, which ended the Knights' ambitions in the area, and due to advances in warfare techniques and gunpowder, Kaunas Castle lost its strategic military importance and was used as a residence.

During the sixteenth century, the castle was strengthened and adapted to new defensive purposes through the construction of an artillery bastion, near the round tower, with a height of twelve metres and a diameter of forty metres, with a ditch in front. A firing gallery was installed at the bottom of the bastion and linked with the tower.

The castle was used as a prison in the eighteenth century. Later, the Russian administration granted permission for houses to be built in and around the castle, resulting in significant damage to the castle itself. For many years, Kaunas Castle stood abandoned. In the 1960s, the round tower was opened as a museum but due to the tower's structural deterioration, the museum was transferred elsewhere.

Protection of the castle began in 1930 with the demolition of nearby houses and an archaeological investigation of the area. Further efforts to preserve the castle were made in the 1950s: repairs were made to the round tower and the bastion was excavated from beneath several overlying strata.

Archaeological excavations continued at Kaunas Castle. The evidence gathered from these works suggests that the configuration of the castle, excluding the bastion, has remained in the form it took during its reconstruction in 1376.

Major reconstruction work started in 2010, building up the walls and adding floors or roofs to create the castle seen today, in red brick with a red-tiled roof. In 2011, a branch of the Kaunas City Museum was established in Kaunas Castle.

I took a taxi to my next destination, rather than struggle on slow buses, in order to save time and it was a long way out of town. The first driver didn't want to take me as there may not have been a return fare, but I got lucky with the second driver. We arrived at the entrance to the IXth Fort of the Kaunas Fortress. I had toyed with the idea of asking him to wait for me but there was a taxi stand with several taxis.

This fort was the last of a series of similar structures built between 1882 and 1911, on the orders of Tsar Alexander II, to protect both Kaunas and the Russian Empire's western borders. The fortress was battle-tested in 1915, when Germany attacked the Russian Empire and withstood eleven days of assault before capture. After the war, the fortress' military importance declined as advances in weaponry rendered it increasingly obsolete. Some sections have since been restored and the IX Fort houses a museum.

Two major nineteenth-century projects contributed to the city's revival. The Augustów Canal, completed in 1832, linked the Neman River and interior areas, providing another exit to the Baltic. A rail line linking Saint Petersburg, Warsaw and Germany via Kaunas made it an important transport hub and incorporated the first railway tunnel in the empire, completed in 1861.

Russia's western borders needed protection and fortresses existed or were being built in Latvia, Ukraine, and Belarus. The concept of building a fortress in Lithuania was discussed without result in 1796, but became a critical concern after Napoleon's French invasion of Russia in 1812.

The Grande Armée managed to cross the Neman River near Kaunas, on its drive towards Moscow, without major difficulties. An increasingly unified Germany troubled the Russian Empire during the second half of the century. A fortress in Kaunas would present an obstacle to attacks from the west, preventing further incursions towards Riga and Vilnius.

Construction began in 1882 with four thousand workers. The first forts were built using bricks protected by thick ramparts of earth, which were incorporated into the surrounding relief making them harder to breach. The buildings were symmetrical, usually having five faces, with positions for infantry and artillery. These forts were built according to the standard, Russian, brick-fort design of the time. Therefore, the first seven forts were very similar and differed only in the layout of their interiors and their integration into the surrounding relief.

During 1890, work began on the VIII Fort, known as Linkuva, but new construction techniques were introduced as the building progressed; in particular, reinforced concrete. The Linkuva Fort became the most modern, equipped with electricity, sewerage, and space for a garrison of one thousand.

By 1890, seven forts had been completed, supporting roads had been constructed and a railroad bridge over the Neman River had been adapted for military transport. In 1894, construction began on a dedicated narrow-gauge railway.

The IX Fort, begun in 1903, was the first of its kind in the Empire. The structure was a trapezoid, encompassing one infantry rampart, and was equipped with two, armoured watchtowers, electricity, and ventilation. The walls of its cannon casemates were covered with cork to reduce firing noise.

As new building and weapons technologies developed, the fortress was repeatedly renovated in order to maintain its military effectiveness. In 1912, an expansion and reconstruction initiative was launched. This project called for twelve new forts, along with batteries, support buildings and defensive structures. Its completion was scheduled for 1917. The older forts were to be completely encircled by the new project.

Work started on the new plans and the old forts were strengthened with concrete. When action began on the Eastern Front during the First World War, work on the fortress was halted. In 1915 only one fort, the IX Fort, conformed to the new technological criteria, while the X Fort was still under construction. The complex then covered about sixty-five square kilometres and contained a thirty-kilometre dedicated railway, a power plant, a water-supply system, mills, bakeries, a brewery and a telegraph.

Germany and the Central Powers began an offensive against Russia and advanced towards Kaunas. The German army reached Kaunas in July 1915. At that time, about ninety thousand soldiers, commanded by Vladimir Grigoriev, manned the fortresses.

To support this attack, the Germans mobilised four divisions and constructed a railway to transport their forty-two-centimetre Gamma-Gerät howitzer, more popularly known as Big Bertha. The howitzer's shell weighed one ton, and had a range of fourteen kilometres.

The German army concentrated its attack on the I, II and III Forts, which were the oldest structures. They could not surround the entire fortress, so its defenders were able to regroup and resupply. Ultimately, the first two forts were destroyed and the defenders retreated from the third. Like dominoes, the fourth fort's defenders retreated, as did the next fort's. All the forts were captured in under two weeks, with over twenty thousand Lithuanian casualties.

In July 1941, the Germans attacked the Russians in Poland, pushed them back towards Moscow and occupied the Baltic States. The VI Fort became a POW camp for Red Army soldiers. Kaunas's Jewish population numbered over thirty-five thousand. The Nazis, aided by Lithuanian auxiliaries, began massacring the Jewish population.

Acting under orders from the SS, Lithuanian auxiliary police units shot three thousand Jews at the VII Fort. In August over eighteen hundred Jews were shot at the IV Fort. In October, the residents of the Kaunas Ghetto were summoned and over nine thousand men, women and children were taken to the IX Fort and executed.

When Germany began losing the war and the battlefront approached Lithuania, there were attempts to prepare a defensive position in Kaunas. The Neman River was the line that Adolf Hitler called for its defence, at any price, but in August 1944 Kaunas was captured by the Red Army. The minimum number of deaths at the fortress during the war has been estimated at eighteen and half thousand, but other sources suggest thirty thousand Jewish deaths and more than fifty thousand in total.

The IX Fort was opened as a museum in 1958 to depict the crimes that had taken place there. The exhibits were expanded to include the history of the fortress. At one side of the restored fort stands a thirty-two-metre tall memorial to the victims of the Holocaust, constructed in 1984. It is designed in a modern, brutalist Soviet style – ugly as sin in my opinion – and in total contrast to the traditional architecture of the fort.

I walked out of the complex to get a taxi but the taxi rank was empty. I waited a while but no taxis arrived: not surprising, as no one would come this late in the day. I had to phone the hotel and ask them to arrange a lift. Another issue was that I wasn't returning to the hotel but wanted to go from IX Fort to Ąžuolynas, on the opposite side of the city.

It was late in the day but it was summer and would stay light until late into the evening, so I had time. Ąžuolynas (Oak Grove) is an eighty-four-hectare public park and a popular destination. It is known as the largest urban stand of mature oaks in Europe. Most of its trees are oaks ranging in age from one hundred to three hundred and twenty years old, but there are also stands of linden, birch and maple trees. There is a zoo in one corner of the park and attractions for children.

The current park is all that remains of a much larger oak forest that grew around the city. Much of this forest was cut down over the centuries, mainly for construction of buildings, bridges, castles and ships.

I walked back towards the hotel through the streets of the old city. Every now and again I caught glimpses of Pilsotas, a thirty-four-storey building, the tallest residential building in Lithuania and the second tallest building in the country at one hundred and twelve metres, completed in 2007. I didn't walk straight to the hotel but took several loops to see as much of the old city as possible, before settling down in a restaurant to try some local delicacies.

Chapter 11

Vilnius

After breakfast, I was collected by minibus for my tour to the Open Air Folk Life Museum in Rumsiskes. It is located overlooking the Kaunas Lagoon Regional Park that lies beside a large lake created by a dam providing water and hydroelectricity to the city of Kaunas. This was not far from the Pažaislis monastery, which, had I done sufficient research, would have been on my list of places to see on a longer visit to Kaunas, as was the Hill of Crosses, but there is always a reason to return.

The folk museum is an ethnographical-based museum covering one hundred and ninety-five hectares, displaying more than ninety thousand exhibits collected from all over the country. It is a series of buildings rescued and moved here and filled with contemporary items to show rural life throughout the centuries.

Some buildings are residential and others are shops, farms and workshops. Volunteers and staff, in period costume, demonstrate long-forgotten crafts and skills. The gardens have crops growing in them and animals are in the barns or wander the streets.

The group that I was with depleted as the day wore on. A few people had had enough and drifted off to go to the cafe or relax in the sun. Towards the end of the day, we had some free time. Just a couple of other stalwarts and I were all that was left of the original group of twelve. I didn't waste time at the cafe but went exploring some of the areas that we hadn't covered on the tour.

We stopped at a souvenir shop and were promised a short tour of the old city. I wasn't interested in the souvenirs and had walked around the old centre, so I tipped the guide and left.

I had some time before my transfer to Vilnius, so my morning was taken up by visiting the Devil's Museum, also known as the Žmuidzinavičius Museum, named after its originator, artist Antanas Žmuidzinavičius (1876–1966). It is dedicated to collecting and exhibiting sculptures and carvings of devils from all over the world.

In 1982, a three-storey extension was built to house the collection's expansion to more than three thousand items. Most of the devils are sculptures in wood, ceramic, stone, or paper. Others are masks or paintings on silk or canvas.

Many of the devils are art objects, for display only, but some have been incorporated into usable items, such as pipes and nutcrackers. Many of them represent folk myths and others express modern, political ideas. For example, one sculpture depicts Hitler and Stalin as devils in a dance of death over a pile of human bones.

The first floor of the museum contains Žmuidzinavičius's collection, which he acquired despite Soviet law against religious artefacts. On the second floor is a huge, wooden devil donated to the museum by someone who believed that it was causing him bad luck. The third floor contains many devils from former Soviet areas but others come from countries around the world, including Japan, Cuba, and Mexico.

I took the afternoon bus for the ninety-minute transfer to Vilnius. The name of the city originates from the Vilnia River, which is Lithuanian for 'ripple'. According to legend, Grand Duke Gediminas (1275–1341) was hunting near where the Vilnia River flows into the Neris River. Tired after the successful hunt of a bison, the Grand Duke laid down for the night. He fell soundly asleep and dreamed of a huge iron wolf standing on top of a hill and howling as strong and loud as a hundred wolves.

Upon awakening, the Duke asked a krivis (pagan priest) in his entourage to interpret the dream. The krivis told him that the iron wolf represented a castle and a city which would be established on this site. This city would be the capital of the Lithuanian lands and the home of their rulers and the glory of their deeds should echo throughout the world. Therefore, Gediminas obeyed the will of the gods and founded the city. The location of the city was ideal, as it lay in the Lithuanian heartland at the confluence of two navigable rivers, surrounded by forests and wetlands that were difficult to penetrate.

The duchy was continuously invaded by the Teutonic Knights. The future King of England, Henry IV (then Henry Bolingbroke), spent the entire year of 1390 supporting the unsuccessful siege of Vilnius with his three hundred fellow knights, returning as King Henry in 1392 with one hundred soldiers, but Vilnius was not captured.

Vilnius was the flourishing capital of the Grand Duchy of Lithuania. Gediminas expanded the Grand Duchy through warfare, along with strategic alliances and marriages. In 1387, Jogaila, a descendant of Gediminas, acting as Grand Duke of Lithuania and King of Poland Władysław II Jagiełło, granted Magdeburg rights to the city.

Magdeburg rights comprised a set of town privileges first developed by Otto I, Holy Roman Emperor (936–973), which regulated the degree of internal autonomy within cities granted by the local ruler. Named after the German city of Magdeburg, these town charters were perhaps the most important set of medieval laws in Central Europe.

Magdeburg was a major trading city on the River Elbe and part of the Hanseatic League. As with most medieval city laws, the rights were primarily targeted at regulating trade for the benefit of the local merchants and artisans. External merchants coming into the city were not allowed to trade on their own, but had to sell the goods they had brought into the city to local traders.

In medieval Poland's royal city development policy, both German merchants and Jews were invited to settle in cities and often competed with each other. Jews lived with privileges that they carefully negotiated with the king. They were not subject to city jurisdiction. These privileges guaranteed that they could maintain communal autonomy, live according to their laws and be subjected directly to the royal jurisdiction in matters concerning Jews and Christians.

One of the provisions granted to Jews was that they had the right to keep confidential how they had acquired objects in their possession. A Jew with this right could voluntarily divulge who had gifted, sold or loaned him the object but it was illegal to coerce him to divulge. Other provisions frequently mentioned were permissions to sell meat to Christians or to employ Christian servants. Magdeburg rights were granted to more than a hundred cities across Central Europe.

Vilnius's major growth as the capital of the medieval state is attributed to the reign of Grand Duke Gediminas, who sent letters across Europe from 1323 – 1324 inviting nobles, knights, merchants, doctors, craftspeople and others to come to the Grand Duchy to practice their trades and faith without restriction.

As a historically multicultural capital, many languages have been used in Vilnius. The predominant language of conversation in medieval Lithuania was Lithuanian but the language had no literary traditions and instead, Latin and Polish were widely used. The first state documents in the Lithuanian language appeared only at the very end of its existence, such as the Constitution of 1791, although Lithuanian is now the only official language. Today, Lithuanians speak, on average. 2.7 languages, and 97.3% of the population speak at least one foreign language.

The Vilnius city walls were built between 1503 and 1522, with nine city gates and three towers. Its growth was due, in part, to the establishment of a university, thanks to the Polish King and Grand Duke of Lithuania Stefan Bathory in 1579. The university soon developed into one of the most important scientific and cultural centres of the Commonwealth. The city also expanded due to its tolerance of various cultures, religions and language.

The seventeenth century brought a number of setbacks. The Commonwealth was involved in a series of wars, collectively known as The Deluge. During the Russo-Polish War (1654–1667), Vilnius was occupied by Russian forces; it was pillaged and burned and its population was massacred.

During the Great Northern War, it was looted by the Swedish army. An outbreak of bubonic plague in 1710 killed about thirty-five thousand residents. Devastating fires occurred in 1715, 1737, 1741, 1748, and 1749. The fortunes of the Commonwealth declined during the eighteenth century and the area was fought over and occupied by Russia, the Habsburg Empire and Prussia.

In 1812, the city was taken by Napoleon on his push towards Moscow. The Grande Armée was initially welcomed in Vilnius but thousands of soldiers died in the city during the retreat from Moscow, until it was re-taken by Russian forces.

Vilnius had a vibrant Jewish population and according to a Russian census of 1897, out of the total population of one hundred and fifty four thousand and five hundred, Jews constituted sixty-four thousand (approximately forty per cent). It became an independent country in 1918, but suffered incursions by Polish and Russian forces.

The war had irreversibly altered the city, as most of the predominantly Polish and Jewish population had been repatriated or exterminated during the Nazi occupation.

After the war the city began to grow again, following an influx from Poland, Belarus, Russia and Ukraine, as well as Lithuanians. On the previously rural outskirts, industrial areas were designed and large Soviet plants were built. By 1980, the number of inhabitants of Vilnius exceeded half a million.

The global economic crisis led to a drop in tourism and caused many of the planned projects to renovate the city's older buildings and monuments, associated with Vilnius' winning the European City of Culture award, to be scaled back or cancelled. There were also allegations of corruption and incompetence among the organisers, while tax rises for cultural activity led to public protests and riots.

I arrived in the late afternoon, so it was not worth the entry price into any paying tourist sights, but I did have time to do a few quick and cheap options. I walked along the promenade by the Neris River and then up the Vilnia

River. I crossed the river and climbed up the hill in Plikasis Kalnas, Kalnai Park to the Three Crosses monument.

According to a debatable legend, fourteen Franciscan friars were invited to Vilnius, from Podolia, by Petras Goštautas. The friars publicly preached the gospel but disrespected the local pagan gods. Angry city residents burned the monastery and beheaded seven of the friars on the hill, crucified the other seven and threw their bodies into the river.

From this hill, there are views across the city and across the river to the Šnipiškės area, which was developed as the new city centre in the 1960s. It has the first pedestrian zone in the city and included the largest shopping centre, the highest and the largest hotel, planetarium, the museum of Revolution, the Pioneer's Palace, a number of government ministry buildings and more recently, the thirty-three storey Europa business tower. It stands at one hundred and twenty-nine metres, being the highest building in Lithuania. The twenty -seven storey Europa apartment building is the third tallest building in the country, at one hundred and four metres.

I returned to the river and walked alongside it towards the Bernardinai Gardens, formerly the Vilnius Botanical Gardens. It has a place in cinema history: the first public film screening in Vilnius was held here in the summer of 1897. It is notable that such an event was held here so soon after the first film screening in the world was held in Paris in 1895 by Auguste and Louis Lumière. Georges Méliès's film A Trip to the Moon was first shown in the Lukiškės

Square cinema in 1902 and was the first feature film shown in Vilnius.

A little further on, I crossed the Vilnia River again to explore the Užupis district. It used to be one of the more run-down districts of Vilnius during the Soviet era, but is now home to Bohemian artists who operate numerous art galleries and workshops. Užupis declared itself an independent republic on April Fool's Day in 1997. In the main square, the statue of an angel blowing a trumpet stands as a symbol of artistic freedom.

I walked on for a brief visit to St Anne's Church, consecrated in 1500. It is a prominent example of both Flamboyant Gothic and Brick Gothic styles and its facade is spectacular.

The present brick church replaced two earlier churches that had suffered severe fire damage in 1582. According to legend, Emperor Napoleon, after seeing the church in 1812, expressed a wish to carry the church home with him to Paris 'in the palm of his hand'.

On the way back to the hotel, I had a quick visit to the Vilnius Cathedral: it was a totally different architecture to St Anne's Church. Its formal name is the Cathedral Basilica of St Stanislaus and St Ladislaus of Vilnius. The coronations of the Grand Dukes of Lithuania took place inside. Many famous people from Lithuanian and Polish history are buried in its crypts and catacombs.

Cathedral Square is surrounded by a number of the city's most historically significant sites. Lukiškės Square is the largest, bordered by several governmental buildings, such as the Lithuanian Ministry of Foreign Affairs, the Ministry of Finance, the Polish Embassy, and the Genocide Victims' Museum, where the KGB tortured and murdered opponents of the communist regime.

I moved on to Gediminais Avenue, the main shopping street in the city, to find a travel agent and a restaurant. I found a great offer from one travel agent and booked a tour, although it promised to be a long day with an early start.

There were also plenty of restaurants and I was looking for traditional dishes to sample. Some were easier to find than others and I would return several times over the next two weeks.

Lithuanian cuisine features the products suited to the cool and moist northern climate of Lithuania, such as barley, potatoes, rye, beets, greens, berries and mushrooms, plus dairy products, whilst fish dishes are very popular in the coastal region. One dish that I wanted to find was *Cepelinai*, a potato-based dumpling dish characteristic of Lithuanian cuisine with meat, curd or mushrooms. Several versions were available.

Dairy products are an important part of traditional Lithuanian cuisine. I had to learn the local words so that I could read a menu. These include white cottage cheese (*varškės sūris*), curd (*varškė*), soured milk (*rūgpienis*), sour cream (*grietinė*), butter (*sviestas*), and sour cream butter (*kastinis*).

Traditional meat products are usually seasoned, matured and smoked, such as smoked sausages (*dešros*) and smoked ham (*kumpis*). Soups (*sriubos*) include cabbage soup (*kopūstų sriuba*), beer soup (*alaus*), milk soup (*pieno*), cold-beet soup (*runkelių*), or a borscht (*šaltibarščiai*) and various kinds of porridges (*košės*) are part of a traditional and daily diet. Freshwater fish, herring, wild berries, mushrooms and honey are very popular on restaurant menus. Rye bread is traditionally served with every meal.

Lithuanians and other nations that once formed part of the Grand Duchy of Lithuania share many dishes and beverages. German traditions also influenced Lithuanian cuisine, introducing pork and potato dishes, such as potato pudding (*kugel*) and potato sausages (*vėdarai*) as well as the tree cake (*šakotis*).

Farmhouse brewing developed to a greater extent in Lithuania than anywhere else, developing into a commercial brewing culture. Lithuania is in the top five European countries for consumption of beer per capita, with seventy-five active breweries, although thirty-two of them are microbreweries. However, that is a lot of breweries for a population of under three million.

After breakfast, I walked to the base of Gediminas Hill and visited the National Museum of Lithuania, which is housed in the Old Arsenal. They also occupy several buildings around the city. I wanted to see the architecture more than the archaeological exhibits, although the museum also has models of Vilnius castles from the fourteenth to the seventeenth centuries, a collection of armaments and iconographic material relating to Old Vilnius.

I took the funicular up to Gediminas Castle, which sits on the top of the hill. The first wooden fortifications were built by Gediminas. The first brick castle was completed in 1409 by Grand Duke Vytautas but suffered from multiple attacks over the centuries. The three-storey tower seen today was rebuilt in 1933.

My last tourist sight of the day was the Palace of the Grand Dukes of Lithuania. The first building was originally constructed in the fifteenth century. For four centuries the palace was the political, administrative and cultural centre of the Polish–Lithuanian Commonwealth, but the original building suffered a major fire. When the Polish recaptured the city from the Russians in 1661, the palace was uninhabitable: it was abandoned until being demolished in 1801.

Work on a new palace started in 2002 on the site of the original building and took sixteen years to complete. The palace was rebuilt in Renaissance style to match the Cathedral of Vilnius. It looks original and is in keeping with the surroundings, but the use of reinforced concrete detracts from its authenticity. It is interesting to visit but knowing that it is a reproduction detracted from my enjoyment.

I was in Cathedral Square at seven a.m. to join the tour I had booked. There were several other tourists waiting and we got chatting until the minibus turned up. We were crossed off a list by the guide/driver and our tour began.

We drove out of the city against most of the rush-hour traffic that was heading into the city. Our first stop was the Paneriai Holocaust Park. This was the site of the Ponary massacre; a Nazi slaughter of seventy thousand Jews, twenty thousand Polish intelligentsia and eight thousand Russian POWs.

It is an area of gently rolling hills, covered in forest, with several paths leading off into the trees. There are several memorials to those who were murdered here and a small museum. It was a little eerie, and I was glad to leave.

Our next stop was the Pazaislis Monastery and the Church of the Visitation that I had missed on my earlier visit to Kaunas. It sits on a peninsula on the Kaunas Reservoir and is the largest monastery complex in Lithuania.

It was founded in 1662 by noblemen for the Order of the Camaldolese Hermits. Construction continued until 1674 and resumed in 1712. Exclusive architectural solutions were used for the first time in Europe, such as a hexagonal church plan and a concave façade. The interior is clad in marble. Writers of the time wrote that the construction cost eight barrels of gold coins.

The monastery's church, decorated with polished marble, was damaged by Napoleon's military horses based in the complex. In 1832 the monastery was closed by the Russian authorities and later converted into an Orthodox church. Alexei Lvov, the composer of the Imperial Russian national anthem, God Save the Tsar, was interred there in 1870. In 1915-1918, after the Orthodox monks had fled, it was used as a military hospital.

After 1920, the damaged monastery became Roman Catholic again and was restored by the sisters of the Lithuanian convent of St Casimir. After the Second World War, the Soviet authorities converted the church and monastery into an archive, later to a psychiatric hospital and finally an art gallery in 1966. It was only following independence that the complex was returned to the nuns and reconstruction work began.

We had a tour of Kaunas in the minibus and were dropped near the old town for some free time and lunch. After lunch, we headed back towards Vilnius to the other main reason for me booking this particular tour. More than halfway along the main road, with which I was now familiar, as I had travelled along it three times in as many days, we turned off it alongside a lake and reached Trakai Castle, probably one of the top twenty-five castles in Europe.

It sits on an island in Lake Galvė and now has a causeway to connect it to the mainland. Kęstutis began the construction of the stone castle in the fourteenth century and used it as his main residence and treasury. The castle suffered major devastation during an attack by the Teutonic Knights in 1377.

After the assassination of Kęstutis, a power struggle began between Jogaila and Vytautas the Great for the title of Grand Duke of Lithuania and the castle was besieged by both sides.

After the two settled their differences, Vytautas the Great undertook major construction at the castle around 1409 and Trakai became one of the main centres of the Grand Duchy of Lithuania: it was the capital before Vilnius. Two wings were added and a six-storey, thirty-five-metre high keep was added.

The keep was used for several functions, adding defence in depth and incorporating a chapel and living quarters, and was linked to the Ducal Palace, which had an inner yard that had wooden galleries which ran around the inner wall, used to access various facilities without going inside the palace itself.

The principal construction material was red Gothic bricks on foundations of stone blocks. The castle was decorated in a variety of ways, including glazed roof tiling, ornamental bricks and stained-glass windows. Its overall style could be described as Gothic with some Romanesque features.

Further development of the castle occurred in the early fifteenth century, when the walls were strengthened to a thickness of two and a half metres and raised with additional firing galleries, three towers and a large gatehouse.

When the castle was undergoing this expansion, the water level of Lake Galvė was several metres higher than it is today. The castle builders took advantage of this by separating the Ducal Palace and the castle with a moat just wide enough for small boats to sail through.

Soon after the Battle of Grunwald 1410, the castle lost its military importance and was transformed into a residence. Vytautas the Great died in the castle in 1430 without being crowned King of Lithuania. During the wars with Muscovy in the seventeenth century, the castle was damaged and gradually fell into disrepair.

During the nineteenth century, castle reconstruction plans were prepared. In 1905, the Imperial Russian authorities decided to partially restore the castle ruins. During the First World War, the Germans brought in their specialists, who made several attempts to restore the castle. Between 1935 and 1941, parts of the Ducal Palace walls were strengthened and the south-eastern castle tower was rebuilt. However, construction was abandoned until restarting in 1951, taking ten years but maintaining a fifteenth-century style.

Our last stop was in Girija, just twenty-six kilometres north of the city. Several places claim to be the central point of Europe but it depends on the definition of the borders of Europe. The first official declaration of the Centre of Europe was made in 1775 by the Polish royal astronomer and cartographer Szymon Antoni Sobiekrajski, who calculated it to be in the town of Suchowola in modern north-east Poland, but he based his calculation on mainland extremities and ignored islands. There is a monument commemorating that definition in Suchowola.

The only location recognised by the Guinness Book of World Records is located near the village of Girija. The exact point hosts a monument, erected in 2004, consisting of a column of white granite surmounted by a crown of stars.

For my last full day in Vilnius, I visited the Museum of Occupations and Freedom Fights, which was previously called the Museum of Genocide Victims, although it is commonly referred to as the KGB Museum. It is situated in a beautiful building completed in 1890. It has had several uses, including housing the Gestapo Headquarters and later the KGB Headquarters, with an interrogation centre and a prison in the basement.

The museum is dedicated to the Soviet Union's fifty-year occupation of Lithuania, the anti-Soviet Lithuanian partisans and the victims of the arrests, deportations and executions that took place during this period. More than a thousand people were executed in the building.

My last historical visit was to the Gate of Dawn, built between 1503 and 1522 as part of the city's defences and the only remaining gate of the original ten. The Gate of Dawn is one of the most important religious, historical and cultural monuments and it is a major site of Catholic pilgrimage in Lithuania.

In the sixteenth century, city gates often contained religious artefacts intended to guard the city from attacks and to bless travellers. The Chapel in the Gate of Dawn contains an icon of The Blessed Virgin Mary Mother of Mercy, said to have miraculous powers. Thousands of votive offerings adorn the walls and many pilgrims from neighbouring countries come to pray in front of it.

A short walk away is the Bastion of the Vilnius Defensive Wall, a museum in a stone bastion added to the city walls for additional defence. It has been extensively restored and a forty-eight metre, long tunnel descends to the lower firing gallery.

For a completely different experience, I visited the Museum of Illusions in the old town. It had only recently opened but early reports suggested that a lot of people thought it a great place. There was a personal reason to visit as both my father and grandfather had been members of the Magic Circle. It was a fascinating experience, especially as I had no idea what to expect, but it is interactive: you can take photos inside and it's a great way to have some fun.

Chapter 12

Latvia

On the way back to the hotel, I went via the main train station to check on train times and to buy a ticket. More than half of all inland freight transported in Lithuania is carried by rail. The Lithuanian Railways network consists of 1762 kilometres of 1520mm Russian gauge railway; just 122 kilometres are electrified. It also has 115 kilometres of standard gauge lines with more to follow.

The Rail Baltica project is currently under construction with a Trans European standard gauge track. It plans to link Helsinki via an underwater tunnel under the Gulf of Finland with Tallinn in Estonia. An extension of this line will link Riga in Latvia and Kaunas in Lithuania to Warsaw. From there, there are connections to the rest of the European rail network. It is expected to be operational in 2026 and when it opens, I plan to be one of the first passengers.

There wasn't a direct train at the time that I wanted to travel, early in the morning, so the journey would start with a Lithuanian train to Daugavpils, just across the border in eastern Latvia, and then a Latvian train from there to Riga. It would take over five and a half hours, including the change of trains, but being part of the EU, there were no border formalities or delays.

Latvian Railway's main network consists of 1,826 kilometres of 1,520mm Russian gauge railway, plus 54 kilometres of standard gauge, making it the longest railway network in the three Baltic States.

We passed through farmland, wetland, lakes and forests. Farmland comprises twenty-eight per cent of the country: the figure used to be higher until land reform. The abandonment of Soviet collective farms and forest makes up fifty-four per cent. Most of the country has an elevation of under one hundred metres and its highest point is Gaiziṇkalns Hill at 311.5 metres in the centre of the country, so I didn't see vistas; just what was next to the railway line.

I peered into the stands of pine, birch and spruce, hoping to see some wildlife common to the country as we sped past, such as deer, boar, moose, lynx, bear, fox, beaver, wolves and bison.

Several species of flora and fauna are considered national symbols, such as oak and linden, and the humble daisy is the national flower. The white wagtail is the national bird and not to be left out, the two-spot ladybird is its national insect.

The first Christian missionaries were sent by the pope in the twelfth century, sailing up the Daugava River, although the local population were reluctant to convert as rapidly as the church had hoped.

Saint Meinhard of Segeberg arrived in Uexküll (present day Ikšķile) thirty kilometres upriver from Riga, in 1184, on a mission to convert the population from their original pagan beliefs. Pope Celestine III called for a crusade against pagans in Northern Europe in 1193. When peaceful means of conversion failed to produce results, Meinhard plotted to convert the pagans by force of arms.

The main religion today is Lutherism due to German and Swedish historical influences. Adherence to Lutheranism peaked at sixty per cent of the population, with Roman Catholicism concentrated in the south. Orthodox Christianity has fallen: many Russians have left, but twenty-one per cent of the population professes no allegiance to any religion.

The Teutonic Knights soon ruled large parts of what is currently Latvia and formed the crusader state that became known as Terra Mariana, or Livonia. In 1282, Riga, and later other cities, became part of the Hanseatic League with Riga as a major trading centre.

In the seventeenth and early eighteenth centuries, the Polish-Lithuanian Commonwealth, Sweden and Russia struggled for supremacy in the eastern Baltic. After the Polish-Swedish War (1626 – 29), northern Livonia came under Swedish rule. Riga became the capital of Swedish Livonia and the largest city in the entire Swedish Empire.

Several important cultural changes occurred during this time. Under Swedish and largely German rule, most of Latvia adopted Lutheranism as its main religion, although the southern area under Polish influence adopted Catholicism. Despite this split, the ancient tribes assimilated to form the Latvian people, speaking one Latvian language although with many words borrowed from other languages.

During the Great Northern War, up to forty per cent of Latvians died from hostilities, famine and plague. Half of the residents of Riga were killed by plague in 1710–1711. At the end of the Great Northern War in 1721, parts of the area went to Russia and parts to the Polish Lithuanian Commonwealth, until 1795, when the whole area became part of the Russian Empire. However, their local laws, language and Parliament were preserved.

Complete emancipation of the serfs had occurred by 1819, but this was a mixed blessing, favouring the landowners as the peasants were dispossessed of their farms without compensation. This forced them to either pay rent or work for meagre wages.

Meanwhile, Riga expanded and became the largest port in the Russian Empire. It had factories, railways, banks, a university, theatres, museums and as the city expanded, new parks and boulevards were constructed.

Land reform allowed peasants to buy land. Many landless peasants remained, although they moved to urban areas and were employed in the new factories. An increasingly influential Latvian bourgeoisie developed just as the Young Latvians' intellectual movement laid the groundwork for nationalism from the 1850s to the 1880s.

The rise in the use of Latvian in literature and society became known as the First National Awakening. Authorities tried a programme of Russification, starting after the Polish led the January Uprising in 1863. The Young Latvians were largely eclipsed by the New Current, a broad leftist social and political movement in the 1890s, but exploded into nationalism during the 1905 Russian Revolution.

The First World War devastated the area which then came under German control until the Russian Revolution in 1917, followed by the Treaty of Brest-Litovsk between Russia and Germany in March 1918. With the armistice in November 1918, Latvia declared independence.

Widespread civil war developed and by the spring of 1919, there were actually three governments. A provisional government backed by the Allies, the Latvian Soviet government supported by the Red Army, and another provisional government supported by the Baltische Landeswehr, a local volunteer force, and the German Freikorps unit Iron Division, with volunteers from the former German army with promises of land and to counter Bolshevism, each fighting for their own interests.

Estonian and Latvian forces defeated the Germans at the Battle of Wenden in June 1919 and again, against the West Russian Volunteer Army in November. Eastern Latvia was cleared of Red Army forces by Polish troops supported by Latvian troops in early 1920, during the Polish–Soviet War (February 1919 to October 1920). They were led by Polish dictator Józef Piłsudski, whose aim was to grab as much land as possible and push the borders deep into Soviet Ukraine.

By 1923, the extent of cultivated land surpassed the pre-war level. Innovation and rising productivity led to rapid growth of the economy, but it soon suffered from the effects of the Great Depression. There was a bloodless coup in 1934 and the country was led by an authoritarian regime under Kārlis Ulmanis.

The start of the Second World War saw Germany invade Poland on 1st September 1939, with Russia attacking on 17th September. In the Molotov–Ribbentrop Pact agreed between Germany and Russia, just a week before, Latvia, Finland and Estonia had been assigned to the Soviet spheres of influence.

After the conclusion of the Molotov-Ribbentrop Pact, most of the Baltic Germans left Latvia by agreement between Ulmanis' government and Nazi Germany. A total of fifty thousand Baltic Germans left by the deadline of December 1939, with one thousand six hundred remaining to conclude business and thirteen thousand choosing to remain in Latvia. Most of those who remained had left for Germany by summer 1940.

Latvia was forcibly incorporated into the Soviet Union in October 1939. State administrators were liquidated and replaced by Soviet cadres. The Soviets dealt harshly with their opponents and more than thirty-four thousand two hundred and fifty Latvians were deported or killed. Most were deported to Siberia where deaths were estimated at forty per cent, but officers in the Latvian army were shot on the spot.

In June 1941, German forces attacked Soviet positions despite their Molotov-Ribbentrop Pact, ten-year non-aggression agreement in Operation Barbarossa. There were some spontaneous uprisings by Latvians against the Red Army, which helped the Germans to occupy the country.

The invasion was followed immediately by SS Einsatzgruppen troops, who were to act in accordance with the Nazi Generalplan Ost, requiring the population of Latvia to be cut by fifty per cent.

Latvian paramilitary and Auxiliary Police units were established and participated in several Holocaust atrocities, with more than thirty thousand Jews murdered in the autumn of 1941. Another thirty thousand Jews from the Riga ghetto were killed in the Rumbula Forest in November and December 1941, to make room for more Jews being brought in from elsewhere.

In June 1944, Soviet troops entered Latvia and captured Riga in October 1944. More than two hundred thousand Latvians died, including seventy-five thousand Jews, during the Second World War, until the country was re-occupied by Soviet forces.

Latvians fought on both sides of the conflict, partly due to conviction, also due to conscription by their occupiers but mainly on the German side with one hundred and forty thousand men in the Latvian Legion of the Waffen-SS.

When the Red Army re-occupied the country, they began to reinstate the harsh Soviet system. Latvian national partisans, soon joined by some who had collaborated with the Germans, began to fight against the new occupier.

As many as three hundred thousand Latvians fled from the Soviet army by moving to Germany or Sweden. Up to one hundred thousand anti-Soviets were captured by the Soviets and were executed or deported as rural areas were collectivised and strict Soviet rule imposed.

In March 1949, forty-three thousand rural residents, known as kulaks and Latvian nationalists, were deported to Siberia in Operation Priboi, which was carefully planned and approved in Moscow, and dealt a blow to partisan activity. Between one hundred and thirty-six and one hundred and ninety thousand Latvians, depending on the sources, were imprisoned or deported to Soviet Gulag concentration camps in the post war years to 1952.

An extensive programme was imposed limiting the use of the Latvian language in official capacity in favour of Russian as the main language. All of the minority schools teaching in other languages, such as Hebrew, Polish, Belarusian, Estonian and Lithuanian, were closed. An influx of new colonists, including labourers, administrators, military personnel and their dependents from Russia began.

The sole official language is Latvian but due to its history, Russian is the most widely used minority language by far and in 2011, thirty-four per cent of the population spoke it at home, including people who were not ethnically Russian.

Moscow used the well-developed Latvian infrastructure, skilled craftsmen and educated specialists to develop advanced industries such as train, aircraft and ship building, agricultural equipment, chemicals, food and oil processing. These developments pulled in more migrant Russian workers, thereby reducing the percentage of Latvians in the country.

By 1959, about four hundred thousand Russian settlers had arrived and the ethnic Latvian population had fallen to sixty-two per cent, but Russians had risen to twenty-five per cent. The population of Latvia reached its peak in 1990 at just under 2.7 million people, compared to the current 1.9 million.

In the 1980s, as the population of Riga city approached one million, the city became eligible, under the erstwhile Soviet rules, for the construction of an underground mass-transit system, funded by the Soviet government. However, the population decline and shortage of funding following Latvian independence put an end to this plan. The population is now about six hundred and twenty-eight thousand.

In the second half of the 1980s, Soviet leader Mikhail Gorbachev introduced political and economic reforms in the Soviet Union that were called *glasnost* and *perestroika*. The Latvian SSR, along with the other Baltic Republics were allowed greater autonomy. The so-called Singing Revolution intensified in the 1980s until Latvia declared independence and the Latvian SSR was renamed Republic of Latvia in 1991.

Citizenship was granted to those who had been citizens of Latvia at the day of the loss of independence in 1940, and their descendants. As a consequence, the majority of ethnic non-Latvians did not receive Latvian citizenship. By 2011, more than half of non-citizens had become naturalised or had left, but even today there are still two hundred and ninety thousand six hundred and sixty non-citizens in Latvia, representing 14.1% of the population.

Latvia's population had been multi-ethnic for centuries, though the demographics shifted dramatically in the twentieth century due to the World Wars, emigration, expulsion of Baltic Germans, the Holocaust and occupation by the Soviet Union. The share of ethnic Latvians had fallen from seventy-seven per cent in 1935 to fifty-two per cent in 1989. In 2011, there were even fewer Latvians, though their share of the reduced population was larger, at sixty-two per cent.

It was a difficult transition from a state controlled to a liberal economy and its re-orientation towards Western Europe, yet Latvia became one of the fastest-growing economies in the European Union.

Today, Latvia is a developed country, with a high per-capita income and an advanced economy. It performs favourably in measurements of civil liberties, press freedom, internet freedom, democratic governance, living standards and peacefulness.

After passing through some marshalling yards, the train slowed and pulled into the central station. I walked into the centre of the old city to find my hotel. I had been on two trains for nearly seven hours, with a short break in Daugavpils, and I needed to stretch my legs.

There was some of the afternoon left but not enough time to visit any attraction with an entry price to get your money's worth. The only thing that I had sort of planned was to go for a walk, visit St Peter's and check out local restaurants.

I signed in and immediately went for a walk in order to orientate myself. I walked through a park adjacent to Pilsetas Kanals (City Canal), which was originally a medieval moat that protected the city, and then cut inland to walk the length of Audēju Iela, the main shopping street.

Latvian cuisine has been influenced by the neighbouring countries. Meat and fish feature in most local dishes, so it can be difficult for vegetarians to taste local foods other than potato pancakes and mushrooms. Common ingredients in Latvian recipes are all found locally, such as potatoes, wheat, barley, cabbage, onions, eggs and pork. I had been warned that Latvian food is generally quite fatty and uses few spices, but dill is used extensively.

Speck is a type of smoked bacon. One of the most traditional dishes made with speck is *pelēkie zirņi ar speķi*. It is a simple dish made from many different types of peas, mixed with fried onions and speck.

Fish may be fresh or smoked and the most popular are cod, eel and pike, which we consider a coarse fish but is widely eaten in Eastern Europe. I was hoping to find some *Liepajas menciņš*, the signature dish of Liepaja, a fishing port in the south west of the country, which is made from smoked cod, potatoes and onions.

Mushrooms are a big part of Latvian cuisine and culture. During the autumn, people rush to the forests to go mushroom picking. There are plenty of traditional Latvian dishes made from mushrooms but the most widely acclaimed is fried boletus with salt, rye bread and herb-flavoured butter.

Rupjmaize is a dark bread made from rye and is considered a national staple. It is served with most main courses, including breakfast. Rye bread is extremely popular in Latvia and there are plenty of different types, including dark or sweet sourdough rye bread.

As for soups, sorrel soup is popular, as is beetroot soup but this is a unique Latvian dish which is also very popular in Lithuania. Every recipe differs and there are as many version as chefs, but it is often prepared using beetroots, cucumbers, eggs and served with kefir (a fermented milk product, like drinking yoghurt).

Another local soup is bread soup made from rye bread mixed with sugar, dry fruits and whipped cream. All these dishes can be washed down with *kvass* made from rye bread. *Kvass* is not considered to be an alcoholic drink but it can contain up to 1.2% alcohol.

After walking along Audēju Iela, I made my way towards Riga Cathedral. As I walked through the centre, I passed St Peter's Church. It had an unusual facade and an octagonal spire. The doors were open so, on impulse, I entered. It was built in 1209 and had a one hundred and thirty-six metres tall spire which was added in 1477. It collapsed in 1491 and was replaced and completed in 1677. The original church was destroyed in 1941, but rebuilt between 1967 to 1983.

I moved on to the Riga Cathedral, part of the Evangelical Lutheran Church of Latvia. It was built in 1211 by Livonian Bishop Albert of Riga and is considered the largest medieval church in the Baltic states.

An interesting anecdote about the church concerns the Reformation that Riga accepted in 1522, ending the power of the archbishops. In 1524, iconoclasts targeted a statue of the Virgin Mary in the cathedral to make a statement against religious icons. It was accused of being a witch and given a trial by water in the Daugava River. The statue floated so it was denounced as a witch and burnt at the stake.

Religious services were prohibited during the Soviet occupation from 1939 to 1989 and the cathedral was used as a concert hall. The Riga History and Navigation Museum was located in the southern wing of the cathedral. The building was reopened for religious services in 1991.

Chapter 13

Riga

The origin of the name of the city is disputed and there are several differing stories. It might be a corrupted borrowing from the Livonian word *ringa* (loop), referring to the ancient natural harbour formed by a loop of the Daugava River that flows through the city. Other theories include that it could be derived from *Riege*, the German name for the River Rīdzene, a tributary of the Daugava.

Another theory suggests that it comes from when Bishop Albert claimed credit for his campaign to conquer and convert the local populace from the Latin *rigata* (irrigated) symbolising an irrigation of dry pagan souls by Christianity.

German historian Dionysius Fabricius suggested, in 1610, that Riga's name comes from its already established role in trade and the name for the granaries found along the banks of the river. So there is plenty of speculation but no definitive answer.

The river Daugava has been a trade route since antiquity. Its inhabitants traded products of fishing, animal husbandry, flax and craft products in bone, wood, amber and iron. It was also offered access to the interior.

Meinhard of Segeberg arrived to convert the Livonian pagans to Christianity. He built a castle and church at Uexküll and died there in 1196, having failed in his mission. In 1198, his successor, Bishop Berthold arrived with a contingent of crusaders and settlers to commence a campaign of Christianisation. Berthold died soon afterwards and his forces were defeated.

The Church mobilised to avenge these setbacks. Pope Innocent III declared a crusade against the Livonians. In 1199, Bishop Albert was proclaimed Bishop of Livonia, by his uncle Hartwig of Uthlede, Prince Archbishop of Bremen and Hamburg. Albert landed in Riga in 1200 with twenty-three ships and five hundred Westphalian crusaders. In 1201, Riga was founded and he transferred the seat of the Livonian bishopric from Uexküll (present day Ikšķile) to Riga.

Albert established the Order of Livonian Brothers of the Sword in 1202, which was open to nobles and merchants with the aim of defending the territory.

Conversion of the local pagans continued. In 1207, Albert started to fortify the town. Emperor Philip invested Albert with Livonia as a fief and principality of the Holy Roman Empire. Crusaders usually served for a year and then returned home. A permanent military presence was encouraged by granting two thirds of the territory to the church and one third to the Order.

Albert had ensured Riga's commercial future by obtaining papal bulls which decreed that all German merchants had to transact their Baltic trade through Riga. In 1212, Albert led a campaign to compel Polotsk, in present day Belarus, to grant German merchants free river passage and also captured more territory.

Albert faced a rebellion from the locals in 1221 and reinforcements could not reach him. He sought the aid of King Valdemar of Denmark. The Danes landed in Livonia, built a fortress at Reval (Tallinn) and set about conquering Estonian and Livonian lands for themselves. Albert was able to reach an accommodation with them a year later and Valdemar returned all Livonian lands and possessions to Albert's control.

Albert's difficulties with Riga's citizenry continued and a settlement was reached in 1225, whereby they no longer had to pay tax to the Bishop of Riga and Riga's citizens acquired the right to elect their magistrates and town councillors. In 1227, Albert expanded the land under his control with the seizure of Oesel (Saaremaa), a large Island at the mouth of the Gulf of Riga and Polotsk.

Albert died in January 1229. He had failed in his aspiration to be anointed archbishop but the German influence he established over Livonia would last for centuries.

In 1282, Riga joined the Hanseatic League. The Hansa was instrumental in giving Riga economic and political stability, thus providing the city with a strong foundation. Over time, the influence of the Hansa weakened and Riga became the object of foreign military, political, religious and economic aspirations.

With the demise of the Livonian Order during the Livonian War, Riga became a Free imperial city of the Holy Roman Empire before it came under the influence of the Polish–Lithuanian Commonwealth in 1581.

During the Polish-Swedish War (1621 – 1625), Riga and the outlying fortress of Daugavgriva came under the rule of Gustavus Adolphus, King of Sweden, in 1621, who intervened in the Thirty Years' War (1618 – 1648) against the Habsburg Monarchy and Spain for political, economic and religious reasons in support of German Lutheran Protestantism.

Riga remained one of the largest cities under the Swedish crown until 1710, a period during which the city retained a great deal of autonomous self-government. In July 1701, during the opening phase of the Great Northern War, the Crossing of the Düna took place nearby, resulting in a victory for King Charles XII of Sweden.

Between November 1709 and June 1710, the Russians, under Tsar Peter the Great, besieged and captured Riga but they retained their privileges. Sweden's northern dominance had ended and Russia's emergence as the strongest Northern power was formalised through the Treaty of Nystad in 1721.

During these many centuries of war and changes of control in the Baltic, and despite demographic changes, the Baltic Germans in Riga had maintained a dominant position. By 1867, Riga's population was 42.9% German.

Riga's official language was German until 1891, when it changed to Russian as part of the policy of Russification of the non-Russian speaking territories of the Russian Empire, undertaken by Tsar Alexander III.

By the end of the Second World War, Riga's historical centre was heavily damaged because of constant bombing. Huge efforts were made to reconstruct and renovate most of the famous buildings that had been part of the skyline of the city, before the war, to make it the marvel that can be seen today, although, obviously for purists, reconstructions are not the same as originals.

I planned to visit the Ethnographic Museum, located on the outskirts of the city, which occupies eighty-seven hectares and displays one hundred and eighteen buildings and one hundred and fifty thousand artefacts. I am a sucker for this type of tourist attraction. I had planned to set out early and walk there but discovered that it was further than I had thought, at fifteen kilometres, avoiding main roads.

That is nothing to someone who had recently walked more than one thousand kilometres for five weeks along El Camino Frances, from St Jean Pied de Port in France via Santiago de Compostela to Fisterra, on the Atlantic coast in Spain, averaging twenty-eight kilometres a day. But I wanted some time to visit all the exhibits and see the Motor Museum nearby, so I took a bus. The journey time was still nearly an hour but it gave me the opportunity to see more of the city, even though it was mostly modern urban sprawl but every city is different. I had still set off early and arrived a long time before opening time at ten a.m., so I walked along the shores of Jugla Lake, which is overlooked by the museum.

In 1924, the Latvian Council of Monuments planned to create an open air museum in Riga, inspired by other open air museums in Scandinavia, such as Skansen in Stockholm. The plan was to relocate buildings from all over Latvia to the museum. Each of the buildings would represent the crafts and culture of different regions.

In 1928, the first building, a barn from Vestiena, was relocated and rebuilt in the museum. In 1932, the museum was opened to the public with just six buildings. By 1939, there were already forty buildings erected in the museum. Every region had its homestead and several other buildings of architectural or cultural merit.

The museum survived the Second World War but many of the staff had not. The Soviet authorities didn't support the project and even declared it ideologically incorrect. Only in the late 1960s did the museum see a renaissance, when a new generation of museum specialists began work and it re-started its expansion.

There are many buildings to see, arranged in clusters, and each furnished according to their original era of construction. There are farmsteads, residential buildings, farm buildings, windmills, cobblers, blacksmiths and so on. Staff and volunteers dress in period costumes. Various crafts and traditional pastimes are displayed, along with folk music, crafts and local festivals.

It is a large site and there was a lot to see: I spent a lot more time there than I had anticipated. It was late in the afternoon and I had also planned to see the Motor Museum. But weighing the cost of entry against the short time remaining before it closed and given that I am not a petrol head, I decided to give the Motor Museum a miss and I caught the bus back.

It was a Monday morning and in anticipation of museums potentially being shut, I had planned a day of doing something that didn't involve a museum. Riga Central Market claims to be Europe's largest market. It was planned in 1922 and built from 1924 to 1930, taking two years longer than anticipated as construction ceased for two years due to financial issues.

The main structures of the market are five pavilions reusing old German Zeppelin hangars from the nearby Vaiņode Air Base, with glass windows where the doors would have been. There are only nine remaining in the world. Four stand in a row and the fifth, the longest, was built perpendicular to them. The market covers seventy-two thousand three hundred square metres with more than three thousand trade stands.

During the Second World War, farmers had to supply the German army and were limited in what they could sell freely. The market shrank and two of the former hangars were used to house the German 726th supply unit's engine-repair shop.

I walked the two hundred metres to the Latvian Academy Observation Deck, housed in what was originally called the Latvian SSR Academy of Sciences. It was built between 1951 and 1961. It is designed in Stalinist architecture style and is also similar in style to the Seven Sisters in Moscow, especially the Leningradskaya Hotel, which is one hundred and thirty-six metres tall.

The Latvian Academy building, at one hundred and eight metres tall, was the first skyscraper in the republic and was the tallest building in the country until the construction of the Swedbank Headquarters in 2004, standing at one hundred and twenty-three metres. The Z Towers, erected in 2017, are the same height. The building is decorated with several hammer and sickle symbols, as well as Latvian folk ornaments and motifs. The spire was originally decorated with a wreath and a five-pointed Red Star, but this was removed after Latvia regained independence in 1991.

The Observation Deck is on the seventeenth floor at a height of sixty-five metres. There are panoramic views of the city below, and off in the distance to the south east is Riga's radio and TV tower, the tallest structure in the Baltic States and was the tallest in the European Union, reaching 368.5 metres.

Today, this is the thirteenth tallest structure in Europe but it is eclipsed by the number one in Europe, which is the Warsaw Radio Mast at a height of a whopping six hundred and forty-six metres. The current tallest structure in the world is the Burj Al Khalifa in Dubai at eight hundred and thirty metres, although the Saudis are planning the Jeddah Tower at over a kilometre tall. However, with just a third of it built, construction has been delayed by labour issues and COVID-19.

I remember going to a meeting in the Maastoren in Rotterdam. The highest building in the country, it stands one hundred and sixty-five metres high and I was due to visit the forty-fourth floor: the top floor. The lifts at ground level are situated in the middle of the structure but the structure tapers towards the top. I got a shock when I stepped out of the lift.

At the top floor, the vestibule outside the lifts is glass, from floor to ceiling, on three sides. It gives brilliant views across the city but when you are not prepared for it and you are not good with heights, it comes as a big shock.

After visiting the Observation Deck at the Academy of Sciences, I walked back to the old centre and out again, heading up Brīvības Bulvāris past a large green space and was about to pass a large church. I hadn't come across this on my research into things to see in Riga, but it was impressive and I had to have a look as I find the architecture and decoration of Orthodox churches so fascinating.

This is the largest Orthodox cathedral in the Baltic states, called the Nativity of Christ Cathedral, and was built in a Neo-Byzantine style between 1876 and 1883. It is renowned for its icons. During the First World War German troops occupied Riga and turned it into a Lutheran church.

In independent Latvia, the Nativity of Christ Cathedral once again became an Orthodox cathedral in 1921. Soviet authorities closed down the cathedral and converted it into a planetarium. The cathedral was restored when Latvia gained independence. I love the interiors and it was probably the best church that I had seen in the city.

After my unexpected diversion, I returned to walking up Brīvības Bulvāris to my original, next destination, the Corner House; a beautiful art deco structure that used to house the local KGB headquarters from 1940 to 1941 and from 1944 to 1991.

The building was originally designed to house shops on the ground floor, with five levels of apartments above and was completed in 1912. It also housed the music school of the Imperial Russian Society of Music.

In 1920, the new government of independent Latvia took over the building for government use and it saw a number of ministries come and go, plus several civilian occupiers. Since 2015, the building has been used by the Museum of Occupation of Latvia for an exposition concerning the history of KGB in Latvia. I had already seen a KGB museum but until you have, you may not know what you are missing, so I went in. However, I didn't need to linger.

I threaded my way through some of the back streets as a short cut in search of another street, Alberta Iela. Riga has one of the largest collections of Art Nouveau buildings in the world, with at least eight hundred. At the end of the nineteenth and beginning of the twentieth centuries, when Art Nouveau was at the height of its popularity, Riga experienced an unprecedented financial and demographic boom.

In the period from 1857 to 1914, its population grew from two hundred and eighty-two thousand to over half a million, making it one of the top five cities in the Russian Empire, and its largest port. Riga's middle class residents used their acquired wealth to build imposing apartment blocks outside the former city walls.

Local architects, mostly graduates of Riga Technical University, adopted current European movements and in particular, Art Nouveau. Between 1910 and 1913, between three hundred and five hundred new buildings were built each year in Riga, many of them in the Art Nouveau style. They are scattered throughout the city but there is a concentration of them along Alberta Iela.

At the top of the street, I made my way down to the docks. They sprawl for a long way downriver, but I just wanted to see a little of them before walking along the front, back towards the centre of the city. There were railway lines running parallel to the river, with spurs going to wharves. Some areas were fenced off but I doubted that I would have been able to walk along all the wharves. Yet I did get to see some of the port from a distance, with ships towering above the buildings, and walk along the wharves of the passenger terminal.

Roughly half of all the jobs in Latvia are in Riga and the city generates more than fifty per cent of Latvia's GDP, as well as around half of Latvia's exports. The biggest exports are wood products, IT, food and beverages, pharmaceuticals, transport and metallurgy.

It handles large volumes of crude oil, petroleum products, grain and coal: these are not produced domestically but are transit cargoes. The transport sector alone is around fourteen per cent of GDP. It is a major trans-shipment port with links to landlocked Belarus, Russia, deep into Asia and via the Baltic to the West.

The Freeport of Riga handles both cargo and passenger traffic. Ferries connect it to other Baltic ports. It handles over thirty million tons of cargo annually.

I walked along the front overlooking the Daugava River and under the Vanšu Tilts (Vanšu Bridge), a modern suspension bridge designed to relieve traffic pressure in the old city and the first bridge, upstream, crossing the river. On the far side of the river I could see the tower of the Swedbank Headquarters and behind it, the distinctive twin, circular Z Towers, plus several other tall structures.

After an early breakfast, I walked along the river front to fill in time until I was back in the Town Hall Square at opening time, outside the House of the Blackheads.

I had walked past it several times but now I was going inside. The original building was erected during the first third of the fourteenth century for the Brotherhood of Blackheads: a guild for unmarried merchants, shipowners, and foreigners in Riga.

The building looks to be in very good condition but it was totally destroyed during the Second World War by Nazi bombing during the first week of Operation Barbarossa in 1941. The Soviets demolished what remained and cleared the site in 1948.

The building today is a replica that was rebuilt between 1996 and 1999 with funds provided by Valērijs Kargins, the president of Parex Bank, and augmented by public donations.

Today the House of the Blackheads is a museum telling the story of trade in Riga and the tale of the Brotherhood of Blackheads. In the upper level are grand ballrooms, where historically many luxurious events took place, such as welcoming ceremonies for kings, queens and presidents, and cultural events, such as balls, classical music concerts, theatre and opera.

The historical cellar is the only original part of the building that survived the war and the Soviet occupation. The cellar is one of the unique places where it is possible to walk through the authentic underground area of Old Riga, where the remains, some walls, floors and even the wooden stairs are original.

Across the old city, sitting inside the Medieval moat, lies the Latvian War Museum, whose building is a mixture of old and recent construction. It first opened in 1916 as the Latvian Riflemen Battalion Museum at another location, displaying artefacts from the First World War. In 1917, the war had reached Riga: it was shelled and the museum was evacuated. In 1919, the museum restored operations at the present-day building, known as the Powder Tower, and re-opened to the public in 1921.

In 1936 the museum acquired the neighbouring plot and started work on an extension. The artefacts were put into storage. The building was completed in 1940 but occupied firstly by the Red Army, followed by the Nazis.

At the beginning of 1945, the building housed the Riga Nakhimov Naval School and later, from 1957 to 1990, the premises were occupied by the Latvian SSR Revolution Museum, which interpreted twentieth-century Latvian history from the point of view of Soviet ideology.

With independence, the Latvian War Museum was restored in the Powder Tower and its extension, displaying many of its original artefacts. I didn't know what to expect but given the lack of space, there is not the range of military vehicles displayed at some war museums, but it was still interesting.

Another day I went to the former Stock Exchange building, which now houses the Riga Bourse Art Museum. I was more interested in the architecture than the art. It was originally established in 1920 and contains an extensive collection of world art, spanning Ancient Egyptian and Middle Eastern art, dating from 5000 BC to the present.

In the first half of the nineteenth century, as Riga's trade developed, the cramped conditions of doing business within City Hall was not conducive to efficient trade. Therefore, in 1847, the members decided to build a new building that could contain the Guild itself and the Stock Exchange.

The Bourse was constructed between 1852 and 1856 in the Venetian Renaissance palazzo style, as a symbol of wealth and abundance. The façade incorporated a terracotta décor, allegorical sculptures and decorative elements. It was opened in the presence of the Russian Tsar Alexander II.

After the Second World War, it hosted the House of Science and Technology Propaganda and the façade was repainted in lighter colours of pale pink and brown. In 1980, there was a fire on the upper floor and remedial work started but stopped in 1982. It was only in 2011, after a three-year re-construction project was completed, that it was ready to open its doors as the Riga Bourse Art Museum.

The collection of the Riga Bourse Art Museum had been assembled and donated by several art collectors during the nineteenth and twentieth century. The collection contains more than twenty-two thousand works of art.

On my way to the next venue, I passed the Grand Palace Hotel. I had not come across this in my research but it is a magnificent building, built in 1877 to house a bank. It is a five-star hotel now and since entrance was not restricted, I walked in to gawp at the architecture and decor. I had lunch there and both architecturally and cuisine-wise, I wasn't disappointed. Next time I visit Riga, despite the cost, I will stay here.

Just a stone's throw away is Riga Castle. The first castle was built in 1330 but it has been demolished, rebuilt, extended and adapted several times. Although it has 'castle' in its name, the building seen today is more of a palace than a building with the thick stone walls associated with a Medieval castle.

It was destroyed in a revolt in 1484, although it was rebuilt between 1497 and 1515. When it was captured by Sweden in 1621, numerous extensions were added in 1641. The fortress was continually augmented and reconstructed between the seventeenth and nineteenth centuries. Since 1922, it has been the official residence of the President of Latvia. The Latvian government declared the castle its residence in 1938, as well as home to several museums, and some of the fascinating building is open to the public.

I often incorporate an extra day into my schedule every now and again to take care of unexpected delays or some fabulous-sounding visit that I hadn't discovered online. My research for Estonia was flawless and there were no hidden gems in the hotel's tourist brochure stand or advertised as I walked past several travel agents. Top candidates would have been the Jeglava or Rundale Palace with its ornate formal gardens but both were fresh in my mind from a recent earlier trip through Riga.

Instead, I had a day off from being a tourist and went for a walk and sat in the sun in a local park. At lunch time, I picked up my laptop from the hotel and settled in a bar I had discovered that served local dishes and a range of locally brewed beers.

Chapter 14

Estonia

The quickest overland way to reach my next stop in Tallinn was by coach, but I wasn't in a hurry. I like to travel by train and I had all day. On my last day in Riga, before lunch, I bought my ticket and reserved my seat on the train.

I could have taken the 'express', a seven-and-a-half hour journey up the coast for just over three hundred kilometres, a distance that you could easily drive in less than four hours. Instead, I was taking a slower route via Valga in southeast Estonia. There is only one train a day on this route. It leaves at a socially acceptable time of 10.46 a.m. but there is an almost four-hour break in Valga to change from a Latvian train to a local Estonian train, and it only arrives in Tallinn at 20.52. Oddly, despite being a much longer distance, it was significantly cheaper than the 'express' but I would get to see a lot more of the countryside.

In Valga, I made a dash to the Military Museum, then took a fast walk along the river front to the city centre to look at both the beautiful town hall and church. Then it was back to the railway station to board my connection to Tallinn.

I had booked my preferred seat on a train: a window seat facing the direction of travel. The country was even flatter than Latvia. Average elevation is only fifty metres and the country's highest point is the Suur Munamägi in the southeast, at three hundred and eighteen metres.

It may be a small country but it has two thousand two hundred and twenty-two islands along its three thousand seven hundred and ninety-four kilometres of coastline. The largest is Saaremaa, known for its cluster of meteorite craters. It also has over one thousand four hundred lakes with the largest, Lake Peipus, covering three thousand five hundred and fifty-five square kilometers. The train passed several of them as we sped through farmland and forest which covers half the country, the most common trees being pine, spruce and birch.

It is a thinly populated country with large open spaces and as we travelled through the countryside, I was on the lookout for a lucky sighting of any wildlife, such as grey wolf, lynx, brown bear, red fox, badger, wild boar, moose, red deer, roe deer, beaver and otter.

Estonia is the smallest of the three Baltic states and much of its history is similar to Lithuania and Latvia. Its name has been connected to the Aesti ancient people, first mentioned by Roman historian Tacitus around 98 AD. It featured in many of the same events as Lithuania and Latvia, so I will not go into detail but will give a brief overview for context.

During the crusades to turn the pagans into Christians, fighting reached Estonia in 1208. There were raids but no decisive battle until the Estonians suffered a major defeat at the Battle of St Matthew's Day in 1217, and again in 1219 as Danish king Valdemar II started conquering Northern Estonia. Despite setbacks, the country was conquered by 1227 and the German Teutonic Knights minority became the ruling elite.

The Reformation in Europe began in 1517 and by the 1530s, a majority of the population had adopted Lutherism.

In 1558, Tsar Ivan the Terrible of Russia invaded at the start of the Livonian War until being expelled in the 1570s by Polish-Lithuanian and Swedish armies. The war ended in 1583 with Northern Estonia becoming the Swedish Duchy of Estonia. Southern Estonia became the Polish Duchy of Livonia and Saaremaa, with the large island at the mouth of the Gulf of Riga remaining under Danish control.

By 1629, Sweden had gained control of the whole area, covering approximately modern Estonia, but the war had halved the population from two hundred and seventy thousand to just one hundred and twenty thousand. The population of Estonia grew rapidly for a seventy-year period, until the Great Famine of 1695–97 in which a fifth of the population died, leaving two hundred and eighty thousand. In the Great Northern War, Estonia was captured by the Russians and again the population suffered, with just one hundred and sixty thousand in 1712.

The Estonian national awakening began in the 1850s, as the leading figures promoted an Estonian national identity, greater use of Latvian and demands for greater rights. Moscow reacted by imposing a policy of Russification. In the 1905 Revolution, five hundred people were executed and hundreds more were jailed or deported to Siberia.

Towards the end of the First World War, the Russians retreated and Estonia declared independence in February 1918. German occupation followed until the end of the war in November 1918, and after just a few weeks of independence, Soviet forces invaded. However, they were repulsed in January 1919. Allied with White Russian forces who supported Latvian independence, invaded Russia until fighting ceased in February 1920.

In 1940, the country was occupied and annexed by Russia with executions and the deportation of eleven thousand people to Siberia. When the Nazis invaded, thirty-four thousand were forcibly drafted into the Red Army and political prisoners were executed by the NKVD.

The Nazis occupied the area and the economy was subservient to military needs: the one thousand Jews who had not escaped were quickly murdered.

As the Nazi military situation worsened, forced conscription was instituted in 1943, eventually leading to the formation of the Estonian Waffen SS division. Thousands of Estonians secretly escaped to Finland, where many volunteered to join the Finnish army, a reluctant alley of the Nazis against the Soviets. Many also fled to

Sweden before the Soviets re-occupied the country. Estonia again suffered in the war and lost about twenty-five per cent of its population through deaths, deportations and evacuations.

Thousands of Estonians opposing the second Soviet occupation and forced collectivisation joined a guerrilla movement known as the Forest Brothers. The armed resistance was strongest in the first few years after the war, but Soviet authorities gradually wore it down through attrition, deportation of twenty thousand to Siberia, and resistance effectively ceased to exist in the mid-1950s.

The introduction of perestroika in 1987 made political activity possible again and during the coup attempt in Moscow, Estonia declared independence on 20th August 1991, now a national holiday known as the Day of Restoration of Independence.

Since re-establishing independence, Estonia has styled itself as the gateway between East and West and has aggressively pursued economic reform and integration with the West. Because of its rapid growth, Estonia has often been described as a Baltic Tiger.

In 2010, after the global effects of the banking crisis, the economic situation stabilised and started a growth phase based on strong exports. In the fourth quarter of 2010, Estonian industrial output increased by twenty-three per cent compared to the year before. The country has been experiencing economic growth ever since.

It is a well-developed country with an advanced, high-income economy that was among the fastest-growing in the EU since its entry in 2004, with a competitive cost structure and a highly skilled labour force giving the country major comparative advantages. The government has pursued tight fiscal policies, resulting in balanced budgets and low public debt, reducing drag on the economy.

The country ranks very high in the Human Development Index, and compares well in many measures of political and economic indicators, such as being sixth in the world on the Index of Economic Freedom in 2017.

It also scores well on civil liberties, education and press freedom. Estonian citizens receive universal health care, free education and it has the longest paid maternity leave in the OECD. However, there are still vast disparities between different areas, as over half of the country's GDP is created in Tallinn.

Surprisingly, Estonians only make up sixty-nine per cent of the population, although it had been as low as sixty-one per cent in the period 1945 - 1989, but it continues to rise while the proportion of Russians, at 24.8% continues to fall. The proportion of Baltic Germans in Estonia has been falling steadily from 5.3% in 1881 to 1.3% in 1934 and continued to decline due to emigration, because of Russification, Soviet occupation and independence.

Unsurprisingly, languages spoken follow similar percentages, while common foreign languages learnt are English, Russian, German, and French. Religion also follows similar proportions and the country has a rich and diverse religious history, but in recent years it has become increasingly secular. The largest group are the various Christian denominations, principally Lutheran at thirteen per cent of the population and Orthodox Christians at sixteen per cent with changes in proportions reflecting the changes in ethnicity. There are very small numbers of adherents of non-Christian faiths, although polls suggest many are non-religious.

My train from Valga arrived dead on time at 20.52 at the main station in Tallinn. It was late in the evening but it was still light. I had noticed that dusk was already getting earlier as the summer solstice had passed some time before. I went straight to the hotel restaurant to order before they closed for the night.

I was hoping to try some local dishes. *Mulgipuder* is the national dish of Estonia, made with potatoes, meat and typically barley, but other grains can be used, such as oat, wheat or rye and served like a porridge. It is a very traditional food in the south of the country.

Historically, the cuisine of Estonia has been heavily dependent on seasons and simple peasant food. The most typical traditional foods in Estonia are black bread, pork, potatoes, and dairy products. Traditionally, Estonians like to eat everything fresh from the garden, the farm, or scavenged from the forest, such as vegetables, herbs, berries and fungi. Hunting and fishing have traditionally supplemented the diet, although today they are enjoyed mostly as hobbies.

Traditionally in winter, jams, preserves and pickles were brought to the table to accompany the main meal.

Gathering and preserving fruits, mushrooms, and vegetables for winter has always been popular, but today gathering and preserving is becoming less common because everything can be bought from supermarkets, whether in season or not.

Other foods that I was looking out for included *Kohuke*, a curd-cheese snack covered in chocolate but not something that I was likely to find on a hotel restaurant menu.

For a starter, I wanted to find *seljanka*, the Estonian version of *solyanka*; a sour soup that originated in Russia made of meat and pickled vegetables, usually cucumbers, but an Estonian variation replaces the meat with fish. Some versions include vegetables such as cabbage, onion or potatoes.

A dish that can be either a starter or a main course is *pirukad*, an Estonian version of an *empanada*. A main course option might be barley sausage, where the sausage meat is mixed with barley or sometimes it can be a blood sausage with barley. Fish features in cooking and popular dishes are sprats or herrings.

I don't have a sweet tooth and can ignore the sweet trolley but anything claiming to be traditional will catch my eye and I will try it. Local dishes include *vastlakukkel*, a cream bun traditionally served on Shrove Tuesday but available for several weeks around Easter, so I would be very lucky to find it in summer.

Kirju Koer consist of pieces of broken biscuits, marmalade, fruit, butter and chocolate; an odd combination but I am told that it is delicious. *Kama* is a flour-based dessert sweetened with sugar or honey and served with forest fruits. Lastly there might be an option to try some local cheese with rye bread. I was deeply disappointed as the hotel menu had no local food and just a bland list of international dishes available in every international hotel.

For my first day as a tourist in Tallinn, I caught the bus to the Tallinn TV Tower. I had been up several towers and belatedly reasoned that having a bird's eye view of the city at the start of the week would be of more benefit than taking in the view in mid-week.

The site is at the base of a peninsula that juts northwards into the Gulf of Finland, an arm of the Baltic. I was disappointed on two counts, as it was expensive to get in and being located so far from the city centre, it was difficult to pick out any of the detail of the city.

At three hundred and fourteen metres, it is the tallest structure in Tallinn. It took five years to build and opened in 1980. The structure consists of a one hundred and ninety-metre, slender, tapering concrete reinforced tower and a one hundred and twenty-four-metre steel mast on top of it. The Observation Deck is on the twenty-first floor, at one hundred and seventy metres, plus the restaurant and plant rooms housed in several floors that overhang the edges of the tower. Bullet holes dating from the Soviet coup attempt of 1991 are still visible at the base of the tower.

I might have been disappointed with the detailed view of the old town, but there were great views of the Botanical Gardens at its base, which I would walk around later, and a view of two harbours at the base of the peninsula. One is a small harbour on the western side, and to the east are great views of the larger and busy ice-free port of Muuga, with ships sailing to and fro, or moored at its wharves. It has modern facilities, featuring good storage and transhipment capability, a high-capacity grain elevator, chilled and frozen storage warehouses and roads and railway lines radiating outwards to the hinterland.

I also had a good view of the Iru Power Station with its giant turbine hall, massive water-cooling tower and its red and white-painted chimney. It provides electricity, hot water for a district heating system and processes two hundred and twenty thousand tonnes of municipal waste.

Estonia produces about seventy-five per cent of its electricity domestically: of that, eighty-five per cent is generated with locally mined oil shale. Alternative energy sources, such as wood, peat, and biomass, make up nine per cent and wind energy contributes six per cent, although that proportion is rising as more wind farms are developed. There is 60MW installed and 399MW worth of projects are being developed and more than 2800MW worth of projects are being proposed in the Lake Peipus area and the coastal areas of Hiiumaa. The country imports all its non-oil shale petroleum products from western Europe and Russia and it gets one hundred per cent of its natural gas from Russia; a heavy dependence meaning, since recent

Russian aggression, it is desperate to find alternative energy supplies.

The oil shale-based mining industry is concentrated in Eastern Estonia and is one of the most developed in the world. Although the amount of pollutants emitted to the air have been falling since the 1980s, the air is still polluted with sulphur dioxide from the industry that was developed in the early 1950s.

Estonia is, in general, energy dependent and resource poor but the mining sector does have opportunities. In addition to oil shale, there are deposits of limestone plus large reserves of phosphorite, pitchblende and granite that are not currently exploited.

Significant quantities of rare-earth oxides are found in tailings accumulated from fifty years of uranium ore, shale and loparite mining at Sillamäe. Because of the rising prices of rare earths, extraction of these oxides has become economically viable. The country currently exports around three thousand tonnes per annum, representing around two per cent of world production.

I returned to the centre but I didn't have time to visit any paying attractions and get my money's worth, so I walked around the old town to get my bearings, check out the shops and find some restaurants. I was particularly looking for Cafe Maiasmokk (Sweet Lip), which claims to be the oldest cafe still operating in the country and its internal decor hasn't changed in over a century.

I passed the Great Guild Hall, which houses the Estonian History Museum. It wasn't a large building and the cafe was open until late, so I changed my plans and bought my ticket to see both the architecture and the exhibits before entering the cafe.

The museum was initially established by chemist Dr Johann Burchart (1776 – 1838), who ran the local pharmacy. It was opened here in 1987 and carries on the story where its counterpart museum began in the mid-nineteenth century to cover the political and social upheavals of the twentieth century. Its exhibits include historically dressed mannequins and recreations of domestic interiors from the Second World War and the 1950s, represented by army uniforms and weapons plus an original hut used by the Forest Brothers.

Then it was time to see the interior of the cafe and stop for some refreshments to have time to absorb the atmosphere. The history of the coffee house goes back to 1806, when sugar baker Lorenz Cavietzel established the first sugar bakery. Later, in 1864, it was redeveloped by the Baltic German confectioner Georg Stude and he opened a café. During the late nineteenth century, it became renowned for its marzipan production: those buying marzipan included the Russian Imperial family.

Apart from the café, the premises also contains a room with an exhibition concerning the history and uses of marzipan. The Kalev Marzipan Museum Room has around two hundred marzipan figures, made from moulds over one hundred years old and features marzipan-painting demonstrations and lectures.

Chapter 15

Tallinn

I walked the couple of kilometres out of town to reach the Kadriorg Palace, a magnificent red and cream-painted palace under a green roof overlooking ornate, formal gardens. Tzar Peter the Great of Russia captured Tallinn in 1710 during the Great Northern War.

He bought a small Dutch-style manor house in nearby Lasnamäe for his wife Katherine. The house seen today is the result of a drastic renovation ordered by Nicholas I of Russia in 1827. The manor house was a little cramped and construction of a new palace at Kadriorg was started in 1718.

Peter and Katherine visited the unfinished residence on several occasions but after the emperor's death in 1725, Katherine showed no interest in the property. The great hall with Katherine's initials and profuse stucco decor survives, while many other interiors have been altered.

It was sporadically visited by members of the Imperial family, such as the empress Elisabeth and Katherine the Great. Between 1741 and 1917, the palace hosted the civilian governor of the Governorate of Estonia.

After the declaration of independence of Estonia in 1919, the palace became state property, and between 1921 and 1928 it housed what would eventually develop into the Art Museum of Estonia. The collections were moved in 1929 to allow refurbishments to take place to convert it into the official residence of the first President of Estonia, Konstantin Päts. It was completed in 1934.

During the Nazi occupation of Estonia, the palace was the residence of the civilian governor of occupied Estonia. After 1944, during the Soviet occupation, the palace once more served as the main venue for the Art Museum of Estonia, although the buildings were neglected and by the time of the restoration of Estonia's independence in 1991, they were completely run down. Restoration works began and the palace was re-opened in 2000 and is used to display foreign art works. It was also decided that a new building would be established nearby for the section of the museum devoted to Estonian art.

After wandering through the stunning interiors of the palace and viewing the artefacts and furnishings, I made my way to the Kumu Art Museum within the palace grounds.

In complete contrast to the classical and historical style of the palace, the Kumu Art Museum is an ugly, angular, glass and steel building. It has five-storeys but since it is built against a limestone escarpment, it doesn't intrude on the historical palace's ambience.

It was founded in 1919 and was housed in several different buildings before becoming established here in a purpose-built museum opened to the public in 2006. The third storey houses classics of Estonian art from the eighteenth century until the end of the Second World War. The next level displays Estonian art from 1945 to independence in 1991 and the top level displays temporary contemporary art exhibitions.

I caught the bus back towards the centre but got off on the outskirts of the old city centre. I was going to see the KGB Museum in the original Hotel Viru, originally run by Intourist, opened in 1972. It was the first high-rise building in Estonia.

It was a hotel with a difference: during the Soviet era, it was also an espionage centre. On the twenty-third floor of the hotel was a KGB radio centre, used to eavesdrop and spy on the hotel guests. The hotel rooms and tables in the restaurant had concealed microphones. The KGB left the hotel in a hurry immediately before the independence of Estonia in 1991, but the secret rooms were not found until 1994.

But this was not a revelation to me as decades before, on my first trip behind the Iron Curtain before the re-unification of Germany, I had heard a similar story. I was always suspicious of mirrors in case they were two-way with someone watching, and I often checked behind paintings and the inside of lamps for listening devices.

That evening, I walked through Tower Square Gardens, overlooked by some of the old town walls and towers, before going to find a restaurant. In the morning I was back at the same place to visit the Toompea Castle.

In 1219, the castle was taken by Danish crusaders led by Valdemar II. According to a popular Danish legend, the flag of Denmark fell from the sky during a critical stage of the battle. It fluttered out of the sky and turned the invasion in favour of Valdemar II and then became the flag of Denmark, known as the Dannebrog.

In 1227, the castle was taken over by the Order of the Brethren of the Sword, who instigated a lot of rebuilding and created much of the castle that is visible today. The castle again fell to the Danes just ten years later but was sold to the Teutonic Order in 1346 and would remain in their hands for the remainder of the Middle Ages. They were also responsible for erecting several towers, including one known as Tall Hermann at forty-eight metres high, which dominates the skyline.

By 1561, northern Estonia had become a Swedish dominion. The Swedes transformed the castle from a crusaders' fortress into a ceremonial, political and administrative centre, a purpose the castle has served ever since.

In 1710, Sweden lost the area to the Russian Empire. The Russian administration eventually carried out large reconstruction schemes and turned the castle into a palace. A new dominating wing in Baroque and Neoclassical style was added in the eastern part of the castle complex.

The castle was used to house the first parliament and despite different periods of occupation, it still serves as the seat of government. For the modern visitor, both the old and new parts can be seen. There is a long section of wall with a covered walkway, plus three towers that can be climbed, which also hold exhibits. From the tops of the towers, there are views across the rooftops of the city and across the park in front of the walls.

Many of the gates and towers still survive as do many of the walls, although some parts are missing. One of the artillery towers that can be visited is Kiek in de Kök (Peep into the Kitchen) built in 1475: it gained the name as the occupants could see into the kitchens of nearby houses. It is thirty-eight metres high with walls four metres thick. Cannon balls dating back to 1577 are still embedded in its outer walls.

Work in the sixteenth and seventeenth centuries saw the two lowest floors become hidden by protective earth works and the upper floors had new gun openings. By 1760, the tower had become obsolete and was used for storage and living space. Twentieth-century restoration work saw the tower and surrounding area returned to a more historical look. The tower now serves as a museum and photographic gallery.

Next door is the Alexander Nevsky Cathedral, a Russian Orthodox cathedral built in a typical Russian Revival style between 1894 and 1900 as part of the Russification of the area. It is dedicated to Saint Alexander Nevsky, who, as Prince Alexander Nevsky of the Novgorod Republic, defeated the crusaders of the Livonian Order and the Kingdom of Denmark.

In 1242, he won the Battle of the Ice on nearby Lake Peipus, so named as it was covered with ice and it forms part of the modern border between Estonia and Russia.

The cathedral has a large, central, onion dome surrounded by four smaller domes, each topped with gilded crosses and ornately decorated on the inside. I had departed from my usual theme of going to see the cathedral in the evening, as it was light until late and it didn't have restricted opening times, but I had seen many churches already on my tour and many Orthodox churches on my many visits through Russia, so it was just a quick visit to cross it off the list.

As the Soviets were communist and non-religious, many churches, including this cathedral, were left to decline. There were even plans in 1922 to use explosives to demolish the building but they were never carried out due to lack of funds and the amount of work required to demolish the massive structure. Since Estonia regained independence, the church has been meticulously restored. It has a peel of eleven bells, the largest of which weighs sixteen tons, more than the other ten combined.

Just a little further on is the Danish King's Garden, where some more of the city walls can be seen. Every year on 15th June, the Day of the Danish Flag is celebrated in the garden.

Overlooking the garden is the Maiden's Tower which houses a cafe and museum exhibits. It was built between 1330 and 1332. There are several stories relating to the name: one is that it was a was a prison for prostitutes.

Another tale is that a virgin was to be buried in the foundations for good luck but she asked whether she could see the view from the top of the completed tower. When it was completed, she threw herself from the top.

My last sight of the day was to continue the old town walls theme and walk along some of the old walls to reach the Viru Gate. At the nearby Helleman Tower, visitors can see the museum and walk along another section of wall on a wooden, covered walkway to another tower.

I caught the bus to the Tallinn Open Air Museum. It was only eight kilometres from the hotel but it took a while to get there as the bus kept stopping. It was also crowded as the route went past the zoo, a popular place to visit for both locals and visitors. I arrived well before opening time so I walked back down the road and along the coast for a while.

It was established in 1957 on a seventy-two hectare site with more than eighty buildings, many of them old. However, the oldest wooden building in Estonia is not here but is the church built in 1644 on Ruhnu Island in the Gulf of Riga.

The buildings are mainly arranged in clusters with forest trails between them. There are several extended farmyards with plenty of ancillary buildings to depict the architecture and culture of different regions in different centuries, plus a rural fishing village which comes complete with a church, schoolhouse, pub, several windmills with both four and five vanes, a fire station and net sheds.

There were staff in period costumes and some of the buildings had small vegetable plots. I was one of the first visitors to enter and I made sure I saw everything and walked along all the trails. I was probably one of the last to leave at closing time.

I had a few more days in the city. I walked across the city centre to the KGB Prison Cells. The building is Art Nouveau style, built in 1912 as a residential building, although it has a dark past.

In March 1918, when the newly declared independence was still extremely fragile, the building housed the Provisional Government of the Republic of Estonia. Later and until 1940, it was the location of the Ministry of War of the Republic of Estonia. With Soviet occupation, it housed the NKVD, the forerunner of the KGB. There were interrogation rooms, offices and prison cells in the basement.

Much of the building has been returned to its original residential purpose, although there is a small exhibition and the basement prison cells have been preserved.

Nearby is St Olaf's Church, which was built in the twelfth century. It was extensively rebuilt during the fourteenth century but a lot of restoration work has been undertaken since, as it has been hit by lightning ten times and been badly damaged by fire three times. Its spire is 123.8 metres tall.

It was the centre for old Tallinn's Scandinavian community before Denmark conquered Tallinn in 1219. Its dedication is to King Olaf II of Norway (also known as

St Olaf, 995–1030). The first-known written records referring to the church date back to 1267.

During the Reformation the church changed to follow the Lutheran tradition. It became surplus to the requirements of the Evangelical Lutheran Church and became a Baptist church in 1950. The Baptist congregation continues to meet at St Olaf's but it has become a Roman Catholic church and has a link with the KGB prison cells. From 1944 until 1991, the Soviet KGB used St Olaf's church spire as a radio tower and surveillance post.

Just up the road, on the very edge of the old city, is a tower which houses part of the Estonian Maritime Museum, with a park on three sides and overlooking the modern port facilities. However, the museum's main building is two kilometres away and is where I went to next, following a quick walk around the tower and its exhibits.

This location is known as the Lennusadam Seaplane Harbour and its main building consists of three giant hangars covering eight thousand square meters, originally housing seaplanes during the Soviet occupation.

Some exhibits are inside the hangars, some are outside in the open and others are in the water, moored to the wharf. The museum considers its main attraction to be the 1936 submarine Lembit, which was ordered by Estonia from the United Kingdom and has been renovated to its original appearance. The museum also has a yellow submarine, where visitors can learn how submarines were operated; there is also a flight simulator.

There is a full-scale replica of a First World War era Short Type 184 seaplane. The restored wreck of the wooden ship Maasilinn dates from 1560 and had plied the route between Saaremaa and mainland Estonia.

Moored against the wharf is the two-funnel, steam-powered icebreaker Suur Töll. It is the largest preserved pre-war icebreaker in the world. It has a chequered and complex history.

It was originally built for the Russian Empire in 1914 by AG Vulcan in Stettin, Germany and christened Tsar Mikhail Feodorovich. In 1917, it was taken over by the Bolsheviks and renamed Volynets.

When Finland captured the ship in 1918, they renamed it Wäinämöinen until 1922, when it was handed over to Estonia under the terms of the Treaty of Tartu and renamed Suur Töll. When Estonia was occupied by the Soviet Union in 1940, the icebreaker rejoined the Soviet fleet and was renamed Volynets.

The Soviet Navy decommissioned the ship in 1985 and it was going to be sold for scrap before being purchased by the Estonian Maritime Museum in 1987. The ship was renamed to her original Estonian name and was extensively renovated.

Chapter 16

Finland

I was back at the port in the morning. The day before, while walking around the port, I had also checked out ferry sailing times from Tallinn to Helsinki. The flight is just half an hour but factoring in the cost and time to travel to and from the airport, plus security, border controls and waiting at the carousel for your luggage, a ferry is the preferred option for many travellers, being quicker and cheaper.

There are several operators with several sailings a day and the journey takes between two and a quarter to four hours. I chose one, not on the basis of cost or speed of journey, that left mid-morning to give me time get to the port.

As part of the Rail Baltica project, a high-speed rail tunnel is being built under the Gulf of Finland. It will connect Tallinn with Helsinki on a standard gauge and will be twice the length of the Channel Tunnel and the longest underwater tunnel in the world. It will link into the rest of the European standard gauge network down to Warsaw. It has the funding and it is being built to cut the journey time to under thirty minutes. However, it is some years away from completion, so it is back to a slow ferry.

I planned to be on deck as we departed and later, on arrival, to see as much as I could as we left one port and approached the next. I wanted to see Helsinki turn from a smudge on the horizon to being able to pick out individual buildings. To fill the time in between, I had been to the supermarket to get something for lunch.

The earliest written appearance of the name Finland is on three runestones. Two were found in the Swedish province of Uppland and the third was found in Gotland and dates back to the thirteenth century. However, the name Suomi – Finnish for Finland – is of uncertain origin.

The archaeological finds from the Wolf Cave overlooking the Gulf of Bothnia suggest Neanderthal activity over one hundred and twenty thousand years ago with more finds dating from 8,500 BC, during the Stone Age, and later when the population expanded in the Iron Age.

The early exports were furs, slaves, iron, castoreum (a product from beaver scent glands) and falcons to European courts. Imports included silk and other fabrics, jewellery and weapons.

Finland became a common name for the whole country in a centuries-long process that started when the Catholic Church established a missionary diocese in Nousiainen, in south west Finland, in the twelfth century. Although distantly related, the Sami retained the hunter-gatherer lifestyle longer than the Finns. The Sami cultural identity and the Sami language have survived in Lapland, the northernmost province.

The twelfth and thirteenth centuries were a violent time in the northern Baltic Sea. The Livonian Crusade was ongoing with raids into Finland and the Finnish tribes were in frequent conflicts with each other, with Novogorod to the south east, against raids from Denmark and incursions by Swedes and Germans.

As a result of the crusades and the colonisation of some Finnish coastal areas with Christian Swedish populations during the Middle Ages, Finland gradually became part of the kingdom of Sweden.

Swedish became the dominant language of the nobility, administration, and education, while Finnish was chiefly a language for the peasantry, lower clergy and local courts. Even today, both are recognised as official languages, although Finnish became officially equal to Swedish only in 1892. Today, eighty-seven per cent speak Finnish as their native language and just five per cent speak Swedish as their native language.

The result of this inequality of language is that Finnish was not widely used in literature until it was given a boost by Mikael Agricola, who translated the New Testament into Finnish during the Protestant Reformation. Only a few works of literature were written in Finnish until the nineteenth century and the beginning of a Finnish national Romantic Movement. This prompted Elias Lönnrot to collect Finnish and Karelian folk poetry and arrange and publish them as the Kalevala, the Finnish national epic.

The most widely recognised Finnish author, who has also had her work translated into more than forty languages is Tove Jansson, best known as the creator of The Moomins. While she is the most translated Finnish writer, she was actually a Swedish speaker.

During the Protestant Reformation, the Finns gradually converted to Lutheranism. Today, sixty-eight per cent of the population identify themselves as supporters of the Evangelical Lutheran Church of Finland. Just one per cent support the Orthodox Church and a surprising twenty-eight per cent of the population claim to be unaffiliated.

In 1869, Finland was the first Nordic country to disestablish its church by introducing the Church Act. Although the church still maintains a special relationship with the state, it is not described as a state religion in the Finnish Constitution or other laws passed by the Finnish Parliament. When Finland gained independence in 1917, religious freedom was declared in the constitution of 1919.

Finland's current capital city, Helsinki, was founded by Gustav I of Sweden in 1550, whereas the capital had previously been Turku. Finland suffered a severe famine from 1696 to 1697, during which about one third of the Finnish population died, compounded by a devastating plague a few years later.

The devastation of Finland during the Great Northern War and during the Russo-Swedish War (1741 – 1743) caused Sweden to begin carrying out major efforts to defend its eastern part from Russia and twice led to the occupation of Finland by Russian forces, known as the Greater Wrath (1714 – 1721) and the Lesser Wrath (1742 – 1743). It is estimated that almost an entire generation of young men was lost during the Great Wrath, due mainly to the destruction of homes and farms and to the burning of Helsinki.

An increasingly vocal elite in Finland soon determined that Finnish ties with Sweden were becoming too costly, and following the Russo-Swedish War (1788 – 1790), the Finnish elite's desire to break with Sweden only heightened. Colonel Sprengporten resigned his commission in the Swedish army in 1777 and for years tried to secure Russian support for an autonomous Finland, but the Finnish national identity had started to become established.

Despite the efforts of Finland's elite and nobility to break ties with Sweden, there was no genuine independence movement in Finland until the early twentieth century. The High Court of Turku condemned Sprengtporten as a traitor in 1793, in absentia, and he died in St Petersburg in 1817.

At the end of the Finnish War in March 1809, after seventeen months of fighting against the Swedes, Russia controlled the autonomous Grand Duchy of Finland but the Finns were already dreaming of independence.

The Finnish famine of 1866 – 1868 killed approximately fifteen per cent of the population, making it one of the worst famines in European history. The famine led the Russian Empire to ease financial regulations and investment rose in the following decades.

The relationship between the Grand Duchy and the Russian Empire soured in 1906, when the Russian government made moves to restrict Finnish autonomy and implement the Russification of the area. For example, the universal suffrage was, in practice, virtually meaningless, since the tsar did not have to approve any of the laws adopted by the Finnish parliament. Desire for independence gained ground, first among radical liberals and socialists.

Significant advances in industrial development occurred after the Russian defeat in the Crimean War 1853 — 56 as the economy sought to catch up with European standards of production. Finland was ideally suited as it had a skilled labour force and natural resources to exploit.

In 1906, Finland became the first European state to grant universal suffrage and the first in the world to give all adult citizens the right to run for public office.

Tsar Nicholas II felt threatened by these developments and introduced a policy of Russification aimed at limiting the special status of the Grand Duchy of Finland, its cultural uniqueness within the empire and possibly the termination of its political autonomy

It was a part of a larger policy of Russification pursued from the late nineteenth to the early twentieth century by successive Russian governments who tried to abolish the cultural and administrative autonomy of non-Russian minorities within the empire.

The campaign evoked widespread Finnish resistance, starting with petitions and escalating to strikes, passive resistance, including draft resistance, and eventually active resistance. Finnish opposition to Russification was one of the main factors that ultimately led to Finland's declaration of independence in December 1917, during the Russian Revolution, although the First World War between Russia and Germany ended only in March 1918.

The German Empire saw Eastern Europe as a major source of vital products and raw materials, and was cognisant of Germany's resources being overstretched by fighting on both the Eastern and Western fronts.

Germany attempted to divide Russia. It provided financial support to revolutionary groups, such as the Bolsheviks, the Socialist Revolutionary Party and to radical, separatist factions, such as the Finnish national activist movement, to get Russia out of the war.

Supporting Finland would allow the German Army to attack Petrograd and the Kola Peninsula, an area rich in raw materials for the mining industry, while they could also utilise Finland's large ore reserves and a well-developed forest industry.

All this encouraged Finnish nationalism and cultural unity, leading to the idea that the Grand Duchy was an increasingly autonomous state of the Russian Empire. During the First World War, Germany used the Finns' eagerness to distance themselves from Russia. From 1915 to 1917, a Jäger battalion consisting of one thousand nine hundred Finnish volunteers was trained in Germany.

The policy of Russification was halted in March 1917 by the February Revolution, which removed Tzar Nicholas II from power. The ultimate collapse of Russia was caused by military defeats caused by inept leadership, war-weariness against the duration and hardships of the First World War and the collision between the most conservative regime in Europe and a Russian people desiring modernisation and freedom. Hence, a civilian government took over.

The autonomous status of 1809 – 1899 was returned to the Finns by the March 1917 manifesto of the Russian Provisional Government, led by Alexander Kerensky.

The February Revolution halted the Finnish economic boom caused by the Russian war economy. The collapse in business led to unemployment and high inflation but those who were employed gained an opportunity to resolve workplace problems. They called for an eight-hour working day, better working conditions and higher wages, leading to demonstrations and large-scale strikes in industry and agriculture.

While the Finns had specialised in milk and butter production, the bulk of the food supply for the country depended on cereals produced in southern Russia. The cessation of cereal imports from a disintegrating Russia led to food shortages in Finland. The Senate responded by introducing rationing and price controls.

The farmers resisted the state control and thus a black market was created, accompanied by sharply rising food prices. Food supply, prices and the fear of starvation became emotional political issues between farmers and urban workers, especially those who were unemployed.

The Bolsheviks' October Revolution in 1917 transferred political power in Petrograd to radical left-wing socialists. An armistice between Germany and the Bolshevik regime came into force in December and peace negotiations began in Brest-Litovsk.

The October Revolution disrupted the informal truce between the Finnish conservatives, socialists and the toppled Russian Provisional Government. Parliament seized power in Finland on 15th November 1917 and ratified proposals of an eight-hour working day and universal suffrage in local elections. The purely non-socialist, conservative-led government of Pehr Evind Svinhufvud was appointed on 27th November.

Svinhufvud's main aspirations were to separate Finland from Russia, to strengthen the Civil Guards and to return a part of Parliament's new authority to the Senate.

The number of Civil Guards tripled in four months. The first attempt at serious military training among the Guards was the establishment of a two hundred-strong cavalry school in Porvoo. German arms arrived in Finland in November 1917 along with fifty Jägers.

Revolution became the goal of the radicalised socialists following the loss of political control. Events in November 1917 offered momentum for a socialist uprising. Both Lenin and Joseph Stalin urged the socialists to take power in Finland. The majority of Finnish socialists were moderate and preferred parliamentary methods, prompting the Bolsheviks to label them as reluctant revolutionaries.

The reluctance diminished as a general strike appeared to offer a major channel of influence for the workers in southern Finland. The strike leadership voted, by a narrow majority, to start a revolution on 16th November. The uprising had to be called in just hours, due to the lack of active revolutionaries to execute it.

The Finnish labour movement wanted a military force of its own but hedged its bets and kept both the parliamentary and the revolutionary routes open. A marked consequence of the events of 1917 was the rise of the Workers' Guards. In three months, the number of trained Guards increased from sixty to three hundred and seventy-five.

The presence of the two opposing armed forces created a rift within Finnish society with the socialists, branded as Reds, facing the conservatives, branded as Whites. The decisive rift between them broke out during the general strike. The Reds executed several political opponents in southern Finland and the first armed clashes between the Whites and Reds took place. In total, thirty-four casualties were reported. Eventually, the political rivalries of 1917 led to an arms race and an escalation towards civil war.

The disintegration of Russia offered Finns an opportunity to gain national independence. After the October Revolution, the conservatives were eager for secession from Russia. The socialists were sceptical about sovereignty under conservative rule but they feared a loss of support among nationalistic workers, particularly after having promised increased national liberty.

Eventually, both political factions supported an independent Finland, despite strong disagreement over the composition of the nation's leadership. The issue of sovereignty also had an economic aspect. The Grand Duchy of Finland benefited from having an independent domestic state budget, a central bank, a national currency, a customs organisation and the rapid industrialisation of 1860 – 1916. Independence would disrupt the economy. On the other hand, the economic collapse of Russia and the power struggle of the Finnish state in 1917 were among the key factors bringing sovereignty to the fore in Finland.

Svinhufvud's Senate introduced Finland's Declaration of Independence on 4th December 1917 and Parliament adopted it on 6th December. The social democrats voted against the proposal and presented an alternative declaration of sovereignty.

The establishment of an independent state was not a guaranteed conclusion for the small Finnish nation. Recognition by Russia and other great powers was essential and Svinhufvud accepted that he had to negotiate with Lenin for the acknowledgement.

In December 1917, Lenin was under intense pressure from the Germans to conclude peace negotiations at Brest-Litovsk and the Bolsheviks' rule was in crisis with an inexperienced administration and the demoralised army facing powerful political and military opponents.

Lenin calculated that the Bolsheviks could win central parts of Russia but had to give up some peripheral territories, including Finland in the geopolitically less important north-western corner. As a result, Svinhufvud's delegation won Lenin's concession of sovereignty on 31st December 1917.

In a short time, Austria-Hungary, Denmark, France, Germany, Greece, Norway, Sweden and Switzerland had recognised Finnish independence, but for very different reasons. The United Kingdom and United States did not approve it but waited and monitored the relations between Finland and Germany, hoping that Lenin's regime would collapse and then get Russia back into the war. In turn, the Germans hastened Finland's separation from Russia to get the country into their sphere of influence.

The final escalation towards civil war began in January 1918, as each military or political action from one side resulted in a corresponding counteraction by the other. Both sides justified their actions as defensive measures. On the left, the vanguard of the movement were the Red Guards. On the right, the vanguard was the Jägers, many of whom had been transferred from Germany back to Finland, and the volunteer Civil Guards. The first local battles were fought during in January 1918 in southern and south-eastern Finland, mainly to win the arms race and to control the industrial city of Vyborg.

Carl Mannerheim, a former Finnish general of the Imperial Russian Army, was appointed the commander-in-chief of the Civil Guards. The Senate appointed the

239

Guards, who were renamed the White Guards, as the White Army of Finland. Mannerheim placed his Headquarters of the White Army in the Vaasa–Seinäjoki area on the coast half way up the Gulf of Bothnia.

The Red Guards, led by Ali Aaltonen, refused to recognise the Whites' authority and established a military force of their own. Aaltonen installed his headquarters in Helsinki and nicknamed it Smolna, echoing the Smolny Institute, the Bolsheviks' headquarters in Petrograd.

A large-scale mobilisation of the Reds began to protect vital positions along the Vyborg-Tampere railway to safeguard a large railway shipment of Bolshevik weapons from Petrograd. More than twenty soldiers died on both sides in a skirmish called the Battle of Kämärä, on the Karelian Isthmus, as White troops tried to capture the shipment.

Chapter 17

Finnish Civil War

At the beginning of the war, a discontinuous front line ran through southern Finland from east to west, dividing the country. The Red Guards controlled an area known as Red Finland, the area to the south, including nearly all the major towns and industrial centres, along with the largest estates and farms. The White Army controlled the area to the north, White Finland, which was largely rural, consisting of small or medium-sized farms and a lot of forest.

Enclaves of the opposing forces existed on both sides of the front line, such as a number of industrial towns within the White area and White strongholds within the Red area, such as Porvoo, Kirkkonummi and Uusikaupunki. The elimination of these strongholds was a priority for both armies in February 1918.

Red Finland was led by the People's Delegation in Helsinki, who sought democratic socialism based on the Finnish Social Democratic Party's ethos, which differed from Lenin's dictatorship of the proletariat.

In foreign policy, Red Finland leaned on Bolshevist Russia. A Finno–Russian treaty and peace agreement was signed in early March 1918. During negotiations, it was implied that nationalism was more important for both sides than the principles of international socialism.

But the Red Finns did not simply accept an alliance with the Bolsheviks without challenge. Major disputes appeared, for example, over the demarcation of the border between Red Finland and Soviet Russia. The significance of the Russo–Finnish Treaty evaporated quickly due to the signing of the Treaty of Brest-Litovsk between the Bolsheviks and the German Empire, also in early March 1918.

Lenin assumed that in war-torn, splintering Europe, the proletariat of free nations would carry out socialist revolutions and unite with Soviet Russia later. However, the majority of the Finnish labour movement supported Finland's independence.

The government of White Finland, under Svinhufvud, relocated to Vaasa, three hundred and thirty-five kilometres up the coast from Turku. In domestic policy, the White Senate's main goal was to return the political right to power in Finland. The conservatives planned a monarchist political system, with a lesser role for Parliament. Social liberals and reformist non-socialists opposed any restriction of parliamentarianism. They initially resisted German military help but the prolonged warfare changed their stance.

In foreign policy, the Whites relied on the German Empire for military and political aid. Their objective was to defeat the Finnish Reds, end the influence of Bolshevist Russia in Finland and expand Finnish territory eastwards to incorporate Karelia, a geopolitically significant home to ethnic Finns, stretching east from current day Finland borders to the White Sea.

General Mannerheim agreed on the need to take over East Karelia and to request German weapons, but opposed actual German intervention in Finland. He recognised the Red Guards' lack of combat skill and the demoralisation of the Soviet army, and he trusted in the abilities of the German-trained Finnish Jägers.

The number of troops on each side varied from seventy thousand to ninety thousand and both had around one hundred thousand rifles, three hundred to four hundred machine guns and a few hundred cannons. The Red Guards consisted mostly of volunteers who were paid wages at the beginning of the war. They were mainly urban and agricultural workers plus two thousand six hundred women recruited from the industrial centres of southern Finland.

The White Army consisted predominantly of conscripts with eleven thousand to fifteen thousand volunteers, such as land-owning farmers and well-educated people, who formed the backbone of the White Army. The main motives for volunteering were socio-economic factors, such as salary, food and political ideology.

The main armaments for both sides were weapons from the previous Imperial army. They were effective and adequately maintained, but there were ten different models of rifle in use, which caused ammunition supply problems.

The Civil War was fought primarily along railways, vital for transporting troops and supplies, as well as for using armoured trains, equipped with light cannons and heavy machine guns. The most strategically important railway junction was Haapamäki, one hundred kilometres northeast of Tampere, connecting eastern and western Finland as well as southern and northern Finland. Other critical junctions included Tampere and Vyborg. The Whites captured Haapamäki at the end of January 1918, leading to the Battle of Vilppula, a Red Offensive attempting to recapture Haapamaki, which was repulsed.

The Red Guards seized the early initiative in the war by taking control of Helsinki in late January 1918 and by undertaking a general offensive, lasting from February until early March 1918. The Reds were relatively well-armed but had a chronic shortage of skilled leaders, both at the command level and in the field, leaving them unable to capitalise on successes. Most of their offensives came to nothing.

Leadership and authority was poor: most of the field commanders were chosen by a ballot of the troops based on popularity rather than military ability. The Red soldiers were also hampered as their military training, discipline and combat morale were both inadequate and low. The

Reds achieved some local victories but better-led White troops forced them back towards the Russian border.

Around fifty thousand of the former Tzar's army troops were stationed in Finland in January 1918. The soldiers were demoralised and war-weary and the former serfs were thirsty for farmland set free by the revolutions. The majority of the troops had returned to Russia by the end of March 1918. Many Soviet soldiers supported the Finnish Reds but only around three thousand were persuaded to fight in the front line.

The White Army had two major advantages over the Red Guards. One was the professional military leadership of Gustaf Mannerheim and his staff, which included eighty-four Swedish volunteer officers and former Finnish officers of the Tzar's army. The other was the Jäger battalion and it was not just the Jägers' numerical strength, but their experts drilled and trained the White troops, who had received only basic training.

The Jäger battalion was not wholly conservative and universally supportive of the Whites. Over four hundred and fifty soldiers, mostly suspected socialist sympathisers, remained stationed in Germany as it was feared they might side with the Reds.

White leaders faced a similar problem when drafting conscripts into the army in February 1918. There were thirty thousand obvious supporters of the Finnish labour movement, who never reported to their draft stations. It was also uncertain whether drafts from the small and poor farms of central and northern Finland had sufficiently strong motivation to fight against the Finnish Reds.

The Whites' propaganda promoted the idea that they were fighting a defensive war against Bolshevik Russians and belittled the role of the Red Finns. Social divisions appeared between both southern and northern Finland and within rural Finland.

The economy and society of the south had modernised more rapidly than that of the north. There was a more pronounced conflict between Christianity and socialism in the north and the ownership of farmland conferred major social status, motivating the farmers to fight against the Reds.

Sweden declared neutrality both during the First World War and the Finnish Civil War. General opinion was divided between supporters of the Allies and the Central powers. The war-time priorities determined the pragmatic policy of the Swedish liberal-social democratic government such as sound economics (with major exports of iron-ore and foodstuffs to Germany) and sustaining the tranquillity of Swedish society's geopolitics. The government tolerated the participation of Swedish volunteer officers and soldiers in the Finnish White Army to block expansion of revolutionary unrest to Scandinavia.

A thousand-strong paramilitary Swedish Brigade took part in the Battle of Tampere. In February 1918, the Swedish Navy escorted the German naval squadron transporting Finnish Jägers and German weapons and allowed it to pass through Swedish territorial waters.

Swedish socialists tried to open peace negotiations between the Whites and the Reds.

In March 1918, the German Empire intervened in the Finnish Civil War on the side of the White Army. Finnish activists had been seeking German aid in freeing Finland from Soviet hegemony since late 1917, but because of the pressure the Germans were facing on the Western Front, they did not want to jeopardise their armistice and peace negotiations with the Soviet Union.

The German stance changed after 10th February when, despite the weakness of the Bolshevik position, Leon Trotsky broke off negotiations, hoping that revolutions would break out in the German Empire and change everything. On 13th February, the German leadership decided to retaliate and send military detachments to Finland.

The Imperial German Army resumed hostilities and attacked Russia on 18th February. The offensive led to a rapid collapse of the Soviet forces and to the signing of the first Treaty of Brest-Litovsk by the Bolsheviks on 3rd March 1918. Finland, the Baltic countries, Poland and Ukraine were transferred to the German sphere of influence.

The Finnish Civil War offered a possible low-cost access route for Germany into Scandinavia. The geopolitical status had just been altered by a British Naval squadron attack on the Soviet harbour of Murmansk on the Arctic Ocean on 9th March 1918. The leader of the German war effort, General Erich Ludendorff, wanted to keep Petrograd under threat of attack via the Vyborg area and to install a pro-German monarchy in Finland.

On 5th March 1918, a German naval squadron landed on the Åland Islands. On 3rd April 1918, the ten thousand-strong Baltic Sea Division launched the main attack at Hanko, the most southerly point of mainland Finland in the far south west of the country and offering the potential to overlook both the Gulf of Bothnia and the Gulf of Finland, followed on 7th April by the three thousand-strong Detachment Brandenstein taking the town of Loviisa, east of Helsinki.

The Germans advanced and on 11th April 1918, the battle for the Helsinki began. Nearly three thousand troops of the German Baltic Sea Division attacked the city from the north west, breaking through the front lines, and advanced on the western part of the city. A German naval squadron blocked the city harbour, bombarded the southern town area and landed marines.

Around seven thousand Finnish Reds defended Helsinki but their best troops fought on other fronts. Within a day, most of the southern parts and all of the western area of the city had been occupied by the Germans. Local Helsinki White Guards, having hidden in the city during the war, joined the battle as the Germans advanced through the town.

The city surrendered when the eastern parts of the city raised the white flag on 13th April in the tower of the Kallio Church. In total, sixty Germans, four hundred Reds and twenty-three Whites were killed in the battle. Around seven thousand Reds were captured.

On 19th April 1918, Detachment Brandenstein captured the town of Lahti. The battle was minor but strategically important as it cut the connection between the western and eastern Red Guards. Local engagements broke out in and around the town for the next two weeks, as several thousand western Red Guards and Red civilian refugees tried to push their way to safety in Russia. In total, six hundred Reds and eighty German soldiers died, and thirty thousand Reds were captured.

Meanwhile, Mannerheim advanced on Tampere. He launched the main assault on 16th March 1918, at Längelmäki, sixty-five kilometres north-east of the town, through the right flank of the Reds' defence. At the same time, the Whites attacked through the north-western frontline.

Although the Whites were unaccustomed to offensive warfare, some Red Guard units collapsed and retreated in panic under the weight of the offensive, while other Red detachments defended their posts to the last and were able to slow the advance of the White troops. Eventually, the Whites surrounded and laid siege to Tampere.

The Battle for Tampere was fought between sixteen thousand White and fourteen thousand Red soldiers. It was Finland's first large-scale urban battle and one of the four most decisive military engagements of the war. The White Army did not achieve a decisive victory in the fierce combat, suffering more than fifty per cent losses in some of their units. The Whites had to re-organise their troops and battle plans while continuing the pressure on the Reds.

After a heavy, concentrated artillery barrage, the White Guards advanced house to house as the Red Guards retreated. In the late evening of 3rd April, the Whites reached the eastern banks of the Tammerkoski rapids. The Reds' attempts to break the siege of Tampere from the outside, along the Helsinki-Tampere railway, failed. The Red Guards lost the western parts of the town by the 5th of April. The battle ended on the 6th of April 1918 with the surrender of Red forces in the city.

The remaining Reds, now on the defensive, showed increased motivation to fight. General Mannerheim was compelled to deploy some of the best trained Jäger detachments, initially conserved for later use in the Vyborg area.

The Battle of Tampere was the bloodiest action of the Civil War. The White Army lost nine hundred men, including fifty Jägers, the highest number of deaths the Jäger battalion suffered in a single battle of the civil war. The Red Guards lost one thousand five hundred soldiers, with a further twelve thousand captured. The eastern parts of the city, consisting mostly of wooden buildings, were completely destroyed.

After the defeat in Tampere, the Red Guards began a slow retreat eastwards and the White Army shifted the military focus to Vyborg where eighteen thousand five hundred Whites advanced against fifteen thousand defending Reds. General Mannerheim's war plan had been revised as a result of the Battle for Tampere, which was a civilian and industrial town. He aimed to avoid new, complex city combat in Vyborg with its old military fortress.

Jäger detachments tried to tie down and destroy the Red force outside the town, while other White forces were able to cut the Reds' connection to Petrograd.

The final attack began on 27th April with a heavy Jäger artillery barrage. The Reds last-stand defence finally collapsed and they were defeated. In total, four hundred Whites and six hundred Reds died, and fifteen thousand were captured.

Behind the major battles, as territory changed hands, both sides carried out political violence, called White Terror and Red Terror, with beatings, imprisonment and executions. Large-scale terror operations had developed during the First World War and were common in the February and October Revolutions, initiated by Russian soldiers mutinying and executing their officers, and later between the Finnish Reds and Whites, with summary executions.

The main goals of the terror were to destroy the command structure of the enemy, to clear and secure the areas occupied by an army and to create shock and fear among the civil population and the enemy soldiers. But the plan had a drawback, as it gave additional motivation to fight against an enemy perceived to be inhuman and cruel. Both Red and White propaganda made effective use of their opponents' actions, increasing the spiral of revenge.

The Red Guards executed influential Whites, including politicians, landowners, industrialists, police officers, civil servants and teachers and White Guards. Ten priests of the Evangelical Lutheran Church and ninety moderate socialists were killed. The two major centres for Red Terror were Toijala and Kouvola, where three hundred and fifty Whites were executed between February and April 1918.

The White Guards executed Red Guards and party leaders, socialist members of the Finnish Parliament and local Red administrators. During the zenith of the executions, between the end of April and the beginning of May, two hundred Reds were shot per day.

In total, one thousand six hundred and fifty Whites died as a result of Red Terror, while around ten thousand Reds perished by White Terror, which turned into political cleansing. White victims have been recorded exactly, while the number of Red troops executed immediately after battles remains unclear.

The civil war ended on 15th May 1918, when the Whites took over Fort Ino, a Russian coastal artillery base on the Karelian Isthmus. The Red Guards had been defeated and had either escaped to Russia or were in prison camps.

Casualties of Finnish Civil War were three thousand four hundred and fourteen Whites killed in battle, against five thousand one hundred and ninety-nine Reds; missing Whites, forty-six; Reds, one thousand seven hundred and sixty seven; executed: Whites, one thousand four hundred and twenty-four; Reds, seven thousand three hundred and seventy. Another stark statistic detailed those who had died in prison camps, such as just four Whites but eleven thousand six hundred and fifty-two Reds.

The White Army and German troops captured around eighty thousand Red prisoners, including five thousand women, one thousand five hundred children and eight thousand Russians. The largest prison camps included Suomenlinna (an island facing Helsinki), Lahti, Tampere and Vyborg. The Senate decided to keep the prisoners detained until each individual's role in the Civil War had been investigated.

In the anti-Red atmosphere of liberation, a total seventy-six thousand cases were examined. As many as twelve thousand five hundred died of starvation, malnutrition or disease, including the Spanish flu, while in prison. Of those cases that were reviewed, sixty-eight thousand were convicted, primarily for treason, with thirty-nine thousand released on parole. The average length of punishment for the rest was two to four years in jail. Five hundred and fifty-five people were sentenced to death but despite the Terror, only one hundred and thirteen were executed.

The end of the civil war did not end the political debate, especially on the best system of government, essentially between a monarchy with limited parliamentarianism or a democratic republic. The German leadership was able to utilise the breakdown of Russia for the geopolitical benefit of the German Empire. On 9th

October 1918, under pressure from Germany, the Senate and Parliament elected a German prince, Friedrich Karl, the brother-in-law of German Emperor William II, to become the King of Finland.

Finland's economic condition had deteriorated drastically from 1918, and recovery to pre-conflict levels was achieved only in 1925. Starvation had been averted, but it was only when the Allies were persuaded to relax their blockade of the Baltic that food shipments improved the situation. German forces left the country in December 1918 and a few days later, the as-yet uncrowned Prince Friedrich Karl also left.

The first free parliamentary election took place on 3rd March 1919. The United States and the United Kingdom, slow to acknowledge realities, finally recognised Finnish sovereignty on 7th May 1919.

Following the First World War, the weakness of both Germany and Russia empowered Finland and made a peaceful, domestic Finnish social and political settlement possible. A reconciliation process led to a slow and painful, but steady, national unification.

Chapter 18

Winter War

The period after the Finnish Civil War until the early 1930s was a politically unstable time in Finland due to the continued rivalry between the conservative and socialist parties. In 1918 and 1919, during the Russian civil war, Finnish volunteers conducted two unsuccessful military incursions across the Soviet border – the Viena and Aunus expeditions – to annex Karelian areas occupied by ethnic Finns.

In 1920, Finnish communists based in the USSR attempted to assassinate the former Finnish White Guard Commander-in-Chief, Marshal Mannerheim.

The Finnish Government allowed volunteers to cross the border to support the East Karelian uprising in Russia in 1921, and Finnish communists in the Soviet Union staged a cross-border raid into Finland, called the Pork Mutiny, in 1922. The Communist Party of Finland was declared illegal in 1931, and the nationalist Lapua Movement organised anti-communist violence. In 1932, the USSR and Finland signed a non-aggression pact.

I believe that Joseph Stalin regretted allowing Finland to become an independent country, especially when the revolution faltered. It was not an ally but a non-communist state and the pro-Finland movement in Karelia posed a direct threat to Leningrad.

When Stalin gained absolute power through the Great Purge of 1938, the USSR changed its foreign policy towards Finland and began to pursue the reconquest of the provinces of Tsarist Russia, lost during the chaos of the October Revolution and the Russian Civil War, especially near Leningrad which was just thirty-two kilometres from the Finnish border.

Russia approached Finland in 1938, as they didn't trust Germany and suspected war, but Finland stressed its neutrality, hoping for a deal with Sweden and privately didn't agree with the violent collectivisation and Soviet purges, including the execution of many of the Finnish communist elite.

The Soviet Union and Nazi Germany signed the Molotov–Ribbentrop Pact in August 1939 – a non-aggression treaty – but it included a secret protocol in which Eastern European countries were divided into spheres of interest. Finland fell into the Soviet sphere. On 1st September 1939, Germany invaded Poland. Two days later, Great Britain and France declared war on Germany. On 17th September, the Soviet Union invaded Eastern Poland.

Finland started a gradual mobilisation under the guise of additional refresher training. The Soviets had already started mobilisation near the Finnish border and assault troops were deployed in October 1939.

On 5th October 1939, the Soviet Union invited a Finnish delegation to Moscow for negotiations. The Soviets made several demands:

1) the border on the Karelian Isthmus to be moved westward to a point only thirty kilometres east of Vyborg,

2) Finland must destroy all existing fortifications on the Karelian Isthmus,

3) the cession of islands in the Gulf of Finland,

4) the cession of the Rybachy Peninsula, to move the border further away from Murmansk, cutting Finland's access to the Artic Ocean,

5) to lease the Hanko Peninsula for thirty years and permit the Soviets to establish a military base there.

In exchange, the Soviet Union would cede Repola and Porajärvi municipalities from Eastern Karelia, an area twice the size of the territory demanded from Finland.

The Finnish counter offered part of the area between the border and Leningrad, plus some Baltic islands. A false flag shelling of a Soviet border post by the NKVD gave them the casus belli and they invaded.

The Red Army had just completed the invasion and occupation of eastern Poland at a cost of fewer than four thousand casualties. Stalin's expectations of a quick Soviet triumph were backed up by some sycophantic politicians and generals suggesting their war aims could be achieved in just two weeks.

The reality was a long way from their aspirations. Stalin's purges in the 1930s had devastated the officer corps of the Red Army with less than half of the officers remaining. Promotion was based on party loyalty, rather than military ability, and any order could be countermanded by political commissars. The troops were poorly trained and poorly led.

Another factor was the terrain. Soviet Generals were impressed by the Nazi Blitzkrieg tactics, but that was in an area with tarmac roads, known depots and communication centres. In contrast, Finnish Army centres were small and deep inside the country. There were no paved roads; even gravel or dirt roads were scarce and most of the terrain consisted of trackless forests and swamps.

The Soviets planned to push the Finnish forces away from Leningrad, attack the centre of the country from the east and cut the country in half. They would then attack Petsamo to cut off access to the Arctic Ocean and advance southwards.

The Finnish strategy was dictated by geography. The one thousand three hundred and forty kilometre-long frontier with the Soviet Union was mostly impassable, except for a handful of unpaved roads. Despite overwhelming Soviet numbers with estimated ratios of twelve-to-one, north of Lake Lagoda, any movement would be slow.

Finland had a small force of full-time professional and technical soldiers, supported by a large force of reservists, trained in regular manoeuvres. They were trained in basic survival techniques in winter snow conditions, including skiing, and had warm winter clothing and snow suits.

Reservists knew their local area and were often on first-name terms with their officers, who were from the same village. Ammunition was an issue but supplies were supplemented by raiding Russian depots and foraging for spare ammunition and weapons from the Russian dead. Their strategy was not to stop enemy forces on the border but wear them down as they advanced into the forests with deadly hit-and-run tactics.

On 30th November 1939, Soviet forces invaded Finland with four hundred and fifty thousand men, bombed Helsinki and formed a puppet government. The Red Army advanced towards the Mannerheim Line, an array of Finnish defence structures stretching across the Karelian Isthmus, some way back from the technical border.

The Red Army soldiers on the isthmus numbered a quarter of a million, facing one hundred and thirty thousand Finns, with twenty-one thousand Finnish troops deployed in front of the Mannheim Line to harass and delay the Soviet advance.

The Finns had few anti-tank weapons and insufficient training in modern anti-tank tactics. The favoured Soviet armoured tactic was a simple, mass frontal assault, which could be dealt with by logs and crowbars jammed into the bogie wheels to immobilise a tank, or by use of the Molotov cocktail bombs which were mass-produced by the Finnish Alko alcoholic beverage company, whose product destroyed more than eighty Soviet tanks in the border-zone engagements.

Within a week, the Red Army had reached the Mannerheim Line and began its first major attack against Taipale, on the shore of Lake Ladoga. The Finnish artillery had scouted the area and made fire plans, in advance, in anticipation of a Soviet assault. The Battle of Taipale began with a forty-hour Soviet artillery bombardment. After the barrage, Soviet infantry attacked across open ground but was repulsed with heavy casualties.

For two weeks the Finns repulsed multiple attacks and the Red Army suffered heavy losses. One typical Soviet attack during the battle lasted just an hour, but left one thousand dead and twenty-seven tanks strewn on the ice.

In Central and Northern Finland, roads were few and the terrain hostile. The Finns did not expect large-scale Soviet attacks, but the Soviets sent eight divisions, heavily supported by armour and artillery, but made little headway.

The winter of 1939–40 was exceptionally cold with the Karelian Isthmus experiencing a record low temperature of minus forty-three degrees centigrade on 16th January 1940. At the beginning of the war, Soviet tanks were painted green and men dressed in regular khaki uniforms. It was not until late January 1940 that the Soviets painted their equipment white and issued snowsuits to their infantry.

The Red Army lacked proper winter tents and troops had to sleep in improvised shelters. Some Soviet soldiers had proper winter clothes, but this was not the case with every unit. In the Battle of Suomussalmi, they fought for a month from 7th December 1939, as part of the Soviet advance to cut Finland in half, between the White Sea and the top of the Gulf of Bothnia. Thousands of Soviet soldiers died of frostbite, with estimates of casualties from frostbite alone passing sixty thousand. Soviet troops also lacked skills in skiing, so soldiers were restricted to movement by road and were forced to move in long, slow columns.

The Finnish Army were experts at guerrilla tactics. The Red Army was superior in numbers and material but Finns used the advantages of speed, manoeuvring and independence of action. They would often isolate a detachment of numerically superior Soviet forces and successfully attack from all sides.

For many of the encircled Soviet troops in a pocket (called a *motti* in Finnish, yet nothing to do with a pocket; it means siege and is also a reference to one cubic metre of firewood), staying alive was an ordeal. The men were freezing, poorly nourished and endured poor sanitary conditions. The common Russian soldier had little choice: if he refused to fight, he would be shot. If he tried to sneak out into the forest, he would freeze to death. Surrender was no option for him as Soviet propaganda had told him how the Finns would torture prisoners to death. They felt trapped.

The terrain and distances on the Karelian Isthmus near Leningrad did not allow guerrilla tactics, so the Finns were forced to resort to the more conventional Mannerheim Line, stretching from the Gulf of Finland on the Baltic to Lake Lagoda.

Soviet propaganda claimed that it was as strong as the Maginot Line. In reality it was just a series of conventional trenches and log-covered dugouts, and even the most fortified section of the Mannerheim Line had only one reinforced concrete bunker per kilometre. According to the Finns, the real strength of the line was the stubborn defenders with a lot of *sisu*: a Finnish idiom roughly translated as guts and fighting spirit.

During the First Battle of Summa, a number of Soviet tanks broke through the line on 19th December, but the Soviets could not exploit the situation because of insufficient co-operation with no infantry support. The Finns remained in their trenches and therefore the tanks, stranded behind enemy lines, attacked positions at random until twenty were eventually destroyed.

North of Lake Ladoga, two Finnish divisions, totalling over thirty thousand, faced three times as many Soviets with a five-to-one advantage in artillery and air supremacy, with two thousand five hundred aircraft supporting the troops (against just one hundred and fourteen Finnish planes). There were, however, few strategic targets to hit and whilst railways were bombed, they were easily repaired. Helsinki was bombed a few times but Vyborg was completely flattened by twelve thousand bombs. The Soviet air force lost four hundred planes.

Finnish forces retreated to a ridge, up to ten metres high, across a small stream known as Kollaa: they held the ridge for the rest of the war. Further contributing to the legend of Kollaa was the sniper Simo Häyhä, dubbed the White Death by the Soviets, who was credited with over five hundred kills.

In the south, the Finns had surrounded some Red Army units. Contrary to their expectations, the encircled Soviet divisions did not try to break through to the east but dug in to repel the attacks as they were expecting reinforcements and supplies to arrive by air. As the Finns lacked the necessary heavy artillery equipment and were short of men, they rarely attacked the mottis but worked to eliminate only the most dangerous threats.

In Northern Karelia, Soviet forces were outmanoeuvred by Finnish guerrilla tactics using their superior skiing skills, use of white clothing and undertaking surprise ambushes and raids. By the end of December, the Soviets decided to retreat and transfer these forces to more critical fronts.

The Suomussalmi–Raate engagement was an operation which would later be used by military academics as a classic example of what well-led troops and innovative tactics can do against a much larger adversary. Suomussalmi was a town of four thousand, with long lakes, wild forests and few roads.

The Finnish command believed that the Soviets would not attack there, but the Red Army committed two divisions to the area with orders to cross the wilderness, capture the city of Oulu and effectively cut Finland in two. There were two roads leading to Suomussalmi from the frontier, the northern Juntusranta road and the southern Raate road.

The Battle of Raate Road, which occurred during the month-long battle of Suomussalmi, resulted in one of the largest Soviet losses in the Winter War. A Soviet force of more than fourteen thousand were ambushed and surrounded, suffering nine thousand casualties against Finnish losses of just four hundred. The Finnish troops captured dozens of tanks, artillery pieces, anti-tank guns, hundreds of trucks, almost two thousand horses, thousands of rifles, and much-needed ammunition and medical supplies.

In Lapland, straddling the Arctic Circle, the Finns expected nothing more than raiding parties and reconnaissance patrols, but the Soviets attacked in force with thirty-five thousand men. On 17th December, near Salla, a Soviet force was outflanked and retreated, abandoning much of its heavy equipment and vehicles.

Following this success, the Finns shuttled reinforcements to the defensive line in front of Kemijärvi. The Soviets attacked and the Finns counter-attacked, and the Soviets retreated to a new defensive line, where they stayed for the rest of the war.

Petsamo was an ice-free port, but the Finns lacked the manpower to defend it effectively. When they were attacked, they abandoned it and concentrated on delaying actions. Their tactics here were guerrilla attacks against

Soviet supply lines and patrols. Despite the Soviet advantage of a five-to-one ratio in numbers, the Finns successfully restricted the Red Army's movements.

The Red Army had been humiliated in the first weeks of the war with Soviet propaganda blaming bad terrain, the harsh climate and falsely claiming that the Mannerheim Line was stronger than the Maginot Line. Troop numbers were increased from ten divisions to twenty-six divisions and seven tank brigades, totalling six-hundred thousand soldiers. On 1st February, the Red Army began a large-scale offensive.

The situation led quickly to war exhaustion among the Finns, who lost over three thousand soldiers in trench warfare on the Karelian Front. After ten days of constant artillery barrage, the Soviets achieved a breakthrough on the Western Karelian Isthmus in the Second Battle of Summa.

By 11th February, the Soviets had approximately four hundred and sixty thousand soldiers; three thousand, three hundred and fifty artillery pieces; three thousand tanks and one thousand three hundred aircraft deployed on the Karelian Isthmus, against a Finnish strength of one hundred and fifty thousand. On 15th February, Mannerheim authorised a limited retreat to a fallback line of defence.

It became clear that the Finnish forces were rapidly approaching exhaustion. For the Soviets, casualties were high, the situation was a source of political embarrassment to the regime and there was a risk of Franco-British intervention. With the spring thaw approaching, the Soviet forces risked becoming bogged down in the forests and swamps.

Peace terms were negotiated with the Soviets through the Swedes, although the terms were harsh. Both Germany and Sweden were keen to see an end to the Winter War, as the Germans feared losing the iron ore shipments from Northern Sweden.

On 5th March, the Red Army advanced up to fifteen kilometres past the Mannerheim Line, entering the suburbs of Vyborg, and established a beachhead on the Western Gulf of Vyborg. The Finnish government, realising that the hoped-for Franco-British military expedition would not arrive, with ammunition running low and increasing casualties, was forced to agree terms and fighting ended on 13th March 1940.

Finland lost territory in the southeast, including its fourth largest city, Vyborg, lost access to Lake Lagoda and had to cede all of the vessels in the Lagoda Naval Detachment. It also lost territory in the central area, in the far north and several islands in the Baltic.

These areas included much of Finland's industrialised areas, about eleven per cent of its total territory and thirty per cent of the economic assets of pre-war Finland. Twelve per cent of Finlands population, about four hundred and fifty thousand Karelians, were evacuated and lost their homes. The Hanko peninsula was leased to the Soviet Union as a military base for thirty years.

The Finns were not alone in their fight: there were also foreign volunteers, forming the Volunteer Corps. The largest contingent was eight thousand seven hundred and sixty from Sweden; followed by one thousand and ten Danes; seven hundred and twenty-seven Norwegians; three hundred and fifty American nationals of Finnish background, and other nationalities totalling twelve thousand.

Finland distrusted Germany as it was an ally of Russia, but still established close ties with Germany in the hope of a chance to reclaim areas ceded to the Soviet Union in the one-sided peace treaty. This later brought Finland into the arms of the Axis powers to gain revenge on the Soviet Union. The Finns didn't support Germany's ideological views but needed a strong friend against a big bully. They had lost twenty-six thousand killed and forty-three thousand five hundred wounded.

Soviet casualties vary considerably, according to source, but perhaps up to one hundred and sixty-seven thousand were killed and one hundred and ninety thousand wounded. There were reforms made to the Red Army with the reduced influence of political commissars, officer reforms, with clothing, equipment and tactics for winter operations improved. Not all of the reforms had been completed by the time Germans initiated Operation Barbarossa, fourteen months later, but their confidence was boosted by the lessons learnt by the Red Army from the Winter War.

Chapter 19

Continuation War

The Finnish government declared national defence to be its first priority: military expenditure rose to nearly half of public spending after the defeat of the Winter War. Finland developed relations with Western powers but after the attack on Poland, the occupation of the Baltic states and the fall of France, Finland had to face reality and change its foreign policy.

On 23rd June 1940, Soviet Foreign Minister Molotov contacted the Finnish government demanding that a mining licence be issued to the USSR for the nickel mines near Petsamo, but a licence to mine the deposit had already been granted to a British-Canadian company.

He then demanded that Finland destroy the fortifications on the Åland islands and grant the USSR the right to use Finnish railways to transport Soviet troops to the newly acquired Soviet base at Hanko. The Finns, very reluctantly, agreed to these demands.

German plans to invade the Soviet Union meant that Germany had to reassess its position regarding Finland. Its policy of refusing arms sales to the Finns was reversed.

Secret sales and shipments started and German troops were allowed to transit through Finland in violation of the Molotov-Ribbentrop Pact.

The plan to invade Soviet Russia, made between Finland and Germany, started with Finland's war aims to reclaim its lost territories and possibly also include the Russian area of East Karelia, populated by ethnic Finns. Another claim by historians was a desire for shorter borders to push Finland's eastern borders to the White Sea. Some claim that Finland was not an ally of Nazi Germany but a co-belligerent.

The Soviets had four hundred and fifty thousand soldiers in the Finnish region. Their plans to invade Finland were ditched as they needed their best troops and materiel elsewhere to resist the Nazi invasion. The Northern Front also had eight aviation divisions of seven hundred aircraft, unaffected by the initial German strike against the Soviet Air Forces at the start of Operation Barbarossa.

The Finnish Army mobilised half a million soldiers, commanded by Field Marshal Mannerheim. Although initially deployed for a static defence, the Finnish Army was later to launch an attack on both sides of Lake Ladoga, putting pressure on Leningrad and thus supporting the advance of the German Army Group North.

Finnish intelligence had overestimated the strength of the Red Army, when in fact it was numerically inferior to Finnish forces at various points along the border. The army, especially its artillery, was stronger than it had been during the Winter War but included only one armoured battalion and lacked motorised transportation. The Finnish Air Force had two hundred and thirty-five aircraft in July 1941, and three hundred and eighty-four by September 1944, despite losses. Even with the increase in aircraft, the air force was constantly outnumbered by the Soviets.

The German Army of Norway, totalling sixty-seven thousand soldiers, held the Arctic Front, stretching five hundred kilometres through Finnish Lapland and tasked with striking Murmansk and cutting the Kirov railway connecting it to Leningrad. It was originally called the Murman Railway, but was renamed the Kirov Railway in 1935 in honour of Sergei Kirov, a prominent Bolshevik leader of the Russian revolution, who had been assassinated the year before.

In the evening of 21st June 1941, German mine-layers, hiding in the Archipelago Sea, deployed two large minefields across the Gulf of Finland, and German bombers flew along the gulf to Leningrad, mining the harbour and the river Neva as the first offensive action of Operation Barbarossa.

The Soviet Union sent seven bombers on a retaliatory airstrike into Finland, and a few days later four hundred and sixty fighters and bombers targeted nineteen airfields in Finland, losing twenty-three Soviet bombers. However, poor intelligence and inaccurate bombing caused damage to civilian targets. The Finns lost no aircraft but used the civilian damage to justify a defensive war against Soviet Russia.

A Finnish offensive started on 10th July and broke through Russian lines, reaching Lake Lagoda, and the Red Army rushed reinforcements into the area. Three Soviet divisions to the northwest of the lake were caught in a motti, and had to be evacuated across the lake.

By 23rd August, the Finns had reached the Vuoksi River to the east and encircled the Soviet forces defending Vyborg. Retreating Red Army forces abandoned equipment. By 2nd September, the Finnish Army had reached the old 1939 border.

A week later, Finnish Headquarters ordered a halt to the advance and settled into defensive positions. The front on the isthmus stabilised and the Siege of Leningrad began.

Meanwhile, the Finnish Army of Karelia started its attack in East Karelia towards Petrozavodsk on Lake Onega and the Svir River on 9th September. Soviet forces repeatedly attempted to dislodge the Finns from their bridgehead, south of the Svir, during October and December but were repulsed. However, the advance had been blunted and offensive operations ceased.

During the five-month campaign, the Finns suffered seventy-five thousand casualties, of whom twenty-six thousand had been killed, while the Soviets had two hundred and thirty thousand casualties, of whom fifty thousand became prisoners of war.

The German objective in Finnish Lapland was to take Murmansk and cut the Kirov railway. The plan was to capture the city in two weeks, starting on 29th June 1941 but a successful defence halted the advance thirty kilometres short of their objective, after months of fighting. Both sides dug in for the winter and undertook a war of attrition, but the front line remained stable until the Soviet Petsamo–Kirkenes Offensive in October 1944.

Murmansk and the Kirov railway were critical to the Russians as it was an ice-free port and handled many Lend-Lease supplies to the Red Army via the Arctic Convoys. The US supplied almost USD11 billion in materials, four hundred thousand jeeps and trucks; twelve thousand armoured vehicles, including seven thousand tanks; eleven thousand four hundred aircraft and 1.59 million tons of food. British shipments of Matilda, Valentine and Tetrarch tanks accounted for only six per cent of total Soviet tank production, but over twenty-five per cent of medium and heavy tanks produced for the Red Army.

The Wehrmacht rapidly advanced deep into Soviet territory early in the Operation Barbarossa campaign, leading the Finnish government to believe that Germany would quickly defeat the Soviet Union. The local name for the war wasn't the Second World War but the Continuation War, created at the start of the conflict by the Finnish government to justify the invasion of Russia, to the population, as a continuation of the defensive Winter War, although the authenticity of the government's claim changed when the Finnish Army crossed the old frontier of 1939 and began to annex Soviet territory.

By the autumn of 1941, the Finnish military leadership started to doubt Germany's capability of finishing the war quickly as their advance had slowed and had been halted at Moscow. The German offensive to Murmansk had stalled and the Finnish Defence Forces suffered relatively severe losses during their advance.

Mannerheim refused to assault Leningrad, believing that he had achieved his objectives, a position that angered the Germans. They would help to encircle the city and cut communications and even threatened convoys supplying Leningrad across Lake Lagoda, but they would not take offensive action to aggravate the Soviets. The Finnish Front settled down to a long stalemate.

Despite fighting with the Nazis, Finland maintained good relations with several other Western powers and stressed its status, not as an ally of Germany but as a co-belligerent and a democratic country.

Finland maintained diplomatic relations with the exiled Norwegian government and more than once criticised German occupation policy in Norway. When Great Britain was forced by Russia to declare war on Finland, Mannerheim repatriated British volunteers via Sweden.

The most sizeable British action on Finnish soil was the Raid on Kirkenes and Petsamo, an aircraft-carrier strike on German and Finnish ships on 31rd July 1941. The attack accomplished little, except for the loss of one Norwegian ship and three British aircraft, but it was intended to demonstrate British support for its Soviet ally.

Finland had a small Jewish population of approximately two thousand three hundred people. Finland was a co-belligerent, not an ally, and didn't support Nazi ideology. Jews fought with other Finns in the ranks of the Finnish Army. The field synagogue in East Karelia was one of the very few functioning synagogues on the Axis side during the war. There were several cases of Jewish officers of the Finnish Army being awarded the German Iron Cross, which they declined, and German soldiers were treated by Jewish medical officers.

Despite several Nazi requests, Finnish Prime Minister Jukka Rangell replied that Finland did not have a Jewish question. In November 1942, the Minister of the Interior and the head of State Police secretly deported eight Jewish refugees to the Gestapo raising protests among Finnish Social Democrat Party ministers. Only one of the deportees survived. After the incident, the Finnish government refused to transfer any more Jews to Nazi detainment.

Finland began to consider an exit strategy from the war after the Nazi defeats at the Battle of Stalingrad in February 1943, the Allied invasion of Sicily in July, and the rout at the Battle of Kursk in August.

Diplomatic advances were made intermittently but no agreement was reached. With Red Army forces pushing the Nazis back, Stalin decided to force Finland to surrender with a bombing campaign on Helsinki, starting in February 1944.

Over six thousand sorties were flown but Finnish anti-aircraft defence repelled many raids and only five per cent of the bombs hit their intended targets. In Helsinki, decoy searchlights and fires were placed outside the city to deceive Soviet bombers into dropping their payloads on unpopulated areas. Major air attacks also hit Oulu and Kotka but the number of casualties was low.

The Soviet Leningrad–Novgorod Offensive finally lifted the Siege of Leningrad on 26th January 1944 and pushed the Germans back to the Estonian border. Field Marshal Mannerheim had reminded the German command, on numerous occasions, that should German troops withdraw from Estonia, Finland would be forced to make peace, even on extremely unfavourable terms. Finland would abandon peace negotiations in April 1944 due to the unfavourable terms the USSR demanded.

On 9th June 1944, the Soviet Leningrad Front launched an offensive against Finnish positions on the Karelian Isthmus and in the area of Lake Ladoga, timed to coincide with Operation Overlord in Normandy, as agreed during the Tehran Conference.

The main objective of the offensive was to force Finland out of the war. The Red Army concentrated three thousand guns and mortars along the twenty-kilometre front. An intense artillery bombardment crushed the main Finnish defence line and the Red Army penetrated the second line of defence and recaptured Viipuri. The Soviet breakthrough on the Karelian Isthmus forced the Finns to reinforce the area, thus allowing the concurrent Soviet offensive in East Karelia to meet less resistance and to recapture Petrozavodsk by 28th June 1944.

The Finnish Army had retreated around one hundred kilometres to approximately the same line of defence they had held at the end of the Winter War. Finland still lacked modern anti-tank weaponry that could stop Soviet heavy armour.

German Foreign Minister, Joachim von Ribbentrop, offered German hand-held Panzerfaust and Panzerschreck antitank weapons in exchange for a guarantee that Finland would not seek a separate peace with the USSR. With the new supplies of weapons and assistance from German units, the Finnish Army halted the numerically and materially superior Soviet advance at Tali-Ihantala on 9th July 1944 and stabilised the front.

More battles were fought towards the end of the war, the last of which was the Battle of Ilomantsi, fought between 26th July and 13th August 1944 and resulting in a Finnish victory with the destruction of two Soviet divisions. However, resisting the Soviet offensive had exhausted Finnish resources.

Despite Nazi support, it was clear that the country would be unable to blunt another major offensive. With multiple Soviet victories and losing territory, Finland wished to leave the war. President Ryti was replaced by Field Marshal Mannerheim and sought peace terms.

Finland was required to return to the borders agreed in the 1940 Moscow Peace Treaty, demobilise its armed forces, pay war reparations, cede Petsamo, break off diplomatic relations with Germany and expel German forces from Finnish territory by 15th September 1944.

Finnish casualties amounted to sixty-three thousand dead and one hundred and fifty-eight thousand wounded. German losses were sixteen thousand four hundred killed and sixty thousand four hundred wounded. But the armistice between Finland and Russia did not bring immediate end to hostilities as there were still many German soldiers on Finnish territory.

The requirement to disarm or expel any German troops remaining on Finnish soil by 15th September 1944 eventually escalated into the Lapland War between Finland and Germany and the evacuation of the two hundred and fourteen thousand-strong 20th Mountain Army to Norway.

As early as the summer of 1943, the Nazi high command began to plan for the eventuality that Finland might negotiate a separate peace agreement with the Soviet Union. The Nazis planned to withdraw their forces northward to protect the nickel mines near Petsamo, and occupied Norway. During the winter of 1943–1944, the Germans improved the roads from northern Norway to Finland by extensive use of prisoner-of-war labour.

Even with the previously planned German withdrawal operation, the Finns estimated it would take three months for the Wehrmacht to fully evacuate and they were under Soviet pressure to disarm remaining German troops and to demobilise at the same time.

The 20th Mountain Army had been fighting along the seven hundred-kilometre Karelian Front from the Oulu River to the Arctic Ocean since the start of Operation Barbarossa. The army had thirty-two thousand horses and mules, twenty-six thousand vehicles, as well as one hundred and eighty thousand tons of rations, ammunition and fuel: enough to last for six months. It was starting to withdraw to Norway.

Following the announcement on 2nd September 1944 of the Finnish-Russian ceasefire, large amounts of materiel were evacuated from southern Finland. As the Finns wanted to avoid devastation of their country and the Germans wished to avoid hostilities, each side strove for the evacuation to be performed as smoothly as possible.

However, as they evacuated, Nazi mine-laying operations, the destruction of bridges and railways and pressure from the Soviets to complete the evacuation on time caused friction, but the last convoy left southern Finland on 21st September 1944, a week past the agreed armistice deadline.

The lack of Finnish aggression did not go unnoticed and there were still Nazi forces in Lapland. Under pressure from Moscow, the Finns attacked the rear-guard force. After the incident, the Nazis told the Finns they had no interest in fighting them but would not surrender.

The next incident took place on 29th September at a bridge crossing the Olhava river, between Kemi and Oulu. Finnish troops had been ordered to take the bridge, intact, and were attempting to disarm explosives rigged to it when the enemy detonated them, demolishing the bridge and killing several Finnish soldiers, including their commander.

Three Finnish transport ships landed troops at Tornio, at the top of the Gulf of Bothnia, on the border with Sweden, on 1st October. More landings were made over the next few days but the garrison in Kemi, twenty-five kilometres by road along the coast, was stronger than anticipated and counter-attacked several times.

It was only after a week of fighting that the Nazis retreated, destroying several bridges over the local rivers as a Finnish overland advance from Oulu worked its way up the coast. The German High Command had anticipated a major offensive and planned to retreat to a strongly defendable line, near Lyngen in Norway, a narrow belt of land between the sea and neutral Sweden, abandoning the nickel mines near Petsamo. Rear-guard actions delayed Finnish movements and the destruction of roads and bridges prevented the Finns from bringing up artillery.

The Finns' slow advance was co-ordinated with the Soviet Petsamo-Kirkenes Offensive, which started to push the Nazis back into Norway. Russian forces crossed the border into Norway and stopped. With a few small exceptions, most of Finland and northern Russia had been cleared of Nazi troops.

There was never an official peace agreement signed between Finland and Germany. It was not until 1954 that the government of Finland officially noted that the hostilities had ceased and interaction between Finland and

Germany, since then, had developed peacefully. Thus, the war had ended.

The 20th Mountain Army successfully withdrew most of its two hundred and fourteen thousand men, as well as a substantial amount of supplies and equipment from Lapland. The rear-guard delaying operations left Lapland devastated. In addition to three thousand one hundred buildings demolished elsewhere in Finland, estimates of destroyed infrastructure in Lapland were:

- 14,900 buildings, 46 percent of Lapland's property
- 470 kilometres of railways
- 9,500 kilometres of roads
- 675 bridges
- 3,700 kilometres of phone lines.

The reconstruction of Lapland took place until the early 1950s, although the railroad network was not functional until 1957. By 1973, over eight hundred thousand cartridges, seventy thousand mines and four hundred thousand other explosives had been identified and made safe in Lapland. The Soviet demand for six hundred million US dollars in war indemnities was reduced to three hundred million (equivalent to USD5.4 billion in 2019).

After the end of hostilities, Finland largely remained an agrarian country with forty-six per cent of workers employed in agriculture and a third living in urban areas. Finland rejected Marshall aid, in deference to Soviet desires, in the hope of preserving Finland's independence, but the United States provided secret development aid and the country rapidly industrialised. It developed an advanced economy, while building an extensive welfare state based on the Nordic model, resulting in widespread prosperity and a high per-capita income.

Chapter 20

Helsinki

The ferry from Tallinn sailed past several islands, including the Soumenlinna (Castle of Finland, from *Soumi* for Finland and *linna* for castle), with good views of its massive fortifications, which were on my list of things to see. We passed several ships moored in the harbour and docked opposite Market Square. I was looking forward to revisiting Finland. Finnish and Swedish are both official languages and while I don't speak Swedish, I knew some Finnish as I had worked in Israel for a year and had a Finnish girlfriend.

We had Hebrew lessons but explanations were in English so, as we learnt Hebrew, she also improved her English and not to be outdone she translated words and phrases into Finnish for me, so I was learning two languages at the same time. And we were surprised about some odd similarities such as *makkara*, which means 'What is the matter?' in Hebrew, but 'sausage' in Finnish or *talo*, which sounds like 'tallow' in English but means 'house' in Finnish.

Nearly eighty per cent of the citizens speak Finnish as their first language, and six per cent speak Swedish, while ninety-three per cent of citizens can speak a second language: this was great if their second language was one that I could also speak. The remainder of the population speak a native first language other than Finnish, Swedish or one of the three Sami languages spoken in Finland.

Foreign citizens make up 9.6% of the population, while the total immigrant population making up sixteen per cent. The largest groups of residents of non-Finnish background come from Russia (19,600), Estonia (12,900), which is the largest Estonian population outside Estonia and thirdly, Somalia (11,400).

Helsinki is the third most northernly capital after Nuuk in Greenland and Reykjavik in Iceland. Finland is known for its lakes and forests. It has one hundred and eighty-seven thousand lakes larger than five hundred square meters and seventy-five thousand islands larger than half a square kilometre. Its largest lake, Saimaa, in the Lakeland area of southeast Finland, is the fourth largest in Europe. The greatest concentration of islands is found in the southwest, in the Archipelago Sea between Turku and the large island of Åland, but even Helsinki is built on three hundred and fifteen islands.

Most of Helsinki's older buildings were built after a massive fire in 1808, but the oldest surviving building in the centre of Helsinki is the stone-built Sederholm House, dating from 1757, on the corner of Senate Square, which now houses the Helsinki City Museum. As I walked around the city, I saw many Art Nouveau-style buildings, making it a delight to wander along the main thoroughfares.

Helsinki opened the world's northernmost metro system in 1982, which also serves the neighbouring city of Espoo. It is a great way to get about but as an inquisitive visitor with time, I like to walk to see much more of the city, whether it is an iconic sight or just humdrum urban sprawl.

I walked through Market Square and past the beautiful, ornate, old market hall and despite carrying a rucksack, I just had to go in and have a look at the architecture and the stalls selling all sorts of goods. On my way to the hotel in the old town centre, I also passed the City Hall and Presidential Palace. I had done some sightseeing from the outside before I had even found my hotel.

I queried whether the tap water was fit for drinking but of course, with typical Nordic efficiency, it was of excellent quality. It was supplied by the one hundred and twenty kilometre-long Päijänne Water Tunnel, completed in 1982 – the world's second longest continuous rock tunnel, named after Finland's second largest lake. The water takes nine days to reach Helsinki under gravity. It has a dimension of sixteen square metres, large enough to drive a truck through. The longest tunnel is the Delaware Aqueduct at one hundred and thirty-seven kilometres, completed in 1945 to bring fresh water to New York.

I checked out the Lutheran Cathedral. After Helsinki was made the capital of Finland in 1812, Alexander I decreed, in 1814, that fifteen per cent of the salt-import tax was to be collected into a fund for two churches – one Lutheran and one Orthodox. The cathedral was built on the site of the smaller 1724-1727 Ulrika Eleonora Church, named after its patroness, Ulrika Eleonora, Queen of Sweden.

The original church was demolished and the new cathedral was built from 1830-1852 as a tribute to the Grand Duke of Finland, Tsar Nicholas I of Russia, so it was also known as St Nicholas' Church until the independence of Finland in 1917.

It is a distinctive landmark in the Helsinki cityscape, with white walls topped with a tall, central green dome surrounded by four smaller domes. This emphasizes the architectural connection to the cathedral's inspiration from the Saint Isaac's and Kazan Cathedrals in St Petersburg, built in the neoclassical style. The church's footprint is a Greek cross, a square centre and four equilateral and symmetrical arms, with each arm's facade featuring a colonnade and pediment.

I walked back through Market Square, along the front, and crossed a bridge to reach the Uspenski Cathedral, the main Orthodox Church of Finland. This was the other church that Alexander I ordered to be built, although it was largely funded by parishioners and private donors.

The cathedral was built from 1862 to 1868. In complete contrast to the previous cathedral, this was built of red brick under green roofs in orthodox traditional style. More than seven hundred thousand recycled bricks were brought in barges from the Bomarsund Fortress on Åland Island that had been demolished in the Crimean War. Following the wish of Alexander II, the church was dedicated to the Dormition of the Mother of God (the Virgin Mary).

The crypt chapel of the cathedral is named after Alexander Hotovitzky, who served as vicar of the Orthodox parish of Helsinki 1914-1917 and who had died a martyr's death in the Great Purge. He was canonized by the Russian Orthodox Church in 1994.

The Cathedral is set upon a hillside on the Katajanokka peninsula, overlooking the city. At the back of the cathedral, there is a plaque commemorating Russian Emperor Alexander II, who was the sovereign of the Grand Duchy of Finland during the cathedral's construction.

The cathedral claims to be the largest orthodox church in Western Europe with an interior area of one thousand square metres, but it is a long way down the list of all orthodox cathedrals and doesn't even reach the top twenty. The largest is the Hagia Sophia in Istanbul at seven thousand nine hundred and sixty square metres (although it was a museum, but was rededicated as a mosque in July 2020).

The cathedral has several historical icons. The icon of St Nicolas, The Wonder Maker, was stolen on 16th August 2007 in broad daylight, while hundreds of tourists were visiting the cathedral. It had been given to the Orthodox Cathedral of Vyborg and dates from the nineteenth century. It has not been recovered.

Another icon, Theotokos of Kozeltshan, was stolen in June 2010. Two robbers had twice broken into the church through a window; on the second occasion, in August, they had been caught. Although they didn't admit to having committed the first robbery, DNA-testing through a blood stain left during the first robbery confirmed it. Nevertheless, they continued denying having done it.

However, in February the next year, one of the jailed robbers had a change of heart, admitted the theft and revealed the location of the icon. It had spent eight months buried in the ground but luckily had remained almost immaculate.

Across the water, to the north, soars a tall tower known as Majakka (Lighthouse), a one hundred and thirty-four metre-tall residential tower of thirty-five floors; Finland's tallest building. Across the water, to the northeast, is Korkeasaari Zoo. It stands on its own island, established in 1889, and claims to be one of Europe's oldest, surviving zoos.

However, it is a crowded space with many competing contenders claiming to be the oldest. In my pedantic mind, merely claiming to be 'one of the oldest' is a damp squib and they should do the research and claim a definitive number. The oldest zoo is the Tiergarten Schönbrunn (Schönbrunn Animal Garden), located in the grounds of the famous Schönbrunn Palace in Vienna, Austria. It was founded as an imperial menagerie in 1752 and it is the oldest, continuously operating zoo in the world.

I moved on back to the centre of the city to explore the main shopping streets of Aleksanterinkatu, Pohjoisplanadi and Eteläesplanadi. I was checking out the shops and the restaurants and looking out for local cuisine. Amongst the dishes that I particularly wanted to try was the Karelian pastry, a traditional Finnish dish made from a thin, rye crust with a filling of rice, often mixed with boiled egg, which is spread over the hot pastries before serving.

Modern Finnish cuisine is notable for generally combining traditional country fare and haute cuisine with contemporary-style cooking. Fish and meat play a dominant role in traditional Finnish dishes from the western part of the country, while the dishes from the eastern part have traditionally included various vegetables and mushrooms. Refugees from Russian Karelia contributed to food variety in Finland.

Finnish foods often use wholemeal products (rye, barley, oats) and berries (such as bilberries, lingonberries, cloudberries, and sea buckthorn with a long list of alleged uses and benefits). Milk and its derivatives are commonly used in various recipes. Turnips were common in traditional cooking but were replaced with the potato after its introduction in the eighteenth century.

Many regions have strongly branded traditional delicacies: Tampere has *mustamakkara* (*musta* being 'black' and *makkara* 'sausage'), a type of Finnish sausage made from pork, blood, rye and flour, traditionally eaten with lingonberry jam. *Mustamakkara* is at its best when bought and eaten fresh and hot from market stalls, as a snack. I tried it while passing through Market Square.

When buying *mustamakkara* in the Tampere region, it is customary to specify the amount of money one wants to spend instead of weight, length or the number of pieces. Often people also choose by simply pointing at the preferred piece. The shape and moisture of *mustamakkara* varies: by this means, the buyer can get the piece best suiting their taste.

Kalakukko is a traditional food from the Finnish region of Savonia, in central Finland, made from fish baked inside a loaf of bread. Traditionally, *kalakukko* is prepared with rye flour (like *ruisleipä*) but wheat flour is often added to make the dough more pliable. Traditional Western Finnish rye bread is dried near the kitchen ceiling and preserved, over the long winter, in many forms.

The fillings consists of fish, pork and bacon. After being baked, traditionally in a masonry oven, *kalakukko* looks much like a large loaf of rye bread. If prepared correctly, the bones of the fish soften and the meat and fish juices cook thoroughly inside. This results in a moist filling without inedible bones.

Traditionally, the fish used in *kalakukko* is either vendace or European perch, but any fish can be used and salmon is popular. In southern Savonia, the vendace is advocated as the only fish for the true *kalakukko*, whereas in the northern parts of the province the same is said of the perch.

Instead of fish, combinations of potato and pork or – in times gone by – *rutabaga*, a type of local turnip was often used in local dishes. *Kalakukko* will keep for a long time when unopened. It used to be a practical lunch for workers away from home, much as the tradition concerning the Cornish pasty.

Some Finnish speakers today find the name *kalakukko* somewhat amusing: *kalastaa* is Finnish for fish and *kukko* means rooster, leading to the often used but non-morphological translation, 'fish cock', especially on poorly translated menus. However, the archaic form of *kukko* is derived from the same root as *kukkaro* meaning purse, from where the name is derived.

I was rather disappointed not to find any restaurants serving traditional Finnish dishes other than reindeer. I would have to look harder and check out restaurants on the internet. I was surprised to see a lot of coffee shops but I should not have been that surprised as Finland has the world's highest consumption of coffee at twelve kilograms of coffee beans per capita. The world's top ten nations of coffee consumers are European, plus Canada, gratefully supplied by Tim Horton, amongst others.

As I had arrived by ferry and would be taking a train later, I checked out the Central Railway station. Helsinki's first railway station was built in 1862. As the popularity of railways grew, the station turned out to be too small and a contest was organised in 1904 to produce plans for a new station.

The contest received twenty-one entries and was won by Eliel Saarinen with a pure, national romanticist design, sparking off a vigorous debate about the architecture of major public buildings, with demands for a modern, rational style. Saarinen himself abandoned romanticism altogether and reworked his offering. The new design was finished in 1909 and the new station building was opened in 1919.

In the 1960s, the underground Asematunneli pedestrian underpass and underground shopping-centre complex was built south of the station. The first electric train arrived at the station on 13th January 1969. The Rautatientori metro station, connected to the railway station via Asematunneli, was opened in 1982.

In 2000, a glass roof, which had featured in Eliel Saarinen's original drawings but not built as part of the original construction project, was built over the railway station's central platforms, although to an updated design.

Helsinki Central hosts a private fifty square-metre waiting lounge for the exclusive use of the President of Finland and official guests. The lounge, featuring furniture designed by Eliel Saarinen, has two entrances – a large one leading in from Rautatientori Square and a smaller one leading in from the main station hall.

The lounge was completed in 1911 and was originally intended for the private use of the Emperor of Russia but the First World War delayed its official inauguration to 1919, at which point it had been converted into a temporary military hospital, and was afterwards given over to the use of the Finnish President.

The station is clad mostly in red Finnish granite under a green roof. Its main distinguishing features are its clock tower and the two pairs of statues holding spherical lamps on either side of the main entrance. In 2013, the BBC chose Helsinki Central as one of the world's most beautiful railway stations.

On my way to the railway station, I had swung by the Kamppi Chapel, located on Narinkka Square. I was going to have a day of testing my views on modern art and architecture. The building is also known as the Chapel of Silence, since it is intended to be a place to restore calm and have a moment of silence in one of the busiest areas in Finland. The chapel is ecumenical and welcomes everyone, irrespective of religion, philosophy of life or background.

The chapel's overall design (both on the interior and exterior) is very austere and simplistic, as well as mostly neutral, bearing some semblance to a multi-faith prayer room. The chapel was constructed as a part of the build-up to the World Design Capital programme in 2012 and won the International Architecture Awards in 2010.

The chapel became popular immediately after it was opened, with around a quarter of a million people visiting by January 2013. A year later the chapel received its five-hundred-thousandth visitor. The building is the shape of an egg on its side with its walls leaning out from the base and covered in wood.

I quickly moved on to the railway station to visit the Ateneum Art Museum, diagonally opposite the railway station and housed in a beautiful old building. It contains an extensive collection of traditional and modern Finnish art. There is a lot to see but for me, it was a quick walk through.

Overlooking the side of the railway station, I could see the Oodi Central Library. In complete contrast to the Ateneum Art Museum building, in my opinion, it is an ugly modern construction completely out of character with the Art Nouveau style of the station but it was the winner of a competition attracting five hundred and forty-three entries, and opened in 2018.

I walked along Mannerheimintie. It was originally called Henriksgatan but was renamed after the Winter War by a grateful nation. I passed the bronze statue of Carl Mannerheim astride a horse perched on a plinth erected in 1960 after his death in 1951.

There was a public fund-raising campaign for the statue and so much money was raised that there were sufficient funds to purchase the Louhisaari mansion in Askainen, in the very south-western corner of the country, Mannerheim's place of birth, and to convert it into a museum.

I entered the Kiasma Museum of Contemporary Art, opposite the statue, which is housed in a modernist building in keeping with its modern exhibits. There was a competition for a design with five hundred and sixteen entries and the building was opened in 1998. I prefer old, cold and draughty traditional buildings but its style matches its exhibits.

I walked further up Mannerheimintie until I was level with Finlandia Hall. This is another modern-style building which was part of a grand plan for a major centre around the Töölö Bay area, designed by Alvar Aalto in 1959-1976. However, only the Finlandia Hall and its Congress wing were built.

The main feature of the Finlandia Hall building is a tower-like section with a sloping roof. Aalto used Italian Carrara marble for both indoor and outdoor surfaces and for Aalto, the marble was a tie to the Mediterranean culture, which he wanted to bring to Finland.

The interior design of the building is a tribute to the principle of the Gesamtkunstwerk, meaning the total work of art. The design of each lamp, piece of furniture, panel, flooring material and decorative board is a result of Aalto's long career as an architect, as well as a designer of furniture, lamps and fixtures such as door handles.

The Main Auditorium was originally designed as a concert hall and it is a simplified version of the concert hall in the Aalto Theatre, the Essen Opera House in Germany. It seats seventeen hundred people and has an oak parquet floor. It has served as a venue for several international summit meetings.

However, it wasn't my aim to walk around the building at length but merely to use it as a distinctive landmark – more distinctive than the National Museum opposite – as it provided my cue to turn left and work my way through the back streets to find the Temppeliaukio Church.

The Temppeliaukio Church is a Lutheran church opened in 1969, built directly into solid rock that was formally a rocky hill in the suburbs. It is also known as the Church of the Rock and Rock Church.

Plans for the Temppeliaukio began as early as the 1930s, when a plot of land was selected for the building and a competition was held for the design. Progress, however, was interrupted by the Second World War. After the war, there was a second competition. The interior space of the church was reduced to about one quarter of its original plan, due to cost. Construction finally began in February 1968 and the church was completed for consecration in September 1969.

The interior was excavated out of solid rock and is bathed in natural light entering through the skylight above the central area. The church is used frequently as a concert venue due to its excellent acoustics created by the rough, virtually unworked rock surfaces and is circular in plan. There is also no tower or spire and no bells but a recording of bells is played via loudspeakers.

The iconic rock walls were not included in the original competition entry as it was thought too radical for the competition jury. But when conductor Paavo Berglund shared his knowledge of acoustics from some of the best music halls, and the acoustical engineer Mauri Parjo gave requirements for the wall surfaces, the designers discovered that they could fulfil all the requirements for the acoustics by leaving the rock walls bare. The Temppeliaukio church is one of the most popular tourist attractions in the city, appealing to half a million people visitors annually, comprising forty per cent of all visitors.

Chapter 21

Suomenlinna Fortress

During one of my wanderings along the city's shopping streets, several tourist agencies' adverts had caught my eye and I investigated the details against my planned schedule. I booked a tour out of town for a change of scene, away from the urban area.

I was picked up early from my hotel and after stopping to pick up a few other passengers, the mini-bus left Helsinki. We were on our way to Hanko, one hundred and thirty kilometres away.

We were only half way there when we had a break in Ingå, at the Cannons of Torp military museum. It is a small, privately run museum with Soviet-era exhibits of military vehicles, artillery, uniforms, guns and a helicopter, providing a chance to stretch your legs, buy some souvenirs and visit the toilet, or just sit and watch the world go by, over a cup of coffee.

Then we were back on the road to stop at the Hanko Front Museum, another military museum but on a larger scale. It is located just one hundred metres from the border, where the Soviet-leased area of Hanko started. We watched a film on the March 1940 evacuation of the city.

Some of the exhibits are indoors: the Artillery Hall displays exhibits from the Finnish Air Force. Other exhibits, such as several tanks and other military vehicles and guns, are outside or in the surrounding forest, together with trenches, dug-outs and bunkers. There is a walk through the forest and part of the area was defended by the Swedish Volunteer Battalion during the Continuation War.

We turned off the main road and drove along the sea front. There are several beautiful sandy beaches in the area. We passed the Hanko Casino, which isn't a gambling den but a banqueting hall and part of the spa complex visited by Russian nobility in the late nineteenth century.

Hanko is located at the end of one of the Salpausselkä Ridges on a peninsula. The Hanko-Hyvinkää railway, connecting the two locations about sixty kilometres north of Helsinki, and the rest of the railway system was the first privately funded railway in Finland. Work started in 1872 and the connection was completed the next year. The city was formally founded in 1874 by Imperial Charter, granted by Tsar Alexander II.

We stopped at the sixty-five-metre tall Water Tower bearing a clock at the top of each of its faces. It has a large central column and four supporting legs and was built after the war to replace an earlier water tower destroyed by the Soviets.

There are great views from the top and many of the local tourist attractions were pointed out. To the north of the peninsula is the site of the naval Battle of Gangut, which was fought between Swedish and Russian navies in 1714. The battle was the first-ever victory of the newly formed Russian regular fleet.

Near the base of the Water Tower is an Evangelical Lutheran Church. It was built in 1892 and repaired after the war in 1953. A little further on is the Emigration Memorial. The harbour at Hanko was where emigrants left Finland during the late 19th and early 20th centuries for a new life in North America. The memorial itself is a ridged column with a flight of birds at the top, a symbol that I have seen elsewhere.

We were driven through part of the harbour and marina, shown the outside of the Hanko Museum, a small museum in the oldest building in Hanko and the main shopping street. We had some spare time to do whatever we wanted until it was time for the return trip to Helsinki.

There was still plenty to explore in Helsinki, but my next day was another trip out of the city for the day. I caught a train to go north to Hyvinkää, for the less-than-one-hour journey to visit the Finnish Railway Museum.

It was founded in 1898 in Helsinki but relocated to Hyvinkää in 1974. The museum is in the marshalling yards of the terminus of the Hanko–Hyvinkää railway. It is a large site with the station, warehouses and other buildings, a turntable and dozens of locomotives and carriages of all types, dating from the 1870s to the present day. Some locomotives are steam, some diesel or electric. There are also ancillary exhibits, such as uniforms, sales offices and waiting rooms decorated and furnished as they would have been originally. There is also the only surviving imperial train of the Russian Emperor.

For the real 'greaser', the museum fires up some of the steam engines and offers short trips on special run days in the summer months. I am interested in the engineering but wouldn't describe myself as a greaser. I reasoned that it would be more crowded on one of the special run days, so I had made sure that I didn't visit then. It was a great day out until it was time to return to Helsinki to search out my evening culinary experience.

After a welcome lie-in, it was a short walk from my hotel to the Hakaniemi Market Hall, the largest and liveliest of three markets in the capital. It was opened in 1914 and built of brick, containing two floors with food, especially seafood, on the ground floor and speciality stalls on the first floor. There are more than seventy stalls.

I wasn't going shopping to buy anything in particular but I find the colours, shapes and smells of local food markets fascinating with their large range of different offerings. I wanted to see the architecture as much as seeing the different stalls and I purposefully went early in the day to see the bustle and hustle, rather than towards the end of the day when stalls would be closing.

I walked down to Market Square and the harbour to pick up the water bus to get to see the Suomenlinna Fortress. As I was approaching, I saw the boat motoring away from the bus stop, so I had just missed it. I wandered around the market keeping an eye out for the next water bus. The Suomenlinna district consists of eight islands, five of them interconnected by bridges, and covers a total of eighty hectares.

The fortress is a fantastic star fort accompanied by many fortified positions on the other islands. The military history of the islands stretches back a long way through many conflicts. Early on in the Great Northern War, Russia took advantage of Swedish weakness in Ingria (the present day locality of St Petersburg) and captured the area near the Neva River, as well as the Swedish forts of Nyen and Nöteborg.

In 1703, Peter the Great founded his new capital, St Petersburg, on the easternmost arm of the Gulf of Finland. In the approaches stood an island, where he built the fortified naval base of Kronstadt.

Russia soon became a maritime power and a force to be reckoned with in the Baltic Sea. The situation posed a threat to Sweden which, until that time, had been the dominant power in the Baltic. The Swedes lacked significant defences in Finland and its main naval base at Karlskrona, in southern Sweden, was too far away to meet Sweden's needs for its navy in the eighteenth century. This situation often resulted in Swedish ships reaching the coast of Finland only after Russian ships and troops had already started or even completed their spring campaigns.

After the war ended, the first plans were set in motion in Sweden to construct an archipelago fleet and its base of operations in Finland. However, nothing with regard to Sveaborg (the then-name for Suomenlinna) took place until the end of Russo-Swedish War of 1741–1743.

That war quickly turned from a Swedish attack into a Russian occupation of Finland and again underlined the importance of developing fortifications in Finland. After lengthy debate, the Swedish parliament decided, in 1747, to both fortify the frontier and establish a naval base in Helsinki, then called Helsingfors, as a counterweight to the threat posed by the new naval base at Kronstadt.

Sweden started the construction of defences in January 1748. The plan was for a series of independent fortifications across several linked islands and a naval dockyard at the very heart of the complex. In addition to the island fortress itself, there would be supporting fortifications on the mainland. Additional plans were made for fortifying the Hanko Peninsula but these were postponed.

Due to repeated Russian threats in 1749 and 1750, more effort was made concerning the island fortifications at the expense of those of those on the mainland, so that a safe base of operations could be secured for the Swedish navy. Much of the planned fortifications were operational by 1754, although incomplete.

This did not reduce the pace of construction: in 1755, there were seven thousand workers constructing the fortifications outside Helsingfors, which at the time had just two thousand residents. Swedish participation in the Seven Years' War (1756-63) halted the construction effort, which also marked the end of the rapid construction phase of Sveaborg.

Facilities for constructing ships for the Swedish Archipelago Fleet had been built at Sveaborg, and in 1764 the first three archipelago frigates were launched from there. Naval-officer training was started there in 1770 but it was not until 1779 that a naval military school was formally founded there.

However, it was not an ideal site as the sea froze in winter and Russian forces attacked or blockaded it several times. The facilities for treating the sick and wounded were inadequate and the lack of supplies and the icing-over meant that Swedish ships could not overwinter there.

Following a treaty between Alexander I and Napoleon, Russia launched a campaign against Sweden and occupied Finland in 1808. By the Treaty of Fredrikshamn (1809) in northern Denmark, Finland was ceded by Sweden and became an autonomous Grand Duchy within the Russian Empire.

After taking over the fortress, the Russians started an extensive building programme constructing extra barracks, extending the dockyard and reinforcing the fortification lines.

A long period of peace following the transfer of control was shattered by the Crimean War (1853–56). The French-English-Ottoman alliance decided to engage Russia on two fronts and sent an Anglo-French fleet to the Baltic Sea. For two summers during the Åland War, the fleet shelled the towns and fortifications along the Finnish coast.

The bombardment of Sveaborg, by the forces of Richard Saunders Dundas and Charles Pénaud on 9th–10th August 1855 lasted forty-seven hours. The fortress was badly damaged but they were unable to knock out the Russian guns. Despite the bombardment, the Anglo-French fleet sent no troops ashore and instead, they set sail for Kronstadt.

After the Crimean War, extensive restoration work began at Sveaborg. A new ring of earthworks with artillery emplacements was built. The next stage in the improvement of Sveaborg's defences and the Gulf of Finland came in the build-up to the First World War.

The fortress and its surrounding islands became part of Peter the Great's naval fortification designed to safeguard the capital, Saint Petersburg, which was the capital of Russia from 1712 until 1918. After the Finnish Civil War, the fortress was officially renamed Suomenlinna as part of the wave of nationalism and independence that swept the country.

No longer very practical as a military base, Suomenlinna was turned over to civilian administration in 1973. It is a popular site and attracts nearly three-quarters of a million visitors a year, over the summer. What many of the visitors don't know is that there is a minimum-security penal labour camp on Suomenlinna, whose inmates work on the maintenance of the fortifications.

It is a massive site and it would take the rest of the day to walk around all the viewable areas: I was not going to miss anything. There are exhibits inside the fortifications and well-preserved naval guns, both inside the fortress and located on the more open slopes on top of the ramparts. Many of the information signs are in English, so I didn't have to struggle with Finnish and was well informed.

Overlooking the water on the seashore is the Vesikko Submarine, launched in 1930 as a prototype. It was bought by Finland and was one of five submarines that served in the navy until the end of the Continuation War, before it was retired and kept in storage until being turned into a museum ship.

I caught the water bus back to Market Square and wandered up the road to find a local restaurant that claimed to serve traditional local dishes. I had found it on the internet the night before.

The next morning I walked up Mannerheimintie to the National Museum, located opposite the Finlandia Hall. It is a fascinating building which was designed by the architect company Gesellius, Lindgren & Saarinen – the same Saarinen who designed the railway station. The appearance of the building reflects Finland's medieval churches and castles, but the external architecture belongs to national romanticism and the interior mainly to art nouveau.

The museum was built 1905-1910 and opened to the public in 1916. It was renamed the Finnish National Museum following Finland's independence in 1917. There are many different exhibitions, both temporary and permanent, plus collections of coins, medals, decorations, silver, jewellery and weapons.

There is the prehistory of Finland; the development of Finnish society and culture from the Middle Ages to the early twentieth century, through the Swedish Kingdom Period to the Russian Empire Era; and Finnish folk culture in the eighteenth and nineteenth centuries, with exhibits of life in the countryside before industrialisation.

The exhibitions include the Mesa Verde artefacts from the cliff dwellings of Colorado. These were donated to the museum by the Finland Swedish explorer Gustaf Nordenskiöld and comprise the most-extensive collection of Mesa Verde items outside the United States. In 2019 it was decided to return a portion of the artefacts to the representatives of the indigenous people of the United States of America, who agreed that some six hundred items could be retained by the museum.

It was just a short walk to the Sibelius Park on the seashore. Sibelius is Finland's most famous composer who lived at Ainola (Aino's Place), located forty kilometres north of the capital. It was his home with his wife, Aino, and their family from the autumn of 1904 until his death in 1957 and her death in 1969. The property was opened to the public as a museum in 1974.

The house stands on the scenic shores of Lake Tuusulanjärvi in Järvenpää. It was designed by the famous architect Lars Sonck. The only requests Sibelius had for

Sonck were to include both a lake-front view and a green fireplace in the dining room.

In the Sibelius Park is the Sibelius Monument, a modern sculpture by Finnish artist Eila Hiltunen entitled Passio Musicae, unveiled in 1967. The sculpture won a competition organised by the Sibelius Society following the composer's death in 1957. It sparked a lively debate about the merits and flaws of abstract art.

It consists of a series of more than six hundred hollow steel pipes, weighing twenty-four tons, welded together in a wave-like pattern. Even as a youngster, I liked his music but for me, this was a ugly mess of stainless steel that should be destined for the scrap heap.

I walked along the shoreline past a marina to the city cemetery, which overlooks a small bay. I am fascinated by funereal architecture and especially by the late nineteenth century craze for monolithic tombstones. A cemetery is not on every visitor's list of things to see but they are often on mine.

Many famous people are buried here, including Carl Mannerheim. There are separate areas for different faiths – Judaism, Islam, Orthodox and the many different Christian denominations. There are multiple war memorials and military grave areas relating to the many wars that have rolled across the Finnish countryside.

For my last day in Helsinki, I made my way to the Seurasaari Open Air Museum, located on its own island to the east of the city centre. I never tire of ethnographical museums, despite having seen several recently, displaying so many similar architectural styles.

It is the home to many mainly wooden buildings transferred from elsewhere in Finland and placed in the dense forest landscape of the island. The island has a wide variety of wildlife and despite the numbers of visitors, there are large numbers of birds, red squirrels and hares.

The casual visitor should note that Seurasaari has one of only two nudist beaches in Helsinki and one of only three in the entire country. Unlike the other nudist beaches, the beach is segregated for men and women, with no unisex nudist area, and is subject to an entry fee, so wandering visitors or families should not be embarrassed by an unintended surprise encounter.

Chapter 22

Turku

I entered Helsinki Central and boarded my train for the two-hour trip, due east, to my next capital on the Baltic of Turku. It took more than half an hour to escape the urban sprawl of Helsinki and its neighbouring city of Espoo, before reaching the open countryside where the train picked up speed.

From the end of the Second World War up until the 1970s there was a massive exodus of people from the countryside to the cities and in particular, Helsinki. Between 1944 and 1969, the population of the city nearly doubled from two hundred and seventy-five thousand to over five hundred and twenty thousand.

The economy of Finland has a per capita output equal to that of other European economies, such as those of France, Germany and UK. The largest sectors are services and manufacturing. In an OECD comparison, high-technology manufacturing and knowledge-intensive services in Finland are ranked second largest, after Ireland.

The largest industries are electronics, machinery, vehicles and other engineered-metal products, forest products and chemicals. Despite having a low population density, the Government annually spends around three hundred and fifty million euros to maintain the five thousand eight hundred and sixty-five kilometres of railway tracks to move people and goods around the country.

The urban sprawl was not surprising as the Greater Helsinki area generates around one third of Finland's GDP. Another interesting economics fact is that Finland has the highest concentration of cooperatives relative to its population. The largest retailer, which is also the largest private employer, S-Group, and the largest bank, OP-Group, are both cooperatives.

Finland rapidly industrialised after the Second World War. Initially, most of the economic development was based on two groups of export-led industries; namely, the metal industry and forest industry. These two broad categories include shipbuilding, metalworking, the automotive industry, engineered products, such as electronics, and the production of metals and alloys, including steel, copper and chromium.

The forest industry includes forestry, timber, pulp and paper, and is often considered a logical development based on Finland's extensive forest resources, as three-quarters of the country is covered by forest.

Finland has significant resources of timber and minerals, such as iron, chromium, copper, nickel, and gold. It produces more than seven tons of gold a year but doesn't even get into the top forty of global produces and production represents just 2.9% of GDP.

Finland's climate and soils make growing crops a particular challenge. It has severe winters and relatively short growing seasons, with the danger of late frosts at the start of the growing season, and dry summers creating the danger of drought. However, because the Gulf Stream moderates the climate, Finland contains half of the world's arable land beyond the sixty-degrees-north latitude.

Farmers rely on quick-ripening and frost-resistant varieties of crops and they have cultivated south-facing slopes to ensure good yields, even in years with summer frosts. Most farmland was originally either forest or swamp and the soils have usually required treatment with lime and years of cultivation to neutralise excess acidity to improve fertility.

Forests play a key role in the country's economy, making it one of the world's leading wood producers and providing raw materials at competitive prices. As in agriculture, the government has long played a leading role in forestry, regulating tree cutting, sponsoring technical improvements and establishing long-term plans to ensure that the country's forests continue to supply sustainable wood to the timber-processing industries.

Once the train was out of the urban landscape, the countryside came into view from the window as we sped towards my next destination. Much of the geography of Finland is a result of glaciation and ice sheets. The ice was thicker and lasted longer here compared with the rest of

Europe. Their eroding effects have left the Finnish landscape mostly flat, with few hills and even fewer mountains. Its highest point, Halti, at one thousand three hundred and tenty-four metres, is in the far north on the border with Norway. Next to it, but completely in Finland, is Ridnitšohkka at one thousand three hundred and sixteen metres.

The retreating ice has left the land covered with boulder clay and glacial moraine, sometimes formed into eskers. These are ridges of stratified gravel and sand, formed by water flowing in tunnels under the ice sheet. Among the biggest of these are the three Salpausselkä Ridges that run across southern Finland.

The enormous weight of the ice depressed the land, which is slowly rising by a process of isostatic readjustment. The effect is strongest around the Gulf of Bothnia, where the land is steadily rising at one centimetre a year. As a result, the surface area of the country is expanding by seven square kilometres a year.

The landscape is covered mostly by coniferous taiga forests and wetland. Of the total area, ten per cent is covered by lakes and rivers, and seventy-eight per cent by forest. The forest is largely pine, spruce and birch. Where the land isn't covered by glacial moraine or forest, the typical rock is granite.

Hiding in the forests are some large animals, such as the brown bear, which is Finland's national animal, the largest carnivore in Finland. The bear is also nicknamed as the King of the Forest by the Finns and appears on the coat of arms of the Satakunta region, just to the north of Turku, as a bear wearing a crown and carrying a sword, possibly referring to the regional capital city of Pori, whose Swedish name *Björneborg* and the Latin name Arctopolis literally means 'bear city' or 'bear fortress'.

Other large mammals lurking in the forest are the grey wolf, wolverine and elk. The endangered Saimaa ringed seal, one of only three lake-seal species in the world, exists only in the Saimaa lake system of south-eastern Finland with a population estimated at just three hundred and ninety seals. Ever since the species was protected in 1955, it has become the emblem of the Finnish Association for Nature Conservation, but today it is found only in two Finnish national parks, Kolovesi and Linnansaari, and neighbouring areas.

My train rolled into Turku. The Finnish name Turku originates from an Old East Slavic word, *tŭrgŭ* (market place), and is still used in some Finnish dialects although in modern Finnish, market place is *markkinapaikka*.

Historically, for many decades Turku was Finland's largest city. It is the oldest city in Finland and was the country's first capital. Early literary sources, such as Al-Idrisi's world map from 1154, mention Turku. The town of Turku was officially founded in the late thirteenth century and its cathedral was consecrated in 1300.

After the Finnish War in 1809, Sweden ceded its eastern third of the country to Imperial Russia under the Treaty of Fredrikshamn. Turku briefly became the official capital of the Grand Duchy of Finland. Tsar Alexander I believed that it was too close to Sweden and too far from St Petersburg and the capital of the duchy was moved to Helsinki in 1812.

A great fire in 1827 destroyed much of the city and the last government offices that had remained in Turku were finally transferred to the new capital. A new city plan was drawn up by German architect Carl Ludvig Engel and Turku remained the largest city in Finland for another twenty years. Today, however it is only the fifth largest city in the country.

While having survived relatively intact throughout the years of wars from 1939–1945, the city faced increasing changes in the 1950s due to rising demands for living space and to accommodate the car on city streets. Many of the wooden, one or two-storey houses were demolished in the 1950s, along with many other historical buildings that some people believed should have been saved.

Turku city centre stretches over both banks of the river, near the mouth of the river with the eastern side, where the Turku Cathedral is located. It is referred to as *täl pual jokke* (this side of the river), while the western side is referred to as *tois pual jokke* (the other side of the river).

The oldest of the surviving ten bridges over the Aura River is Auransilta, constructed in 1904. The newest bridge is Kirjastosilta (Library Bridge), a pedestrian bridge built in 2013.

The business district in the city's economy is centred on the Port of Turku and other service-oriented industries. The city is a renowned high-tech centre with the Turku

Science Park hosting over three hundred companies, as well as several institutions of higher learning that work closely with the business sector.

Turku has a longer educational history than any other Finnish city. The first school in the city, the Cathedral School, was founded along with the Cathedral in the late thirteenth century. The first university in Finland, then named the Royal Academy of Turku and now part of the University of Helsinki, was established in 1640. The university is now the second largest in Finland with eighteen thousand students.

My first tourist site was the Qwensel House, overlooking the river. It is the oldest wooden building in the city. It is a single-storey building, painted red, built around 1700 and houses the Pharmacy Museum. The building has been dedicated to representing how a pharmacy would have looked in the nineteenth century. The pharmacy has a herb room, two laboratories, and an office, as well as the shop area.

Just to the north is the Turku Art Museum, housed in a large granite building housing over seven thousand artefacts although it was a quick walk through for me. I passed the city library, an ugly, square concrete building, as I made my way across the river and through a park to visit the cathedral.

In the thirteenth century, the Bishop's see was transferred from its previous location at Koroinen, some distance further up on the Aura River, to the middle of the town. By the end of the thirteenth century, a new stone church had been completed on the site of the former wooden parish church on the Unikankare Mound. It was consecrated in 1300 as the Cathedral Church of the Blessed Virgin Mary and St Henry, the first Bishop of Finland.

Extensions were made to the cathedral throughout the Middle Ages. By the end of that era, there were forty-two side chapels. The roof vaults were also raised during the latter part of the fifteenth century to their present height of twenty-four metres. A major, later addition to the cathedral was the tower, which has been rebuilt several times as a result of repeated fires.

The worst damage was caused by the Great Fire of Turku in 1827, when most of the town was destroyed, along with the interior of both the tower, the nave and the old tower roof. The present spire of the tower, constructed after the great fire, reaches a height of one hundred and one metres and is visible over a considerable distance as the symbol of both the cathedral and the city of Turku itself.

The next morning, I wandered down to the harbour to see the facilities, the ships and the ferries loading and unloading, until it was opening time at the Turku Castle. The first building was started in 1280 but over the following centuries, it was adapted and developed. It served as a bastion and administrative centre in Eastland, as Finland was known during the time as a province of Sweden.

The main part of the castle was extended considerably during the sixteenth century, after Gustav Vasa had ascended the Swedish throne and his son, John, headed the Finnish administration following his promotion to duke. The round tower was added to the bailey at the south-east corner.

Only once did the castle actually figure in the defence of the realm, when Russian invaders from Novgorod destroyed Turku in 1318. On the other hand, it frequently played a role in internal struggles for power within Sweden and the Kalmar Union. Not until the end of sixteenth century did it really enjoy peace.

Many accidents and numerous sieges have assailed the castle. For instance, in 1614, when King Gustav II Adolf visited the castle, a tremendous fire destroyed the wooden structure of the main building. The castle was abandoned as a fortress and used partly as a store, yet otherwise stood empty. A new accident beset the castle in the summer of 1941, soon after the Continuation War had begun, when a Russian incendiary bomb hit the main castle and caused further damage.

The governor-general lived there during the seventeenth century and after the Greater Wrath period, it housed the provincial government for some time. When the Finnish War began in 1808, the castle was used by the Russian navy and handed power over to the Finnish authorities only a couple of decades later, after the country had been granted autonomous status within the Russian empire. The Turku Historical Museum was founded in 1881 and was housed in the bailey.

The castle's serious renovation began in the 1930s but was interrupted by Finland's two wars with the Soviet Union and completed only in 1987. Today the castle is Finland's most visited museum with attendance surpassing two hundred thousand per annum. Some of its larger rooms are still used for municipal functions. However, its charm is interrupted by the sounds of the harbour in front of it and the railway that skirts its southern flanks.

Next was the Forum Marinum Museum. This museum was founded in 1999 by merging the Turku maritime museum, established in 1977, and the Åbo Akademi University museum of maritime history, established in 1936. It is a former shipyard and has a long river frontage with more than a dozen ships, ranging from a small fast police boat, a ketch, a tugboat, a gun boat, and a minelayer to a fully rigged commercial sailing boat.

I reached my last stop of the day by crossing the river using the Föri, a free passenger ferry that carries people and bicycles across the river, so that I could visit the Waimo Aaltonen Museum of Art. In March 1964, the City Council of Turku approved the proposal to establish a museum dedicated to Wäinö Aaltonen, and Aaltonen himself donated a basic collection to the proposed museum. Construction started in October 1965 and the museum was officially opened in September 1967.

The original donation has been supplemented by acquisitions purchased with an annual grant. The number of annual acquisitions varies but during the twenty-first century, approximately sixty new works of art have been acquired annually. The focus of the collection is on the art of the Turku area, the art of Wäinö Aaltonen and on three-dimensional art.

Four kilometres northeast of the city centre is the Kylämäki Village of Living History. I could have taken public transport – it is easy to get to, as it lies on a main road – but it was only four kilometres and I needed the exercise after all the restaurant meals that I had been eating to sample local cuisine and beers. It is yet another ethnographic museum but much smaller than many of the others that I had visited in the last few months.

I was soon making my way back towards the city centre, by public transport, to see the Luostarinmäki (Cloister Hill) Handicrafts Museum. It is an open air museum: I had originally thought that the Kylämäki Village of Living History was the better option but was proved wrong. The buildings date from 1775 in an area of the old city that survived the major 1827 fire and the wooden buildings are preserved in their original locations.

Afterwards, I had just enough time for the short walk through the Vartiovuori Park to visit the Sibelius Museum. It houses many historical musical instruments and memorabilia. Judging from the pictures of the building, I wouldn't need long to walk past the exhibits but I thought that I shouldn't miss out on the opportunity.

Then it was time to repack and take the morning train back to Helsinki, change trains and catch the four-hour train to St Petersburg for my last Baltic capital. I had a free electronic visa to cross through Kaliningrad but the visa for mainland Russia would mean applying in person to the visa-issuing office in London, handing over my passport for two weeks and a fee of £120 – and it was valid for only three months. I had planned and booked my summer trip around the Baltic unaware of this essential piece of knowledge.

However, there was a solution. I could get a five-day and free-transit visa into Russia from Finland on the border. This would leave me little time to see St Petersburg, as my first day would be taken up by travelling to the city and my last day would be taken up travelling out of Russia by train back to Helsinki and its airport. I would travel by train out of St Petersburg, as there were no direct flights to my local airport from St Petersburg, and I would have had to go via a hub airport, thus increasing costs, carbon emissions and time.

It was quicker and cheaper to go back to Helsinki. I have visited Russia and St Petersburg many times for business, research and leisure and I wouldn't feel that I was missing out.

Chapter 23

St Petersburg

The border checks were undertaken on the train, firstly by the Finnish border guards to stamp you out of Finland and then the Russian border guards came down the train and checked your passports and visas. It was about three and a half hours on the train from Helsinki to St Petersburg and we arrived at the Finlyandsky station, the same station where Vladimir Lenin returned to Russia from exile in Switzerland on 16th April 1917 in a sealed train to aid the German war aim of getting Russia out of the war.

The city was named St Petersburg in 1703. It has had several names during its life. In 1914, at the start of the First World War between Germany and Russia, the name of the city was changed from St Petersburg to Petrograd, to remove German sounding parts of 'Saint' and 'burg'.

This wasn't a recent invention but had appeared in the 1830s when Alexander Pushkin translated the 'foreign' city name of St Petersburg to the more Russian Petrograd in one of his poems. In 1924, just five days after Lenin's death, it was changed to Leningrad in his honour. Lastly in

1991, following a referendum which was only narrowly won, it was changed back to St Petersburg.

Tsar Peter the Great founded St Petersburg, formerly a small town called Nyenskans, on 27th May 1703. He had captured it two weeks previously, early on during the Great Northern War, when Sweden's imperial control of northern Europe was being challenged. Peter finally moved the capital from Moscow to St Petersburg in 1712. Between 1713 and 1918, the city was the Imperial Capital. It had a short break in 1728 for four years when Tsar Peter the Second moved it back to Moscow, but Empress Anna of Russia moved the capital back to St Petersburg. In 1918, the Soviets moved the capital back to Moscow.

Peter the Great was interested in seafaring and maritime affairs and founded the Russian navy. He needed a better seaport than Arkhangelsk in the far north. This harbour is located on the White Sea but it was a long way to the north and closed to shipping for months during the winter, due to ice. He built the Peter and Paul Fortress, which became the first brick and stone building in St Peterburg and is the oldest building in the new city.

Thousands of conscripted peasants from all over Russia, and Swedish prisoners of war, were used to start the building of a great new city even before the war finished; it dragged on to 1721. There was an edict that forbade buildings beyond the city from being built in stone, thus freeing local stone masons to work on the new city. Initial city development started around the Peter and

Paul Fortress but later moved to a grand design on nearby Vasilyevsky Island.

This project was not finished as planned, but it established a standard grid pattern and incorporated several canals. During the construction, an estimated twenty thousand peasants and workers died. The Tsar built his Winter Palace in the city but it was not the only palace in the unfinished city, as Peter had ordered his nobles to construct their residences here also and to spend half the year there.

Although it was a good location for a city, as it was on the shores of the Baltic Sea, in geological terms this wasn't the ideal place for a major urban centre as it was an area of soft sediments, scattered across several islands in a low-lying delta area of mud flats. However, that didn't stop further expansion. The edict that nobles build their residences here was unpopular and it was said that only cabbages and turnips would ever grow there.

The city is built on one hundred and one islands linked by three hundred and fifty graceful bridges. The number of canals has also meant that the city has been called the Venice of the North. There have been several floods of the city, which needed further investment, including building up the banks of the islands with stone embankments.

The soft sediments also caused problems for the building and running of the metro. One section was flooded early on in its life. The first line, which had been planned before the Second World War, was finally built after the war and opened in 1955. Some of the lines and stations on the network are the deepest in the world.

My first full-day tour was to the Peterhof Palace on the southern coast of the Gulf of Finland, with St Petersburg to the east and Kotlin Island to the west, also now known as Kronstadt. This island protected the sea approaches to St Petersburg and it has both a large commercial harbour and a naval harbour.

Peterhof means Peter's Court. Peter the Great had noted its ideal position between St Petersburg and Kronstadt in a diary entry in 1705, during the Great Northern War. Peterhof commemorates Russia's victory over Sweden in the Great Northern War and the nation's modernisation. Its name was changed in 1944 to Petrodvorets to eradicate its links with its German-sounding name but was changed back in 1997.

Peter began construction of the Monplaisir Palace (meaning 'my pleasure'), a modest summer palace with gardens and a few other buildings on the shoreline overlooking the gulf. This is the oldest building on the site and was completed in 1721. He used it often en route to Kronstadt and from there went into the rest of Europe by ship.

Further construction halted after Peter's death in 1725 but work was recommenced in 1740, when his daughter Elizabeth came to the throne. She engaged architect Bartolomeo Rastrelli to review the plans. He kept much of the original design but added to it to create the Grand

Palace seen today, standing on higher ground overlooking the more modest Monplaisir Palace down by the seashore.

The Grand Palace is one of the last buildings built in a plain baroque style as it was shortly to be overtaken by the newer, more fashionable neoclassicism. Inside, the décor is opulent and there is gold everywhere.

There is a magnificent and ornate Ceremonial Staircase. Other rooms include the Throne Room, the Ballroom and the Chinese Study, to name just a few, and the Drawing Room with its chinoiserie and fine silk wall decorations.

Outside, to the south of the palace, are the small and formal Upper Gardens. On the northern, seaward side, the palace looks out over the Lower Gardens and from its elevated position it has extensive views across the gulf. This is where the Bolshoi Kaskad (Grand Cascade) was built, along with a series of fountains.

There are fountains running the length of the façade of the palace, a cascade and the Sea Channel, a long canal with more fountains linking the palace through the gardens to the shore. All the statues are covered in gold leaf and when the sun shines, the light twinkles in the spray from the fountains and glints off the gold on the many statues. It is so spectacular that it is a long-lasting memory for many visitors.

There are security guards near all the gold-leaf-covered statues to ensure that visitors don't try to scrape it off. To protect them from the harsh winter weather, some of the smaller statues are removed and placed in storage.

The larger statues are left in situ but are covered with insulation, packed out with polystyrene padding and finally enclosed in purpose-built wooden boxes.

In the afternoon, on the way back to the hotel, I still had some time, so I bought a ticket for a canal tour of the city. There are many canals and lots of pretty bridges crossing them: passengers are warned to duck as the boat approaches each one. I thought that this was a bit obvious and unnecessary, but our first bridge showed me why. There is extremely little clearance and several people had nasty knocks on the head when they hadn't paid enough attention.

There was a commentary in multiple languages as we chugged along the waterways. There were plenty of sights pointed out, with a brief bit of history on each.

Towards the end of the trip, we were on our return journey when a couple of lads shouted and waved to us. They ran to the next bridge and did handstands on the balustrade as we passed underneath. They ran on to the next bridge and did some more acrobatics and handstands, including a one-handed handstand on the balustrade. This continued until the last bridge and they stood by the gang plank with their hands out, looking for tips.

The next day I had booked another coach trip for the twenty-five kilometre drive to the Alexander Palace at Tsarskoye Selo (Tsar's Village). This is the former residence of the imperial family. The estate was originally owned by a Swedish nobleman, but following the defeat of Sweden and the capture of Sweden's Baltic provinces,

Peter the Great gave the estate to his wife, the future Empress Katherine I, as a present in 1708.

There are, in fact, two imperial palaces: the baroque Katherine Palace and the neoclassical Alexander Palace with the adjacent Alexander Park. The Katherine Palace is surrounded by a Garden à la Française, a formal garden and an English landscaped garden. It is a big building and you need to be able to walk quite a long way to see everything and then there are still the gardens to walk around.

Bartolomeo Rastrelli was responsible for the building of the Katherine Palace, which has some of the most extravagant interiors in Europe. Room after room is filled with the highest quality workmanship that artists and craftsmen could produce, and there is an inevitable abundance of gold everywhere.

Next to the Katherine Palace is the Cameron Gallery. Katherine asked Charles Cameron to design a Roman bathhouse modelled on the ruins of the Baths of Constantine, in Rome. The original bathhouse on the ground level has been converted to a temporary art exhibitions space. The upper storey has some fine interior designs, known as the Agate Rooms, covered in semi-precious stones.

The Tsarskoye Selo Railway was the first public railway line to be built in Russia. It ran for twenty-seven kilometres from St Petersburg to Pavlovsk and passed Tsarskoye Selo near the end of the line. Construction began in May 1836 and it opened in October 1837. The second railway line to be built in Russia was the much more ambitious Saint Petersburg to Moscow line, opened in 1851, which was six hundred and fifty kilometres long. Russian economic development was slow and expansion had started from a low base. As a comparison, Britain – a few years earlier, in 1845 – already had over three thousand nine hundred kilometres of railways.

The Bolsheviks renamed Tsarskoye Selo as Detskoye Selo (Children's Village) in 1918. It was renamed yet again in 1937 to Pushkin, to commemorate the centenary of the poet's death. On 17th September 1941, the Germans occupied the area and destroyed or looted many historical artefacts.

The Russian authorities had taken some of the artefacts away for safekeeping, but the Nazi advance was faster than had been anticipated. The Nazis occupied the palace, drove their tanks through the gardens and dug trenches. They used the main ballroom as a garage to repair their vehicles with total disregard for the history of the building.

The Red Army liberated the town and the palace on 24th January 1944 to find an immense amount of damage. Also, there was no sign of the famous Amber Room, which had been plundered and has never been found. It was a room whose walls were completely covered in mirrors and amber. What can be seen today is a modern but exact reproduction of the original. Reconstruction and renovation has taken more than six decades.

There is another imperial residence, just thirty kilometres away, called the Great Gatchina Palace. It was built between 1766 and 1781 for Count Grigory Orlov, who was a favourite of Empress Katherine the Great. When he died in 1783, she liked the palace so much that she bought it and presented it to her son, the future Emperor Paul I. The railway reached this palace in 1854.

After Alexander II's assassination in St Petersburg in 1881, the city's Winter Palace was considered unsafe and Tsar Alexander III was advised to move to Gatchina Palace. There is a beautiful Fabergé egg there containing a miniature reproduction of the Gatchina Palace.

We reboarded the coach for a visit to another nearby palace, crossing the track of the original Tsarskoye Selo Railway line and arriving at the Pavlovsk Palace. Some people had had enough of viewing palaces and a couple stayed on the coach rather than be guided around yet more.

Paul I was the son and heir of the Empress Katherine the Great of Russia. When his wife, Maria Feodorovna, gave birth to the future Alexander I, Katherine gave him a thousand hectares of forest along the winding Slavyanka River, just four kilometres from her residence at Tsarskoye Selo, to celebrate the birth. In 1780, Katherine the Great loaned her official architect, Charles Cameron, to design a palace on a hillside overlooking the Slavyanka River.

Cameron was a close friend of the architect who designed Chiswick House, the home of Lord Burlington who had commissioned one of the earliest and finest Palladian houses in England. This style was the major influence on Cameron when he designed Pavlovsk Palace. He dammed the Slavyanka River to create a lake, which would mirror the facade of the palace.

In September 1781, Paul and Maria set off on a Grand Tour of Europe. They travelled incognito as the Count and Countess of the North and bought enormous amounts of furniture, tapestries, statues, paintings, porcelain and fireplaces in Europe for their new residence.

Tensions grew: Cameron was accustomed to the unlimited budget for materials given him by Katherine the Great, and was annoyed at the European purchases bought without consulting him. Maria wanted more delicate colours than the bright decoration proposed by Cameron and Paul did not want something that was a reproduction of his mother's palace.

In 1786, Cameron left to build a new palace for Katherine in the Crimea. Paul and Maria engaged the Italian architect, Vincenzo Brenna, from Florence, to decorate the interior. Hence, the inside décor is a different style to what the outside design suggests.

When Katherine the Great died in 1796, Paul became Emperor and decided to enlarge Pavlovsk into a palace suitable for a royal residence. Meanwhile, he had alienated many of his government and the elite and he was assassinated in 1801, leaving Maria to look after the palace. Maria died in 1828 but she specified in her will that the building and contents were to be preserved as they were, and her descendants have respected her wishes.

During the Great Patriotic War, Nazi forces captured the palace and some units were garrisoned there. The staff at the palace did their best to box up the valuables and send them somewhere safe, away from the front. The Nazi advance was quicker than they had expected and there were still a lot of items that had not been evacuated.

Some artefacts were tightly packed into the cellar and a false wall was built. Some of the statues were buried in the grounds. They had expected the Nazis to dig trenches, thus accidentally discovering the statues. They expected the trenches to be no deeper than two metres, all the protection that a soldier might need, so the staff dug even deeper pits and buried all the carefully wrapped items three metres deep.

Pavlovsk was liberated on 24th January 1944. The departing Germans had set fire to the palace and the roofs and floors were destroyed, leaving the building an empty shell. Some items that had not been evacuated, such as statues, furniture and the books in the library, had been looted and sent back to Germany. The rest had been destroyed by the fire.

There had been over one hundred thousand trees in the gardens but seventy per cent had either been destroyed by shelling or had been cut down for firewood. The garden structures, follies and bridges had been destroyed.

Even before the war had ended, the debris was carefully sorted through for surviving fragments. Crates that had been sent away for safekeeping were returned. Looted treasures were found as the Nazi armies retreated but had been overtaken by advancing Soviet forces. The statues buried in the gardens were still there and the false wall in the cellar had survived both the occupation and the fire. After the war, the building and its opulent interiors were carefully and faithfully reconstructed to recreate the marvel that is on view today.

I had a tour of the building with an English-speaking guide. It was a large group, which always takes longer, and some of our fellow visitors walked slowly, so it took time to get around the palace. We had reached the gift shop at the end of the tour and had five minutes before we were due back on the coach. I checked with the guide, as we had missed Maria's private apartments.

There was a strict deadline for departure and so to keep on schedule, we had missed out part of the palace. Therefore, I missed the gift shop and went back for a quick walk through her private apartments, marvelling at yet more delicate and elaborate furnishings.

It was a disappointingly quick walk through the rooms without time to ponder and stand in awe, but I was back in time for the allotted departure time. But we still had to wait for stragglers to make their way back, including the two who had stayed on the coach and missed the tour but had gone to the café. After everyone else was back and had been waiting for some time, the guide had to go back to find them to chivvy them along.

Next was the Church of the Saviour on Spilled Blood, built between 1883 and 1907, funded by the imperial family with the support of many private donors. I am sure that it was a pet project: when your Tsar asked whether you would like to donate, you were not in the position of being able to say no without dire consequences, so I wonder how many of the donations were voluntary. . .

The cathedral was built on the site where Emperor Alexander II was assassinated in March 1881. There had been several attempts and one had occurred in the Winter Palace. During some renovations, a terrorist was employed as a carpenter and every day for weeks he smuggled some dynamite into the building and placed it beneath the dining room.

There was a banquet due to be held on 17th February 1880, but a guest arriving from Berlin was delayed and so the start of the banquet was also delayed. When the huge amount of dynamite exploded, it was heard all over St Petersburg. Eleven people were killed and a further thirty injured but the royal family survived uninjured. This incident represents the first use of a time-delay bomb for political purposes.

Just a year later, Tsar Alexander II's carriage was travelling along one of the embankments when a grenade was thrown by an anarchist conspirator and exploded. The Tsar was unhurt but he descended from the carriage and started to remonstrate with the would-be assassin. A second conspirator took his chance, rushed towards the Tsar and detonated his grenade, killing himself and mortally wounding the Tsar, who died shortly afterwards to be succeeded by Alexander III.

The story reminded me of one of my boyhood, historically notable characters, one of whom was just a bit short of being a hero. King Zog of Albania ruled as a self-crowned king of the small country between 1928 and 1939, having previously served as prime minister and president. He was a military dictator but liked the high life, spending a lot of time and his country's money abroad. His popularity can be expressed by the fifty-five assassination attempts.

One such recorded event was in Vienna, as he attended the opera. I remember the story: as the would-be assassin drew his pistol, King Zog I produced his own pistol and shot the assassin.

The incident at the opera is recorded but the story about his retaliation I have not been able to authenticate, so as I have been recounting the story perhaps erroneously at dinner parties for decades, I ought to apologise to all those guests who have received an inaccurate or just an unsubstantiated version of history, but it makes an interesting and unusual story.

We drove through the centre of the city, crossing several bridges and past many beautiful buildings, to the waterfront. We caught a ferry to cross the Neva River to Zayachy Ostrov (Hare Island) on the north bank of the river, the last large upstream island of the Neva Delta. Here we were to visit the Peter and Paul Fortress built by Peter the Great in 1703 and where Nikolay Chernyshevsky had been imprisoned.

The original citadel was completed within a year and built of timber and earth embankments. It was then rebuilt in brick and stone over the next three decades. It was constructed in a star pattern design so that bastions extending from the main walls gave other battlements overlapping firing or killing zones on any attacking army. Over the centuries it served as the city garrison and as a gaol for high-ranking or political prisoners.

During the February Revolution of 1917, it was attacked by the mutinous soldiers of the Pavlovsky regiment on 27th February and the prisoners were freed. Under the Provisional Government that followed the revolution, hundreds of Tsarist officials were held in the Fortress. In 1924, when the Bolsheviks were in control, the site was converted to a museum.

At the centre of the fortress is the Peter and Paul Cathedral, built between 1712 and 1733. It tall bell tower is over one hundred and twenty two meters high, which is the tallest Orthodox bell tower in Russia. It is unusual, as the belfry is not a standalone structure that had been common up to this date. The height is achieved by a tall, slender, golden spire topped with a golden angel, an important symbol of the city. Inside, it is airy with some great marble pillars and gold leaf picking out some of the intricate stone carvings and statues.

The cathedral has a typical Flemish carillon, a gift of the Flemish city of Mechelen in Flanders. The new fifty-one bells were installed in 2001. This is a continuation of a historical quirk of history. When Peter the Great visited the Netherlands in 1690, he heard the perfectly tuned Hemony carillons in Amsterdam and Leiden singing out every quarter hour. The Hemony brothers were talented bell founders whose skills at casting were not matched until the nineteenth century.

Later, in 1717, he visited Flanders incognito and heard the Hemony carillon of the Cathedral of Our Lady in Antwerp. The sound of the carillon so impressed him that he ordered a set of bells for his new cathedral in St Petersburg in 1720. After several disasters, including fires that melted the original bells, they were finally replaced with the carillon that can be heard today.

The cathedral is the burial place of most of the Russian tsars since Peter I. Two exceptions are Peter II, who is buried in the Cathedral of Michael the Archangel in the Moscow Kremlin, and Ivan VI who was murdered and buried in the fortress of Shlisselburg, located where the Neva River leaves Lake Lagoda, during an attempt to free the twenty-three-year-old.

The last tsar, Nicholas II and his family were murdered in Yekaterinburg, and their remains were ignominiously secreted nearby. However, after many decades, the remains of Nicholas II and his family and four of his entourage were interred here in 1998.

The next day, I made my way to the Hermitage, one of the world's most famous museums housed in the former Winter Palace. I had visited it before but always on a group tour. It is a huge place and I am sure that I had not seen all of the exhibits. Therefore, I aimed to walk through the bits that I remembered and concentrate on those parts that I hadn't seen before.

One side of the palace overlooks the Neva River and the other side looks out across the Palace Square, which is surrounded by neoclassical buildings. In the centre of the square is the Alexandrian Column made of Finnish red granite, raised after the Russian victory in the war with Napoleon's France, although not completed until 1834.

The Hermitage museum is located within the baroque white and blue Winter Palace of the Russian tsars, built between 1754 and 1762 although subject to extensive remodelling. The façade facing Palace Square is two hundred and fifty metres long and thirty metres high. The Winter Palace claims to have 1,786 doors, 1,945 windows, 1,500 rooms and 117 staircases. It is, indeed, a huge complex.

Architecturally, the exterior is impressive but inside the decoration of the rooms and the staircases is exquisite. It must be seen to be believed, to admire the craftsmen's handiwork and the lavish use of gold leaf and marble everywhere.

The Hermitage has a vast collection of works of art and was first opened to the public in 1852. It displays many examples of work executed by the great masters, such as Leonardo da Vinci, Picasso and Rembrandt, and that of many other great masters of painting, sculpture, carvings, timepieces, stonework, marquetry and stone inlay. The list is almost endless.

There are fascinating, specialist, historical Russian and Oriental sections in amongst the huge displays on offer. There are so many exhibits that the visitor can be overcome by the opulence. For some people, a couple of hours is enough, but I spent all day there and it was late afternoon when I left, exhausted but awe-inspired.

For my last full day in St Peterburg, I crossed the city and over the bridge to Zayachy Ostrov, to visit the Krassin. The icebreaker was built by Armstrong Whitworth in Newcastle upon Tyne under the supervision of Yevgeny Zamyatin. The vessel was launched as the Svyatogor on 3rd August 1916 and completed in February 1917 and was the most powerful icebreaker in the world for the next four decades.

During the allied intervention against the Bolsheviks in the Russian civil war, she was scuttled by the Royal Navy. Svyatogor was raised from her watery grave in the White Sea and returned to the navy in 1921 to be used for minesweeping duties. In 1927, this icebreaker was renamed to honour a recently deceased early Bolshevik leader and Soviet diplomat, Leonid Krassin.

The most famous duty the Krassin performed was rescuing General Umberto Nobile and his surviving crew, when their airship Italia crashed on the ice whilst returning from the North Pole in 1928. On return from this mission Krassin helped to repair the German passenger ship Monte Cervantes, with one thousand eight hundred and thirty-five passengers on board, after it hit an iceberg, severely damaging its hull.

In 1933, Krassin became the first vessel in the history of navigation to reach the inaccessible northern shores of Novaya Zemlya. In 1938, the Krassin rescued Icebreaker Lenin and her convoy, trapped in ice at the end of the previous summer.

In 1941, the US Government entered into negotiations with the Soviet Government for the purchase or lease of one or more of their modern ice breakers for use by the US Coast Guard on the east coast of Greenland. The Krassin was offered, and crossed the Pacific to Bremerton, Washington. She was surveyed and found to be in need of repairs totalling about half a million US dollars and negotiations collapsed.

She continued her journey through the Panama Canal to Great Britain, where she was armed with surface and anti-aircraft guns and proceeded to Reykjavik, Iceland, to join convoy PQ-15. She escorted the convoy through the North and Barents Seas, around the Kola Peninsula and into Murmansk. In 1942, the Krassin and Lenin were spotted near the Mona Islands by a Kriegsmarine plane during Operation Wunderland. The heavy cruiser Admiral Scheer rushed to find them, but providential bad weather, fog and ice conditions saved the icebreakers from destruction.

Between 1953-60, under the East German war reparations programme, Krassin was extensively reconstructed at VEB Mathias-Thesen-Werft, Wismar, Germany. She then had a chequered history, serving the Arctic Northern Sea Route until 1971, then as an Arctic scientific vessel, followed by being used to import used cars from Europe to Russia and was about to be sold for scrap but rescued to be used as a floating museum.

That evening, I sat in an open-air bar, with a Baltica beer, in the feeble warmth of a setting sun as the night drew in, late summer turning to early autumn, contemplating that I had finally completed my tour of Baltic Capitals.

Books by Norman Handy

The Klondikers

The Klondikers was the name given to the people who took part in the gold rush when they heard about the gold that was to be found near (what was to become) Dawson City. It was just sitting there, waiting to be picked up by anyone who could make the challenging journey to get there.

This is the recreation of the journey that one farmer, from the wheat-growing areas of the prairies around Calgary, may have experienced to get to the gold.

It is the story of crossing the Rockies to the western seaboard, travelling up the coast and making landfall. Then the intrepid potential gold panner had to cross the Rockies on foot and brave blizzards and freezing cold.

When the weather improved and the ice had melted, he then had to paddle his way down eight hundred kilometres of the Yukon River to the goldfields. Once he arrived, that was the least of his problems.

K2, The Savage Mountain

This is the story of travels in northern Pakistan using Gilgit as a centre. The journey heads westward to the fascinating Kalash Valleys and a surviving, unique culture struggling to live and maintain their identity in the harsh and rugged mountains bordering Afghanistan.

In the province of Baltistan and its capital Karimabad, with its iconic forts of Baltit and Altit set high in the mountains, the route follows the infamous Karakoram Highway through the Karakoram Mountains that links the country to China, via the Khunjerab Pass, the highest road border crossing in the world.

Looking eastwards there is the Deosai plateau, which has an average elevation of four thousand metres and the disputed areas of Jammu and Kashmir. Finally, there is the ascent to K2's base camp, below the world's second highest but most deadly mountain.

Overlanding the Silk Road

This is the long journey that follows the Silk Road overland between Europe and China. The journey starts in London with a dash across Europe. There is a pause in Istanbul to view its many treasures and the story winds through the history and countryside of Turkey, then over the border into Iran to experience its rich history and architecture.

There are the bizarre experiences of the beautiful, modern but empty city of Ashgabat, the capital of Turkmenistan. Just north of the city are the Dervasa Gas Craters located in the middle of the desert with its secret spectacular display best seen at night.

A trip to the disappearing Aral Sea is followed by an immense amount of empire building, architecture and history across a land fought over by Alexander the Great, Tamarind and Genghis Khan, to name just a few of the conquerors who have roamed across this landscape.

There is an enchanting wander through the mountains of Kyrgyzstan; this country of beautiful mountains and lakes, known as Asia's Little Switzerland. The scene slowly changes as the Muslim influence gives way to Han Chinese dominance, the Great Wall of China and the end of the Silk Road at the ancient capital of Xian and its famous terracotta army.

Yellow School Bus

This is a trip from Anchorage in Alaska to Panama City in an iconic, yellow school bus. There is the wild frontier landscape in Alaska and a glimpse of the Klondikers' story of panning for gold in the Yukon, always with the potential danger from bears, moose and elk.

Travelling through the United States roughly following the Pan American Highway, there are stops at some of the most famous national parks, such as

Yellowstone and the Grand Canyon, to name just two of many. There are side trips to Antelope Island and Salt Lake City and a stop-off at Las Vegas for the glitz.

A nostalgic ride down Highway 66 relives some of the past and there is a visit to the meteorite crater outside Flagstaff. Over the border into Mexico, there is some relaxation on the beach and a taste of Tequila.

The journey twists through Aztec and Mayan culture, over crocodile-infested rivers and an oasis of English culture in Belize, within an otherwise Latin American environment. There is relaxation on Caribbean islands, hunting for sloths, tasting the high life in spas and some romance as the journey weaves its way through the mountains, history and wildlife of Central America.

Crossing Russia on the Trans-Siberian

Russia is a vast country that covers more than a third of Europe and stretches for nearly nine thousand kilometres across northern Asia. The story takes the reader on a tour through Russian culture, history and geography, starting in the Imperial city of St Petersburg with its spectacular palaces and museums.

A voyage by ship leaves St Petersburg to follow rivers and canals crossing several lakes through the northern pine forests, past wooden cathedrals and monasteries to join the Volga to reach Moscow. There is the Kremlin and

Red Square plus many other sights, including one of the largest and ugliest sculptures in the world.

After Moscow is one of the longest journeys in the world on the Trans-Siberian railway to pass through birch forests, over grassy steppes and through the Ural Mountains.

There are stops en route at Yekaterinburg, where the Imperial family were murdered by the Bolsheviks; horse riding in the Altai Mountains to reach Mount Belukha, Siberia's highest mountain, and at Irkutsk, near Lake Baikal, with its unique biodiversity and the world's largest volume of fresh water, before finally reaching Vladivostok in Russia's far east and its port on the Pacific.

Across the Caspian

This is a tale about a journey through the Caucasus from Europe's lowest point on the shores of the Caspian Sea to its highest point on the summit of Mount Elbrus. The route follows a strand of the Silk Road from Ashgabat, the capital of Turkmenistan, through the desert to reach a ferry across the Caspian to Baku.

From there the journey winds through some of the history of The Caucasus with its ancient kingdoms and the landscape of Azerbaijan and across the border into Georgia. This country is famous for its distinctive and good quality wines, plus a large number of churches and monasteries, an enclave of Christianity surrounded by populations that are predominantly Muslim.

Mount Elbrus is in Russia, to the north, but the border was shut so it meant a diversion through Cappadocia in Turkey and a flight via Moscow before approaching Mount Elbrus from the Russian side of the border for the attempt on the summit, which at an elevation of 5,862 metres is Europe's highest mountain.

Gold, Ivory and Slaves

Travelling down the west coast of Africa, there is a lot of history about how merchants accumulated wealth out of the misery of Africans, captured and shipped across the Atlantic to be sold into slavery. The triangular trade was shipping European-manufactured goods to Africa to buy slaves to ship to the Americas and then trade them for tobacco, sugar and rum to sell in Europe.

Many of the countries didn't exist as states and were known by the products they produced, such as the Pepper Coast, Ivory Coast, Gold Coast and the most emotive name, the Slave Coast.

Slavery was eventually banned, but only after more than twelve million Africans were sold into slavery. But then came the Scramble for Africa, when European powers sought to grab as much African land as they could before one of their rivals got there first. It wasn't slavery but it was economic exploitation, sometimes of the worst type, with arbitrary borders decided by Europeans in Europe without regard to local realities. Then there was independence and the people were exploited by their own leaders.

There is a wealth of detail about the historical origins of every country. He traces the history and the rationale behind the Africa Slave Trade and how it relates to what is happening, politically and economically, in Africa today. It gives us much insight into what is often described as the 'The African Way'. Is this still happening in Africa today? Is it any better today? For anyone thinking of overlanding along the coast of Africa, this is a must-read! This book is a joy to read, for travellers with a taste for adventure and history.

Condors over Chile

The condor is associated with the Andes and this adventure travels down the length of the Andes searching for condors. From the far north of the continent, on the arid Guajira peninsular, the route passes through hotspots such as Medellin and Bogota and a climb up Mount Puracé, an active volcano.

There is a break in Quito to stand on the equator. There is a fascinating visit to the Galapagos and a voyage through the islands that make up the archipelago. There is a huge array of wildlife that is not afraid of humans so you can get really close to its tortoises and its other unique wildlife.

Then there is the experience of seeing some of Peru's ancient civilisations and the country of origin of more than 3,500 varieties of potato, before continuing down the Andes to the windswept wastelands of Patagonia to Ushuaia at the end of the world in the search for the condor.

Land of Ice and Fire

Iceland is a fascinating country with a detailed history recorded in the Book of Settlement and many sagas. The Vikings first started colonisation of the island in 876AD despite its harsh climate and geography. It is covered by ice caps and glaciers. As it sits on the tectonically active, expanding North Atlantic Ridge, it is rocked by earthquakes and suffers frequent volcanic eruptions pouring out ash and poisonous gases.

One eruption from Eyjafjallajökull in April 2010 threw thousands of tons of fine volcanic dust into the atmosphere for weeks. The dust cloud spread across Europe and caused chaos to aircraft flights and many people's travel plans.

Enjoy a journey through the geography, geology, history, and culture of Iceland with widely believed stories of the supernatural and the beautiful but wild scenery of the island and its promises of seeing the Northern Lights.

Danger in the Jungle

The journey starts in the city of Belém, on Brazil's Atlantic seaboard, and traverses thousands of kilometres up the Amazon River through dense jungle to Leticia, reaching an eco-lodge in the depths of the jungle, to experience native village life.

There is the thrill of Carnival to experience in the city of Manaus, cut off by road from the rest of Brazil and only accessible by air or river; cut off despite having a population of over two million, making it Brazil's seventh largest city.

Going north, the journey crosses the border into Venezuela – what a vast difference between Brazilian and Venezuelan culture and society. Colombia used to be known as a basket case but just as Colombia has addressed its issues, Venezuela has taken over as the basket case of South America with alleged widespread corruption, unfunded social programmes, economic mismanagement and security forces cracking down hard on any opposition, making the place unattractive as a tourist destination. So why was I going there?

Carnival

Starting at the southern tip of the continent in Ushuaia, the adventure goes through the windswept plains of Patagonia and past settlements whose immigrants from Wales brought their language and customs with them. The Patagonian plains give way to Pampas before reaching the major urban centre of Buenos Aires for some culture and relaxation.

The journey of 1,200 kilometres northwards reaches the magnificent, thundering Iguazú Falls on the border of Argentina and Brazil and then crosses into the Brazilian jungles. There is a lot to explore in the Pantanal area of wetlands, with piranhas and capybaras to see before heading to Rio de Janeiro for the extravaganza and colour of the carnival, the biggest party on earth. Everyone is invited. But Brazil is a big country and there is a lot more to see and explore before reaching the Caribbean coast of South America.

Reflections on El Camino

El Camino is the pilgrims' route across northern Spain to reach the cathedral in Santiago de Compostela, built on the site where St James' body was buried after he was martyred in Jerusalem in 44 AD. His remains lay unmarked and unknown for eight centuries until a miraculous light led a shepherd to discover the bones in a cave.

A cathedral was built over the spot where the bones were found and it became a vital destination for pilgrims in the medieval era. But the way to Santiago de Compostela was fraught with danger for those pilgrims with the notoriously bad weather in the Pyrenees, warring kingdoms in the north, civil war and the ever-present danger of invasion from the Muslim Moors, who controlled the southern half of the Iberian Peninsula.

This is a long distance walk through the countryside, culture and history of the area, from St Jean Pied de Port on the French side of the Pyrenees to Santiago de Compostela and onwards to the Atlantic coast of Spain, to finally reach Finisterre, at the end of the world, for the known Roman Empire, a journey of 900 kilometres. But what is the route like today for the modern pilgrim?

Cape to Cairo

Starting out from Cape Town, there is plenty to see as the journey heads north: the scenery changes from the green fields and vineyards of Stellenbosch to the deserts and giant sand dunes of Namibia. It is only further north that the desert changes to savannah. There are safaris to see wild animals in their natural habitat, including hippopotamus, the most dangerous animal on the continent, and walking with cheetahs.

There are close encounters with elephants in the Okavango and views of thousands of zebras before crossing the border in Zimbabwe, where the magnificent Victoria Falls can be found, and a railway journey across the Zimbabwe countryside to Bulawayo, with its great industrial centre and railway heritage.

On safari through the Serengeti and the Ngorongoro Crater, there is the opportunity for visitors to see all of the Big Five Game animals, the five most dangerous animals to hunt on foot. There are the Spice Islands, the Bwindi Impenetrable National Park, where there is an opportunity to walk with gorillas and plenty more countries and experiences to enjoy. This was still only half way up the continent to Cairo.

White to Black

An exciting adventure travelling through Russia from the frozen far north, within the Arctic Circle, overlooking the Arctic Sea in Hero City Murmansk and the destination of many Allied Arctic conveys during the Second World War, known in Russia as the Great Patriotic War.

Travelling along the rivers and across the lakes of northern Russia, the adventure passes through many major cities with a wealth of historical and interesting stories to be heard before reaching Moscow, the capital of the Tsar's empire with its Kremlin, cathedrals and palaces.

A trip along the Volga passes through many major historical cities and reaches Stalingrad, where the Russians finally stood firm and turned the tide of the Nazis' advance into Russia during the Great Patriotic War.

There is caviar to experience and a visit to Sochi, widely known for its hosting of the Winter Olympics in 2014. Working my way along the Black Sea Coast, I reach Sevastopol, the largest city in the Crimea, annexed by Russia from Ukraine in 2014 and Putin's latest acquisition to his new Russian Empire. And what is it like today?

Living with Los Madrileños

I was sitting at my desk, minding my own business, keeping my nose clean, until I was summoned to my directors' office. Never a happy moment even if you think that you have done nothing wrong.

I was about to be given a fantastic opportunity to work abroad on secondment on a ground-breaking project based in Madrid, Spain. During my free time there, I would have time to explore and experience the culture, gastronomy, history and geography of both the plains and the mountains – a tempting offer for an adventurous spirit. I love to travel and enjoy a challenge.

However, I would be living and working away from home. How would I survive the challenge of living in a foreign country, in a strange city, not knowing the language, with no local friends, no familiar support network and playing a different role? Was I up to the job?

Other titles by the same author

El Camino Portuguese

North to Black

Cape to Cairo

White to Black

Kiwis and Kakapos

Norwegian Fjords

Cape to Cairo

White to Black

Return to the Silk Road

---x---

Britain's Top 25 Castles

---x---

A Freshman's Travels
A Sophomore's Travels
Gap Year Travels

---x---

Orphan Tales

A request from the author

Whether you have enjoyed the book immensely or found it a useful aid to insomnia, please provide me with a little help and feedback. Amazon Books' algorithms work to advertise books that they think would be of interest to other readers based on their search criteria. But they only work if they have sufficient data, which means at least fifty reviews on the Amazon Books website, or so I am told by a marketing friend.

Therefore, in order to help, please may I ask you to write a review of this book on Amazon Books in a simple three-step process. I am not looking for a five-hundred-word review, so it can be of any length, and write what you felt about the book. Secondly, rate it honestly as you think fit. Lastly, you can use your own name or remain anonymous by using a pseudonym or simply put 'An Amazon customer'.

Thanking you in anticipation.

Norman Handy.